Feature Transfer and Feature Learning in Universal Grammar

Nao Ishino

Kwansei Gakuin University Press

Feature Transfer and Feature Learning
in Universal Grammar

Copyright © 2019 by Nao Ishino

All rights reserved.

No part of this book may be reproduced in any form or by any means without permission in writing from the author.

Kwansei Gakuin University Press
1-1-155 Uegahara, Nishinomiya, Hyogo, 662-0891, Japan
ISBN: 978-4-86283-295-5

はじめに

　本書は関西学院大学大学院文学研究科に出した博士論文 Feature Transfer and Feature Learning in Universal Grammar: A Comparative Study of the Syntactic Mechanism for Second Language Acquisition を基にしたものです。博士論文ではかなり早い段階から、第二言語習得、特に再帰代名詞の現象を扱うという構想は定まっていました。しかしその後、様々な実験をすすめていく過程で、第二言語習得の途上に現れる言語体系の姿を実験で記述する帰納的なアプローチに対して、自分は何を明らかにしていけるのかという自問を繰り返していました。そんな中、指導教授で共同研究者の関西学院大学大学院 浦啓之教授と多くの議論をもつ機会に恵まれ、ミニマリスト統語理論に基づく第二言語習得理論としての素性転移・素性習得仮説（Feature Transfer and Feature Learning）が生まれました。浦教授との実りある議論の中で、研究論文の構成や研究法について学びを深め、理論言語学における研究者としての視点を養うことができました。御指導に心より御礼申し上げます。

　この仮説が従前のものと大きく異なる点は、学習途上の文法体系に対する視点で、本書ではそれを過渡文法と称しています。従来の第二言語習得理論研究では習得途上の言語能力は調査実験によって記述されていますので、その記述対象である言語文法（中間言語文法）は、実験結果によってその体系が変わりうる「動的な」文法体系です。一方、本書でとらえようとする過渡文法とは、理論的にその体系を説明し得る、いわば「静的な」文法体系です。本書の仮説は、語彙や機能範疇に内在する素性の指定を対象として転移や学習が起きていると説明します。最小の道具立てで言語習得のメカニズムに説明を与えようとするアプローチはミニマリズムの精神にそったもので、この仮説の最大の強みにもなっています。

　全体は三部構成で、第一部（1〜2章）では理論的背景や枠組み、そして Feature Transfer and Feature Learning 仮説で用いる基礎的な規定について示しています。次に、第二部（3〜5章）では再帰代名詞の

素性に注目し、各素性を合成することで様々な統語的振る舞いに説明がつけられることを明らかにしています。この仮説の強みの一つに、多様な言語間での習得現象を予測できることが挙げられますが、それらの一部として日本語と英語だけでなく、中国語やドイツ語間での習得についても扱うことができました。第三部（6～9章）では、この仮説が再帰代名詞の習得のみならず、多重主格・多重属格付与構文についても説明可能な仮説であることを明らかにしました。

　この研究の中心は、再帰代名詞や多重指定部構文の第二言語習得ですが、Feature Transfer and Feature Learning 仮説を用いることで、今後取り組むべき新たな課題を見出すことができました。何のためにこの研究をすすめているのか、という迷いにぶつかっていた時に、この仮説を生むことができたことで、自分の研究の見取り図のようなものが納得して描け、大げさではなく霧が晴れたようなすっきりとした気持ちになれたことを今でも思い出します。この仮説は素性の指定というシンプルな道具立てを用いるため、応用力が高い仮説です。まだ他の統語現象の第二言語習得のメカニズムにも説明を与えることができるだろうと考えおり、その可能性を探るという新たな目標につながったことは研究者として歩み始めた私にとって幸いなことでした。

　本書の出版にあたり、大手前大学交流文化研究所より助成を頂きました。出版の機会を下さった大手前大学学長　鳥越皓之教授、大手前大学前学長　柏木隆雄名誉教授、交流文化研究所所長　小林宣之教授、そして所員の先生皆様に心より御礼申し上げます。また、企画及び編集においてご尽力を頂きました関西学院大学出版会　田中直哉氏、浅香雅代氏、装丁を担当下さった松下道子氏に感謝申し上げます。そして、博士論文の執筆から出版まで、子育てと研究の両立において、日頃より体調を気遣い、支えてくれた両親に改めて感謝の気持ちを伝えたいと思います。

　　2019 年 11 月

　　　　　　　　　　　　　　　　　　　　　　　　石野　　尚

ABSTRACT

Under the UG-based theoretical investigations on the Second Language Acquisition, this dissertation aims not only at elucidating the language competence which develops at the intermediate stage of grammar in the way of L2 learning, but also at giving an explanatorily adequate theoretical account to the syntactic mechanism for the L2 learning. It will be demonstrated that ***Feature Transfer and Feature Learning Theory*** (FTFL), which will be proposed in this dissertation, is consistent with crosslinguistic L2 data and is explanatorily adequate on theoretical/conceptual grounds. In line with the minimalist assumptions, which stipulate that the ultimate object of a syntactic operation is not a lexical item per se but ought to be formal features with which the given lexical item is endowed in the lexicon, it will be argued in this dissertation that the L2 learning is the learning of the specification of syntactic formal features within a given item in a target language. The φ-features in a target item at the intermediate L2 learning stage are composed depending on the markedness of their feature specification through *Feature Transfer* from the L1 feature inventory and through *Feature Learning* from a target item. More specifically, it will be maintained that the φ-feature composition of an item/category at the intermediate L2 learning stage will be deduced through FTFL, the validity of which will be confirmed through experimental surveys of the L2 learning concerning reflexive binding and multiple Specifiers. Our theory to be newly proposed in this dissertation will be shown to enable us to provide a necessary and sufficient explanation to all the experimental observations, and we hence argue that it is theoretically superior to previous L2 hypotheses because it gives a theoretically coherent account to the syntactic mechanism for the crosslinguistic L2 learning universally and uniformly.

Acknowledgements

First and foremost, I am indeed grateful to Hiroyuki Ura for his invaluable and constructive suggestions and very encouraging comments on the materials presented in this dissertation. Without extensive and fruitful discussion with him throughout this study, this dissertation would not have been completed. I would also like to express my sincere appreciation to my dissertation committee members, Kiyomi Kusumoto, Noriko Ue, and Keiko Yamamoto, all of whom gave me insightful comments and generous support. Throughout this study, it was my pleasure to discuss the relevant topic with Jun Abe, Tomohiro Fujii, Ken Hiraiwa, Masatoshi Koizumi, Toshifusa Oka, Yuji Takano, Hiroyuki Tanaka, Shigenori Wakabayashi, and Kazumi Yamada. Particular thanks go to a large number of participants in my experimental surveys. I would especially like to thank Daniel Gallimore, Ai Koyama, Ikuyo Morimoto, Hiromi Nakano, and Akio Ogawa, for their generous cooperation in my experimental research. Many thanks are also due to my friends and colleagues in Kwansei Gakuin University: Shin'ya Asano, Eriko Hirasaki, Koyuki Ichida, Kazuya Kudo, Hitohiko Mimura, Saeko Oka, and Hajime Takeuchi. I am very thankful to them for judgments and helpful comments. Portions of this dissertation were presented at Bunkyo University, Doshisha University, Gifu University, Keio University, Kobe University, Kyoto University of Foreign Studies, Kwansei Gakuin University, Osaka University, Osaka City University, Tohoku University, and Yokohama National University. I wish to thank the audience at those meetings.

Finally, I would like to thank my parents Hirohisa and Michiko Ishino, my sister Maki Ura, my grandmother Setsu Takegawa, and my son Keiichirou Ishino for their warm encouragement in every respect and for their smile and love.

CONTENTS

はじめに iii

Abstract v

Acknowledgements vi

Contents vii

Introduction xi

CHAPTER 1
Framework   1

    1.1. Goals 1
    1.2. Theoretical Background of L2 Studies 2
    1.3. Feature Decomposition and Syntactic Parameters 4
    1.4. What is Transitional Grammar? 8
    1.5. Variations in Syntactic Properties of Reflexive Binding 13
    1.6. Major Proposals and Their Conceptual Problems 17
    1.7. Aims 21
    1.8. Theoretical Assumptions 25

CHAPTER 2
Theory of Feature Transfer / Feature Learning   31

    2.1. Three-Way Criterion of Φ-Feature Specification 31
    2.2. Markedness of Learnability 35
    2.3. Feature Transfer and Feature Learning 36

CHAPTER 3
Φ-Feature Specification of Reflexives   47

    3.1. Neutral Interpretation and Φ-Features 48
    3.2. Distributive Reading and *Number*-Feature 48
    3.3. Φ-Defective *vs.* Φ-Complete 50

3.4. Minimalist Account for Syntactic Binding of Φ-Defective Anaphora 51
3.5. Summary on Φ-Feature Specification 57

CHAPTER 4

Φ-Feature Specification of TG Reflexives: Prediction by FTFL and Experimental Results 65

4.1. Prediction of the L2 Learning of the English Reflexives by Japanese Learners of English (JLsE) 65
4.2. Empirical Problems in Predictions by Previous Studies (PRA and LTA) 71
4.3. Experimental Results on JLsE's TG Reflexives 74
4.4. Experiments to Beginner JLsE 83
4.5. Follow-up Experiments to High-Intermediate JLsE 88

CHAPTER 5

Crosslinguistic Investigations on TG Reflexives 91

5.1. Chinese *Ziji* and *Ta-ziji* and Feature Specification 91
5.2. German *Sich* and *Sich selbst* and Feature Specification 118
5.3. Crosslinguistic Variations 145

CHAPTER 6

Multiple Specifiers and Φ-Feature Specification 161

6.1. Multiple Specifiers in L1 Japanese 163
6.2. Φ-Feature Specification of T 166
6.3. Φ-Feature Specification of D 170

CHAPTER 7

Φ-Feature Specification of T/D in Transitional Grammar: Prediction by FTFL and Experimental Results 177

7.1. Prediction by Previous Studies (PRA and LTA) 177
7.2. Prediction by FTFL 178

7.3. Experimental Results on JLsE's Specifiers   182

CHAPTER 8
Crosslinguistic Investigations on Multiple Specifiers in Transitional Grammar   187

8.1. Multiple Specifiers in ELsJ's TG: Prediction by FTFL   187
8.2. Experiments   189

CHAPTER 9
Split Binding in Transitional Grammar   193

9.1. Split Binding through *Agree*   194
9.2. Experiments   199
9.3. Explanation   202

Conclusion   207

References   209

Index   217

Introduction

In the literature on the UG-based study of Second Language Acquisition (SLA), the second language (L2) acquisition of the English reflexives by Japanese learners of English (JLsE) has been extensively investigated. More specifically, it has widely been recognized, since Finer and Broselow (1986) and Hirakawa (1990), that JLsE are apt to misunderstand the locality of the binding dependency for the English reflexives at their intermediate acquisition stage (the grammar of which is called *interlanguage (IL) grammar* (where "interlanguage" is meant to refer to an intermediate stage of grammar in the way of L2 learners to master their second language (cf. White 2003)). It seems, however, that most of the major previous L2 studies have merely succeeded in drawing *descriptive* generalizations about their empirical observations/facts on the basis of their experimental surveys; that is, they have inductively shown how the reflexives in JLsE's IL grammar behave in syntactic respects, but they have failed to explicate the theoretical rationale as to why JLsE's IL reflexives syntactically behave as such.

This dissertation aims to give a universal account to the syntactic mechanism for the L2 learning by proposing a hypothesis with the idea of the φ-feature (de) composition (what we hereinafter call **Feature Transfer and Feature Learning** (FTFL) hypothesis). We will propose that syntactic formal features within a lexical item, but not lexical items per se nor syntactic properties inherent in a particular construction, are to be learned in the course of L2 learning. It will be stipulated that the specifications of formal features are classified into the following three types; that is, *underspecified*, *strictly specified*, and *partially specified*. Then, we will propose that **Feature Transfer** from a native language and **Feature Learning** from a target language should take place at some intermediate acquisition stage (which is referred to as ***transitional grammar*** in order to make a clear distinction from the term *IL grammar*, which has been oft-used in the L2 literature). More precisely, we will distinguish three levels in transitional grammar, and this distinction is, indeed, demanded theoretically by FTFL: (i) For beginners,

FTFL demands that only *feature transfer* should take place; that is, feature specification in the L1 feature inventory should be transferred to transitional grammar at a very early stage of their L2 learning; (ii) for intermediate/advanced learners, FTFL demands that *feature learning* should take place in their transitional grammar; that is, the transferred L1 feature should be overwritten/replaced by the corresponding feature in the target language, when the L1 feature is different from the equivalent one in the target language in terms of the markedness of their feature specification; and (iii) for even more advanced learners, FTFL demands that no *feature learning* should take place in transitional grammar, when both L1 and target features are the same in terms of the markedness; that is, the transferred L1 feature are very likely to fail to be overwritten/replaced by the corresponding feature in the target language.

With FTFL, we can deduce the feature specification of a reflexive item in transitional grammar. Moreover, following the idea about the decomposition of the φ-features, which was proposed by Bouchard (1984) and Burzio (1991), we will reveal whether a reflexive item in transitional grammar is ***φ-defective*** or ***φ-complete***. Then, under the current minimalist assumptions of binding through ***Agree*** (*inter alia,* Gallego 2010), we will give a theoretically consistent explanation to our crosslinguistic observations concerning the various syntactic properties of reflexive items in transitional grammar, which we have obtained through our experimental surveys.

Of theoretically particular significance is that FTFL is applicable simultaneously to the L2 learning of the presence/absence of multiple Specifiers with the assumption that the specification of the φ-features in T(Infl) and D determines whether the relevant head can project more than one Specifier. FTFL therefore is expandable empirically, the application of which is expected to show the validity of FTFL.

This dissertation is organized as follows: The theoretical/conceptual background for this dissertation will be outlined in Chapter 1. In Chapter 2, the definition/criterion of the specification/value of φ-features will be introduced, and the conceptual rationale for the definitions and assumptions embraced in FTFL will be therein discussed in detail. Then we will explain how the mechanism of FTFL works in L2 learners' transitional grammar.

INTRODUCTION

The empirical puroprose of this dissertation is twofold: (I) Part I, which consists of Chapter 3, 4, and 5, aims to argue about the syntactic mechanism for the L2 learning of reflexive binding; and (II) Part II, which consists of Chapter 6, 7, and 8, aims to argue about the syntactic mechanism for the L2 learning of the presence/absence of multiple Specifiers. In Chapter 3, we will define the specification/value of the φ-features in reflexive items in L1 English and L1 Japanese. Then we will explain how the specification/value of the φ-features within a given lexical item is concerned with various syntactic properties of a given reflexive (such as the neutral interpration in *person*, *gender*, and *number*, the distributive reading, the locality for the reflexive binding and the subject orientation of a φ-defective reflexive) under the current minimalist **Binding Theory through *Agree*.** In Chapter 4, we will deductively demonstrate through FTFL the specification/value of each φ-feature within the English reflexives in JLsE's transitional grammar, and we will present the detailed results of our experimental surveys on the precise syntactic behaviors of the English reflexives in JLsE's transitional grammar. Then, we will elucidate the φ-feature composition of the English reflexives in JLsE's transitional grammar and conclude that the English reflexives in JLsE's transitional grammar are φ-defective. With the help of some independently motivated assumptions under the minimalist framework, we will coherently answer to the unsettled question as to why the English reflexives in JLsE's transitional grammar behave as what we have discovered through our experimental surveys. In Chapter 5, we will argue that FTFL is applicable consistently to the crosslinguistic L2 data on Chinese reflexives for Japanese learners, Japanese reflexives for Chinese learners, German reflexives for Japanese learners, Japanese reflexives for German learners, English reflexives for Chinese learners, English reflexives for German learners, and Japanese reflexives for English learners. In Chapter 6, it will be demonstrated that FTFL is applicable coherently to the L2 learning of the presence/absence of multiple Specifiers, the application of which is regarded as a significantly important theoretical consequence of FTFL. In Chapter 7, we will present the detailed results of our experimental surveys on the L2 learning of presence/absence of multiple Specifiers by JLsE, and it will be confirmed that a prediction by FTFL perfectly conforms to our experimental results. In Chapter 8, we will argue that FTFL is also applicable to the crosslinguistic L2 data on multiple Specifiers for ELsJ. In Chapter 9, we will discuss the split binding in transitional grammar. The syntactic mechanism for the L2 learning of the split binding is explainable when we take it into consideration that FTFL is simultaneously applied not only to the φ-features in a lexical item (such as a reflexive item) in transitional grammar but also to the φ-features in a functional category (such as T(Infl)). Finally, we will conclude the present dissertation at the last Chapter.

CHAPTER 1

Framework

1.1. Goals

Numerous researches into the L2 acquisition of reflexive binding have been conducted within the generative framework. As MacLaughlin (1995) correctly points out, one of the theoretically important issues addressed therein is: which one of anaphora in the grammar of L2 learners' native language (L1), when L1 has more than one anaphoric expression (such as *zibun* 'SELF', *zibun-zisin* 'SELF-self', and PRONOUN+*zisin* (e.g., *kare-zisin* 'himself' and *kanojo-zisin* 'herself') in L1 Japanese, and *ziji* 'SELF' and *ta-ziji* 'himSELF/herSELF' in L1 Chinese), is to be selected as the source of consideration for L2 researchers to investigate the syntactic behaviors (or what has often been referred to as *syntactic parameters*) of L2 learners' IL reflexives in the course of the L2 acquisition? More specifically, which one of their L1 anaphora, *zibun*, *zibun-zisin*, or *kare-zisin*, do Japanese learners of Chinese (JLsC) select when they learn the usage of *ziji* or *ta-ziji* in Chinese as their L2? On the other hand, which one of their L1 anaphora, *ziji* or *ta-ziji*, do Chinese learners of Japanese (CLsJ) select when they learn the usage of *zibun*, *zibun-zisin* or *kare-zisin* in Japanese as their L2?

Independent proposals on this issue, each of which has been made so as to argue about an individual case (such as Japanese learners of the English reflexives or Chinese learners of the Japanese reflexives), have been developed in the L2 literature and some of them seem to be descriptively adequate, but no theoretically coherent and explanatorily adequate account has been provided, as far as we can tell, that is applicable simultaneously to crosslinguistic data on the L2 learning of reflexive binding.

What is selected from the grammar of learners' L1 in the course of the L2 learning of reflexive binding? Is it a certain lexical item or its syntactic parameters that is selected? What else is indeed selected? Why is it that the reflexives appearing in the course of the L2 learning do not behave syntactically the same either as reflexives in a native language or those in a target language? What does the UG-constrained grammar of L2 learners look like? Approaching these questions, we aim to give a universal account to the syntactic mechanism of the L2 learning of reflexive binding under the framework of the current feature-based minimalist syntax (Chomsky 1995 and its subsequent work).

1.2. Theoretical Background of L2 Studies

Back in the era from 1920s to 1950s, the L2 research was dedicated solely to describing empirical data, the approach which was called Structural Linguistics. Their contrastive analyses and approaches were extensively espoused in SLA studies and brought a boom of researches in foreign language teaching. Their approaches tried to show how human languages differ by describing a number of differences in their syntactic behaviors in considerable details. In those days, it was considered that languages were acquired through repetitive training. Those SLA researchers have descriptively carried out experiment-based investigations, and they have drawn the conclusion that languages significantly differ from each other and that it turns out to be impossible to acquire L2, because L1 is significantly different from L2 in linguistic properties.

In 1950s, Chomsky (1955/75) hypothesized, in the field of generative grammar, that all human beings are pre-equipped with universal linguistic principles, which is known as Universal Grammar (UG), and have an innate genetic apparatus, what is called Language Acquisition Device (LAD). Under this hypothesis, the mysterious problem can be readily resolved as to why all human beings, despite some differences between individuals, can

CHAPTER 1 FRAMEWORK

homogeneously acquire their native language through the same acquisition process to reach the same level of language ability. It was assumed that all human beings acquire human language unexceptionally through LAD. It was assumed, under the approach of generative grammar, that in addition to UG there are various sub-rules that determine each grammar of a particular language. In contrast with structural linguistics, which aims at the descriptive explanations of differences of languages, generative grammar focuses on eliciting similarities of languages as well as their differences with recourse to UG.

Returning to the topic of SLA, we thus conclude that SLA researchers under the perspective of generative grammar not only need to describe linguistic differences and to classify them, but also need to make an attempt to explain differences in the syntactic behaviors between native language and target language by utilizing abstract, theoretical methods.

After more than 20 years had passed since the inception of generative grammar, SLA studies made a substantial progress in the late 1970's, greatly affected by the Principles and Parameters approach in generative grammar. Under the studies of FLA (First Language Acquisition), children have been considered to have UG innately and its concomitant parameters in LAD. It has also been assumed that certain set of parameter values determine language-particular properties of each language. Children analyze Primary Linguistic Data (PLD) with the use of UG, and they set the parameter values through positive evidence and successfully establish the core grammar of their L1 without fail.

Since the early 1980s, UG-based SLA researches have concentrated their attention on UG accessibility, inquiring whether L2 learners have no access, direct access or indirect access to UG. No Access Hypothesis is represented by *Fundamental Difference Hypothesis* (cf. Bley-Vroman 1990), the hypothesis which supports the idea that UG survives only as the language-specific L1 grammar and is not available at all in SLA. Given the heretofore well-known fact that IL grammar is constrained by UG, No Access Hypothesis has turned out to be inappropriate.

Under the UG-based SLA studies, it is assumed that L2 learners have the grammatically consistent system as their IL grammar at their intermediate acquisition stage, because grammatical errors in the course of acquiring L2 represent rule-governed behaviors, which shows that they are constrained by UG. SLA researchers then have shifted their concern from surveying whether UG is available in SLA to theorizing how UG-constrained IL grammar of L2 learners is affected by learners' L1 grammar (i.e., what is called "parameter (re)setting"); that is, an important issue soon arises as to how L2 learners set the L2 parameter values when a target language has parameters different from their native language.

SLA studies therefore made substantial progress, greatly affected by the Principles and Parameters approach in generative grammar. In the late 1990s, theoretical linguists within the generative paradigm entered the new phase, Minimalist Program, so that the current SLA researches were conducted within the framework of Minimalist Program and aimed to establish feature-based L2 acquisition theories.

1.3. Feature Decomposition and Syntactic Parameters

The principles in UG apply uniformly to every human language, but UG cannot contain everything that explains variations between all human languages. The aspects of UG which specify the systematic, limited ways of language variations are captured with the conception of *parameters* (cf. Crain and Lillo-Martin 1999).[1] It has long been believed/accepted uncritically that parameters indeed exist as a part of UG. Parameters with (usually binary) values therefore are proposed to capture/explain crosslinguistic variations.[2]

On the other hand, several non-binary parameters (which are called "multi-valued parameters") have, indeed, been proposed in the literature. For example, the traditional binding theory, which was proposed in Chomsky (1981), states that an anaphor is bound in its governing category.[3] Anaphors must be bound by its syntactic antecedent, because they are regarded as referentially deficient and cannot be interpreted independently. It has therefore been widely acknowledged that the governing category of an anaphor is five-way parametrized, as initially proposed by Wexler and Manzini (1987) for Governing Category Parameter (GCP).[4]

As stated above, most of the parameters have binary settings/values (which are expressed by [±]) and mutually exclusive. It has often been observed in experimental surveys in the L2 literature that L2 leanrers' non-native grammar has a parameter value which is different either from the value of their native language or from that of their target language. There are two possible ways to show that L2 learners' non-native grammar has values which are expected to be different either from the native language or from the target language (cf. White 2003). When a given parameter has multi-valued settings (e.g., Governing Category Parameter (Wexler and Manzini 1987), and Null Subject Parameter[5] (Saleemi 1990)), it can be logically possible that L2 learners' non-native grammar has the setting other than their native language or their target language. Look at Figure 1 below:

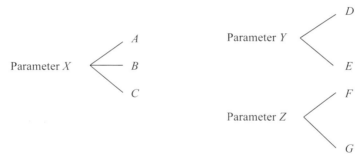

FIGURE 1. **Parameter Setting**
(White 2003: 142)

In Figure 1, parameter X has multi-valued settings; that is, parameter X has the three values of A, B, and C. When, for example, a native language has the value A and a target language has the value C, L2 learners' non-native grammar can have the setting other than their native language or their target language (that is, L2 learners' non-native grammar has the value B).

On the other hand, if we stipulate a different parameter for each syntactic property of a given language, the properties which emerge in the intermediate L2 acquisition stage can be explained with the combination of several parameters. Suppose that a native language has the value D for parameter Y and the value F for parameter Z, and a target language has the value E for parameter Y and the value G for parameter Z, as shown in Figure 1, L2 learners' non-native grammar is expected to behave syntactically differently when it has the value E for parameter Y and the value F for parameter Z or when it has the value D for parameter Y and the value G for parameter Z (see MacLaughlin (1988) for relevant discussion on parameter settings in SLA of reflexive binding with two parameters, such as reflexive parameter and Agr parameter under Progovac's (1992, 1993) Relativized subject framework). It has thus been proposed in the L2 literature that the course of the L2 acquisition is expected to be explained through demonstrating whether seemingly unrelated parameters in a target language and their values can be acquired or not.

Wexler and Manizini's (1987) GCP states that the binding domains of reflexives are parametrically determined; however, it is curious about where do the parametric values stem from? It has been admitted that a reflelxive has its own parameteric value concerning its locality of the binding domain when it is formed in a Lexicon. Given that each reflexive item has its own parameter with respect to its binding domain as its priminitive property, UG admits at least five values for the locality of the binding domain for a reflexive. Then, parameters have been proposed to be more construction-specific, the problem which is referred to as the "atomization of parameters" (Safir 1987). This problem has been correctly pointed out by Bennis and Koster (1984: 6) as follows: "Too often ill-understood differences among languages are simply attributed to some new *ad hoc* parameter". Accordingly, it has been suggested (cf. Borer 1984, Fukui 1986, 1988, Chomsky 1989, and Ouhalla 1991) that all parameters can be reduced to the inflectional system (or functional categories).

Later in the history of the minimalist framework (Chomsky 1995 and its subsequent work), it has been widely acknowledged that parametric differences in crosslingusitic variations stem from some properties of lexical items and functional categories/elements in languages concerned. The spirit of the minimalism advocates exclusion of theoretically unnecessary/redundant devices in order to explain the mechanism of human languages and the process of the language acquisition with less syntactic devices. We will argue in this dissertation that syntactic formal features inherent in a lexical item and a functional category are regarded as the sole locus of syntactic parameters which plays a crucial role in determining the syntactic properties of a given language. We totally agree with the widely-accepted assumption that parameters determine the systematic differences between languages, but a theoretically significant point here is how we can derive parameters. To put it differently, where do parameters come from? Notice here that the problem initially pointed out by Bennis and Koster (1984) is still unsettled if we attribute language differences to some new *ad hoc* "parameters" on formal features.

In this dissertation, we reject the widely-acknowledged idea that parameters indeed exist as a a theoretically existent substance in UG. We make the following hypothesis, essentially following the Minimalist spirit: The feature composition of a lexical item or a functional head determines the syntactic properties of the relevant item. More specifically, when a lexical item (or a functional category) is selected from the lexicon and is inserted/ externally merged in a given syntactic derivation, the syntactic properties of the relevant item (or its maximal projection) are determined by the specification of each φ-feature (i.e., *person, gender,* and *number*-features) in the item. Thus, the syntactic properties of an item in transitional grammar (which have often been referred to, in the L2 literature, as *syntactic parameter values*) ought to be explained only with the specification of the features that the item has in transitional grammar. In this dissertation hereinafter, we aim to argue (i) that all syntactic properties concerning the reflexive binding in transitional grammar can be explainable when we reveal the (de) composition of the φ-feature specification for a given reflexive, and that (ii) the number of Specifiers that are allowed to be projected in transitional grammar can be explained when we reveal the (de)composition of the φ-feature specification for T(Infl) and D in transitional grammar.

Of theoretically/conceptually significant consequence here is that we have the following advantage: It is not necessary to stipulate any theoretically additional device; for, according to our proposal, all syntactic properties are properly explainable without any recourse to conceptually unnecessary syntactic parameter. Now we would like to stress that formal features, to which we attribute language variations, indeed, exist in UG for conceptual grounds; that is, formal features are regarded as virtually essential for semantic interpretation and phonological realization. If we can explain the syntactic varieties in human language without assuming syntactic parameters, they are no longer conceptually necessary in the theory of human language.

We can therefore eliminate the abovementioned problems concerning syntactic parameter values: Are parameters multi-valued or binarily valued? Is a given parameter too construction-specific? In order to explain the syntactic properties of a given language, we are no longer relying on the notion of syntactic parameter for each syntactic property found in the language. Accordingly, it is demanded in this dissertation that language acquisition should be considered as the acquisition of the φ-feature specification in a relevant item in a target language. Recently, the roles of grammatical features in SLA have been investigated extensively (cf. Liceras, Zobl, and Goodluck 2008, Lardiere 2008, 2009, Travis 2008, García Mayo and Hawkins 2009, among others), so that the perspective in this dissertation will surely contribute to the existing L2 studies on theoretical grounds. Trying to share the ultimate goal with minimalist syntax, we will demonstrate that our theory, if reinforced with the idea of the φ-feature (de)composition, is conceptually plausible and theoretically superior to most of the traditional L2 studies, which have long admitted that syntactic parameters with some settings/values are indeed built in UG independently.

1.4. What is Transitional Grammar?

In this dissertation, in order to refer to the grammar which emerges at L2 learners' intermediate acquisition stage, we use a newly-coined term/notion *transitional grammar* instead of *interlanguage (IL) grammar*, which has long been used in the L2 literature. It is not an empirical description but rather a theoretical accout that the goal of this dissertation is to give to the syntactic mechanism for L2 learning. We simply assume that experimental observations are very significant on empirical grounds in analyzing given linguistic data not only in the field of SLA but also in every field of linguistics.

CHAPTER 1   FRAMEWORK

As mentioned in § 1.2, it has widely been acknowledged that L2 learners have a grammatically consistent system as their IL grammar and it is assumed that their IL grammar is more or less constrained by UG. It has often been discussed whether the initial state of IL grammar is fully or partially accessible to UG. Moreover, it has also been extensively discussed whether knowledge in L1 is fully or partially transferred to the initial state of IL grammar, or whether it is not at all transferred to the initial state of IL grammar. Therefore, many proposals about the initial state of IL grammar has been made in the L2 literature (such as *Full Transfer/Partial Access Model* (e.g., Tsimpli and Roussou 1991 and Hawkins and Chan 1997), *No Transfer/Full Access Model* (e.g., Epstein, Flynn and Martohardjono 1996), *Full Transfer/Full Access Model* (e.g., Schwartz 1996, 1998, Schwartz and Sprouse 1994, 1996, 2000, and White 2000), *Partial Transfer/Full Access Model* (e.g., Vainikka and Young-Scholten's (1994, 1996) *Minimal Trees Hypothesis*, (which is made in the context of *the Weak Continuity Hypothesis* for the L1 acquisition (see Pinker 1984 and Clahsen et al. 1994)), and *Partial Transfer/Partial Access Model* (e.g., Eubank's (1994, 1996) *Valueless Features Hypothesis*, and Eubank, Bischof, Huffstutler, Leek and West 1997) (see White 2000, 2003 for comparison of initial state and beyond). We also totally agree that L2 learners' non-native grammar is systematic and rule-governed. This dissertation, however, emphasizes that we should elicit L2 learners' non-native grammar in their intermediate L2 acquisition stage in a deductive manner with some theoretical assumptions. We cannot fully capture their non-native grammar only by experimental observations.

Now, let us schematize our aim in this dissertation. Look at Figure 2 below:

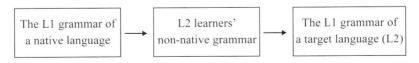

FIGURE 2. **L2 Learners' Non-Native Grammar**

L2 learners' non-native grammar looks like Figure 2. Note that L1 grammar of L2 learners' target language has often been referred to as *L2 grammar*.

The term *L2 grammar* seems to be misleading, because some researchers also refer to L2 learners' non-native grammar at the intermediate acquisition stage as *L2 grammar*. I will not follow either of the above usages. Throughout this dissertation, we will use the term *transitional grammar* for some fixed stage of the state for L2 learners' non-native grammar and use *L1 grammar of a target language* in order to avoid any confusion.

Here, notice that we do not use the term *transitional grammar* only to refer to L2 learners' non-native grammar but also to address a theoretically/conceptually significant issue as to how we should capture/explain the syntactic mechanism for L2 learners' non-native grammar. According to White (2003), we explain, following the widely-accepted notion of the interlanguage (IL) grammar (cf. Selinker 1972), that IL grammar is considered to be steady and systematic and shows rule-governed behaviors. Then, an important question has been posed as to whether IL grammar is constrained by principles and parameters of UG. Notice that it has often been observed in the L2 literature that IL grammar is not steady and is different either from the grammar of a native language or from the grammar of a target language.

Then, how should we explain L2 learners' non-native grammar (which has long been referred to as *IL grammar*)? One method is to describe them *inductively*; otherwise, the other way is a *deductive* explanation. The former method has been developed through most of the previous L2 studies, but the latter one is the approach we should aim at. Look at Figure 3 below:

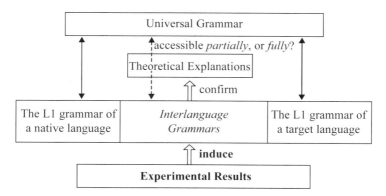

FIGURE 3. Data-based IL Grammars in L2 Studies

Previous/current L2 researchers have given priority to the issue as to how to set out their experiments; that is, how precisely they collect their experimental results is a matter of considerable concern to them. Therefore, as shown in Figure 3 above, before making a hypothesis about the status of IL grammar, they inductively demonstrate, with wide-ranging experimental data, how the theory for IL grammar is formed. Then, they confirm whether or not their L2 data are properly explained through exsting L2 hypotheses. If there is any problem in procedures, given sentences, background of experimental subjects, and a way of setting out experiments, it will be expected that we will obtain a considerably different result from previous experimental data. As long as IL grammar is described according to experimental observations, it cannot help but remain unsteady. Empirically, it seems prima-facie true that a grammar varies somewhat from person to person. It is presupposed therefore that grammars should be idealized as one grammatical system (see Chomsky (1965) for this point). Reconsidering the study on L2 learners' non-native grammar, we have two ways to investigate how to formalize it; that is, the data-based IL grammar (as shown in Figure 3) and the theory-oriented transitional grammar, as shown in Figure 4 below:

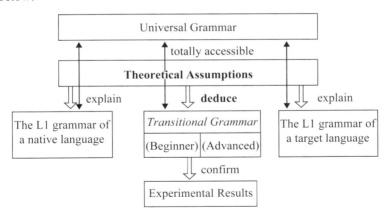

FIGURE 4. Theory-oriented *Transitional Grammar*

Figure 4 depicts our perspective hereinafter; that is, current minimalist assumptions, which are espoused to give a theoretically coherent accout to the mechanism of UG, should also be applied to L2 learnres' non-native grammar (transitional grammar). Crain and Lillo-Martin (1999: 55) state that "Universal Grammar (UG) (is) a theory of the internal organization of the mind/brain of the language learner.... (S)ince UG is taken to be a theory of our biological endowment, the principles of UG should be observed in every natural language." If UG is regarded mistakenly as one of the language acquisition devices, as previous L2 researchers have argued, there soon arises an issue as to whether the initial state of L2 learners' non-native grammar is fully or partially accessible to UG, as shown in Figure 3. Notice that UG is no longer viewed, under the current Minimalist theory, as being a language acquisition device. As long as L2 learners' non-native grammar is a type of the human language system, it is obvious that transitional grammar is totally UG-based (as shown in Figure 4), and the abovementioned issue as to whether the initial state of L2 learners' non-native grammar is fully or partially accessible to UG is no longer the issue we should consider.

This dissertation aims to deductively elucidate and describe the syntactic mechanism for the totally UG-based transitional grammar with theoretical assumptions which are stipulated to explain the syntactic mechanism for L1 grammar. Therefore it is first required to idealize L2 learners' non-native grammar. Moreover, it is naturally expected that each of their non-native grammar can vary according to their level/stage of their L2 learning and we agree with L2 researchers in this respect. Now we strongly stress that we should first idealize L2 learners' non-native grammar as transitional grammar, however. As depicted in Figure 4 (compared to Figure 3), we do not see it as a problem that we do not cover a wide-ranging L2 learners' non-native grammar, which varies from learner to learner. We deduce the syntactic properties of a given item in learners' transitional grammar with some widely-assumed theoretical hypotheses. Then we next set out experiments concerning the syntactic properties and confirm whether our theoretical deduction is consistent with the experimental results. When they are consistent with the experimentally-obtained data from previous studies or from one's own experimental surveys, it can be concluded that the validity of proposed theories/hypotheses is confirmed on empirical grounds as well.

L2 learners' non-native grammar, which has been customarily called *IL grammar*, can mean various states of grammar, depending on experimental results. On the other hand, *transitional grammar* refers to a particular state of grammar for an L2 learner. Therefore, our perspective on L2 learners' non-native grammar in this dissertation is different drastically from the one in the traditional L2 studies. As we have seen in Figure 4, *transitional grammar*, which we regard as theory-oriented, can be explained through UG-based theoretical assumptions universally and uniformly. Consequently, we hereafter call L2 learners' non-native grammar *transitional grammar* and distinguish it from the oft-used term/notion *IL grammar* in the previous L2 studies.

1.5. Variations in Syntactic Properties of Reflexive Binding

Trying to give a universal account to the syntactic mechanism for the L2 learning of reflexive binding, we will briefly overview some various syntactic properties of reflexive binding. Anaphors can be divided into two morphological variations; namely, simplex anaphors (which are often referred to as *SE anaphors*) and complex anaphors (which are often referred to as *SELF anaphors*) (Reinhart and Reuland 1993). English, for example, has SELF anaphors alone, which are morphologically made from a pronoun and the *self* suffix, such as *himself* and *herself*; however, universally, two morphological variants of anaphora can be found in not a few languages. They are, for instance, *zibun*, *zibun-zisin* and *kare-zisin* in Japanese, *ziji* and *ta-ziji* in Chinese, *sich* and *sich selbst* in German, *zich* and *zichzelf* in Dutch, and *seg* and *seg selv* in Norwegian.

Syntactic properties of reflexive binding, which are mainly concerned in this dissertation are exemplified with the following four phenomena: (I) Locality of the binding dependency; (II) existence/absence of the subject orientation; (III) availability of the distributive reading; and (IV) availability of the neutral interpretation in *person*, *gender*, and *number*.

According to the traditional Binding Theory A (cf. Chomsky 1981, and Chomsky and Lasnik 1993), an anaphor must be bound in its syntactically local domain (what is called *binding domain*). Look at the English examples in (1.1) below:

(1.1)   a.   Mary said [that **John** criticized *himself*.]
         b.   Mary made [**John** criticize *himself*.]

The embedded clauses which are in the brackets in (1.1) are regarded as the binding domain of *himself*, and *himself* must be bound within each embedded clause by *John*, which is counted as its syntactic antecedent. The English reflexives, therefore, are regarded as locally-bound. Returning to the well-known observation that more than one reflexive form (simplex *vs.* complex) can be found in quite a few languages, it has widely been observed that a morophologically simplex anaphor not only allows local binding but also allows long-distant binding, whereas a morphologically complex anaphor only allows local binding except for some emphatic use as a logophor as found in the discourse binding (what is called "Pica's (1987) generalization"). Look at (1.2) below:

(1.2)   a.   **John**$_i$-wa [**Bill**$_j$-ga   *zibun*$_{i/j}$-o   hihansi-ta   to]   it-ta.
             John-TOP   Bill-NOM   SE-ACC   criticize-PAST   C   say-PAST
             Lit. 'John said that Bill criticized ^{OK}John/^{OK}Bill.'

        b.   John$_i$-wa   [**Bill**$_j$-ga   *zibun-zisin*$_{*i/j}$/*kare-zisin*$_{*i/j}$ -o
             John-TOP   Bill-NOM   SELF/himself-ACC
             hihansi-ta   to]   it-ta.
             criticize-PAST   C   say-PAST
             Lit. 'John said that Bill criticized *John/^{OK}Bill.'

Among the three forms of the Japanese reflexives, the simplex form *zibun* is regarded as a long-distant reflexive (as shown in (1.2a)), whereas the complex forms *zibun-zisin* and *kare-zisin* are regarded as locally-bound reflexives (as shown in (1.2b)). In the case of an embedded non-tensed clause (such as a causative construction), however, one of the complex forms *zibun-zisin* can be bound over a non-tensed clause boundary, as shown in (1.3a), but the other complex form *kare-zisin* is still locally-bound, as shown in (1.3b) below:

(1.3) a. John$_i$-wa [Bill$_j$-ni   *zibun-zisin*$_{i/j}$-o   hihans]-ase-ta.
        John-TOP   Bill-DAT   SELF-ACC   criticize-CAUSE-PAST
        Lit. 'John made Bill criticize ^{OK}John/^{OK}Bill.'

   b. John$_i$-wa [Bill$_j$-ni   *kare-zisin*$_{*i/j}$-o   hihans]-ase-ta.
      John-TOP   Bill-DAT   himself-ACC   criticize-CAUSE-PAST
      Lit. 'John made Bill criticize *John/^{OK}Bill.'

Why is it that *zibun-zisin* syntactically behaves differently from *kare-zisin* with respect to the locality on binding dependency? It will be discussed in detail in § 3.4.2.

According to Faltz' (1977) typological classification, it has long been recognized that a simplex anaphor with the property of long-distant binding dependency shows the subject orientation, as exemplified by the Chinese example of *ziji* in (1.4) below (Huang 1982, and Huang and Tang 1991):

(1.4) **Zhangsan**$_i$ song   Lisi$_j$ yizhang   *ziji*$_{i/*j}$ de   xiangpian.
      Zhangsan   give   Lisi   one-CLA   SE   DE   picture
      Lit. 'Zhangsan gave Lisi a picture of ^{OK}Zhangsan/*Lisi.'

The simplex form *ziji* can be bound only by *Zhangsan*, which is assumed to be the logical subject, but not by *Lisi*, because *Lisi* does not have subjecthood. It is therefore concluded that *ziji* is regarded as subject-oriented. In the case of *ta-ziji*, however, it also shows the subject orientation even though *ta-ziji* is morphologically complex and locally bound, as shown in (1.5) below (see Xue 1991):

(1.5) Zhangsan$_i$ shuo [**Lisi**$_j$ song gei Wangwu$_k$ yizhang *ta-ziji*$_{*i/j/*k}$
      Zhangsan say   Lisi   give to Wangwu   one-CLA himself

de zhaopian].
DE picture
Lit. 'Zhangsan said Lisi gave Wangwu a picture of *Zhangsan/
^{OK}Lisi/*Wangwu.'

The example in (1.5) shows that *ta-ziji* cannot be bound by *Zhangsan*, because the embedded tensed clause boundary intervenes between *Zhangsan* and *ta-ziji*. In addition, *Wangwu* cannot bind *ta-ziji*, because it does not have subjecthood. What induces the property of the subject orientation of a reflexive? It will be discussed in detail under the current minimalist binding theories in § 3.4.1.

Another highlighted syntactic property of reflexive binding is *distributive reading*. Look at the Japanese reflexives in (1.6) below:[6]

(1.6) [John$_j$ to Bill$_k$]-ga ^{OK}zibun$_{j\otimes k}$/ ^{OK}zibun-zisin$_{j\otimes k}$-o seme-ta.
John and Bill-NOM   SE / SELF-ACC   blame-PAST
Lit. 'John blamed John, and Bill blamed Bill.'

The example in (1.6) is acceptable under the interpretation 'John blamed John, and Bill blamed Bill.' We call the interpretation *distributive reading*, because a reflexive is distributively bound by *John* and *Bill*. On the other hand, *kare-zisin* does not allow the distributive reading, resulting in the ill-formedness of (1.7) below:

(1.7) *[John$_j$ to Bill$_k$]-ga   *kare-zisin$_{j\otimes k}$-o   seme-ta.
John and Bill-NOM   himself-ACC   blame-PAST
Lit. 'John blamed John, and Bill blamed Bill.'

Where does the difference between *zibun-zisin* and *kare-zisin* with regard to the distributive reading come from? It will be explained with the aid of the φ-feature specification in a reflexive in § 3.2.

Whether a reflexive allows the neutral interpretation for each of the φ-features or not is another important point in determining the syntactic properties of the reflexive. For instance, the pronominal part within the

English reflexive *himself* carries the specifications for 3rd person, masculine, singular, and the pronominal part within the Chinese reflexive *ta-ziji* carries the specifications for 3rd person and singular, but it allows the neutral interpretation in *gender*; that is, *ta-ziji* can be bound either by a male antecedent or by a female antecedent. The notion of the (under)specification will be defined in § 2.1, 2.2, and 3.1.

It is obvious from these observations that the abovementioned syntactic properties of reflexive binding are not regarded as *language*-specific, but should be regarded as *lexical* properties. Notice that it is necessary for most of the previous L2 studies to presuppose that an L1 anaphora, when L1 has more than one anaphoric expression (as in Japanese), is to be selected as the source of resetting or transfer, because the syntactic properties of reflexive binding vary from item to item as have been overviewed in this section. In the next section, we will outline some major proposals in the L2 studies of reflexive binding in JLsE's IL grammar and point out conceptual/methodological problems immanent in them.

1.6. Major Proposals and Their Conceptual Problems

In the UG-based studies on SLA, PARAMETER RESETTING APPROACH (hereafter, PRA) (e.g., Finer and Broselow 1986, Hirakawa 1990, Thomas 1995, MacLaughlin 1998, and Watanabe et al. 2008, among many others), and LEXICAL TRANSFER APPROACH (hereafter, LTA) (e.g., Yuan 1994, Ishino and Ura 2009, and Ishino 2010, among others) are widely recognized as a foremost approach to L2 acquisition of reflexive binding. As for the studies on the L2 acquisition of reflexives by JLsE, a question has been much debated as to whether the syntactic parameter value for the binding domain in L1 undergoes resetting or not. According to PRA, which votes for the approach espousing parameter resetting, L2 learners' IL grammar is formed through resetting the parametric values of their L1; on the other hand, according to LTA, it dissents from the idea of parameter resetting, and adopts the idea that the parametric value of a certain lexical item in their L1 grammar forms their IL grammar (see White 2003 for comparative discussion). Under PRA,

L2 development is regarded as a maturational process (cf. Borer and Wexler's (1992) *Linguistic Maturation Hypothesis*). Both of them, nevertheless, agree that UG is available somehow to L2 learners. In this section we will demonstrate that these two approaches, when we take JLsE's learning of the English reflexives into full consideration, turn out to be insufficient on theoretical/conceptual grounds.

1.6.1. Parameter Resetting Approach

First, let us illustrate some empirical deficiencies of PRA, which fails to provide any consistent account to all of the syntactic properties of JLsE's IL reflexives. Advocates for PRA have built their rationale upon the conception of GOVERNING CATEGORY PARAMETER (GCP), which states that the binding domain of an anaphor is alleged to be parametrically determined (cf. Yang 1984, and Wexler and Manzini 1987). The five parametric values determine five different binding domains, which range from the most restrictive English type (i.e., the value (a)) to the least restrictive Japanese *zibun*-type (i.e., the value (e)). Hirakawa (1990), one of the pioneering works of the L2 acquisition of the English reflexives by JLsE, takes only *zibun* into consideration, and still has a considerable influence on the other studies on JLsE's acquisition of the English reflexives. Then, most of the advocates for PRA presuppose that the parameter value for the locality concerning the binding domain of the simplex reflexive *zibun* is identified as the parameter value for the locality concerning the binding domain of their L2 reflexive, ignoring the well-known fact that there are more than one reflexive form in L1 Japanese with the abovementioned distinctive syntactic properties. Notice that, as far as we know, there has been *no* theoretical answer to the question as to why *zibun* (and its syntactic parameter value) is selected as the representative of L1 anaphora for JLsE. This statement can no longer be explanatorily adequate, because it is not provided any theoretical rationale for its selection.

PRA has another more theoretically fatal problem; for, the advocates for PRA adopt the Subset Principle proposed in Wexler and Manzini (1987) (cf., also, Berwick 1985), and try to explain the experimental result that JLsE at their IL stage adopt neither their own L1 parameter value for the binding domain (i.e., the value (e)) nor the L1 English value (i.e., the value (a)); rather, they reset their L1 parameter into the Russian parameter value (i.e., the value (c)), which is intermediate between (a) and (e).[7]

PRA, if reinforced with the Subset Principle, maintains that the parametric value intermediate between the L1 value and the target one is reset in L2 learners' IL grammar when the relevant parameter value in a target language does not include the one in L1 as a subset. More precisely, it is assumed, under GCP, that the L1 parameter value (i.e., the value (e)) subsumes the target parameter value (i.e., the value (a)) as a subset. For the PRA advocates, this plays the most important role of explaining the binding dependency of JLsE's IL reflexives, as we argued above. But it should be noted that there are two values other than the value (c), which lie between the L1 Japanese value (e) and the L1 English value (a); namely, the value (d) and the value (b), in addition to the value (c), lie between them. Then, why is it that there are so many JLsE who adopt the value (c), instead of adopting the value (d) or the value (b)? It seems that there is no consistent explanation of this issue under PRA and no cogent speculation on it without any proviso has yet been provided as far as we can detect.

In addition, according to Pica's (1987) generalization, as we have observed in the previous literature, it has often been claimed that the binding domain of a simplex form is wider than that of a complex form. That is to say, as long as a simplex form with the widest parameter value (e), which is the least restrictive, is selected as the L1 representative anaphora, most experimental results on the L2 learning of reflexive binding turn out to be explained through the methodology espoused in PRA, because the value (e) subsumes all of the other values (i.e., the value (a), (b), (c), and (d)) as its subsets.

The last and most significant theoretically fatal problem immanent in PRA is the following: In PRA, various syntactic parameters are unavoidably stipulated. For example, with respect to presence/absence of subject orientation, advocates for PRA utilize PROPER ANTECEDENT PARAMETER (PAP), which states that whether an anaphor must be bound by a subject or not is alleged to be parametrically determined (cf. Wexler and Manzini 1987).[8] Then, advocates for PRA argue that, if the target parameter value subsumes the L1 parameter value as a subset, it is easy for L2 learners to reset their L1 parameter value to the target value only with positive evidence. PRA is conceptually/methodologicially insufficient, because it needs to stipulate an additional syntactic parameter for each syntactic property of a reflexive. If we stipulate another newly-devised syntactic parameter, though it might be possible, the relevant parameter would be just a paraphrase of what the corresponding syntactic property indicates. In this dissertation, the notion of *syntactic parameters* will be reconsidered. We will argue that the syntactic parameter of language *L* is determined by the specification of formal features in a certain lexical item in *L* and the syntactic structure of *L*.

1.6.2. Lexical Transfer Approach

Advocates for LTA (i.e., Non-Parameter Resetting Approach) have hypothesized (e.g., Yuan 1994, Ishino and Ura 2009, and Ishino 2010) that the syntactic properties of a lexical item in learners' L1 grammar are copied (i.e., transferred) to the corresponding lexical item in their target language. According to LTA, only L1 parameter settings are available in IL grammar. Returning to JLsE's learning of reflexives with this in mind, we are led to predict that the syntactic properties of *zibun* in L1 Japanese are copied to the English reflexives in JLsE's IL grammar in the case where *zibun* is selected as the representative of the Japanese reflexives; in the case where either *zibun-zisin* or PRONOUN+*zisin* is selected as the representative of the Japanese reflexives, its syntactic properties are copied to the corresponding lexical item in JLsE's IL grammar.

LTA, too, is not free from a conceptually serious problem: A reflexive in learners' L1 language must be selected as the representative of their L1 grammar before its syntactic properties are copied (i.e., transferred) to the corresponding lexical item in the target language. Thus, Yuan (1994) proposes that PRONOUN+*zisin* (such as *kare-zisin*) should be selected and transferred to JLsE's IL grammar in the course where they learn the English reflexives, and Ishino and Ura (2009) propose that *zibun-zisin*, instead, should be selected and transferred. Those proposals, no matter how much descriptive adequacy they might have on empirical grounds, have a conceptually fatal problem, however: As correctly pointed out by MacLaughlin

(1995), there is no theoretically/conceptually obvious reason as to which one of the Japanese reflexives is to be selected as the representative of them and transferred to JLsE's IL grammar. Unless this issue is given a lucid solution, LTA is not sufficient in the least on conceptual grounds.

1.7. Aims

1.7.1. Theoretical Aim

The aim of this dissertation is not to give an empirical description, but to give a universally consistent account to the syntactic mechanism of reflexive binding in transitional grammar. The purpose of this dissertation, therefore, is to give a theoretically consistent explanation, by proposing a novel hypothesis utilizing the φ-feature (de)composition of a reflexive, to the syntactic properties of reflexive binding in transitional grammar. This dissertation hypothesizes that the syntactic mechanism of transitional grammar should be recast within the minimalist syntax; that is, we will propose that the syntactic properties of reflexive binding in transitional grammar are determined not by lexical items per se nor syntactic properties inherent in a particular construction (such as syntactic parameters), but by the compositional properties of syntactic formal features within lexical items both in native and target languages. Syntactic formal features which are dealt with in this dissertation are φ-features (such as, *person-*, *gender-*, and *number-*features).

It is important to notice, here, that our main goal is to provide a theoretically adequate explanation to the issue as to why reflexives in a transitional grammar show the syntactic properties which have been noticed through major experiments conducted in the previous literature on the relevant topic. While arguing that two leading approaches (i.e., PRA and LTA) to JLsE's transitional grammar of reflexive binding cannot provide any satisfactory explanation to the empirical/experimental discovery, we will propose, under the feature-based minimalist syntax, a novel theory (which we will call FEATURE TRANSFER / FEATURE LEARNING THEORY (hereafter, we abbreviate it as **FTFL**)) with the idea of the φ-feature (de) composition.

To be precise, we will propose that FEATURE TRANSFER takes place at a very early to intermediate stage in the L2 learning, and, later in the course of the L2 learning, FEATURE LEARNING takes place in L2 learners' transitional grammar. Notice here again that FTFL stipulates that only formal features, but not a lexical item per se nor syntactic properties inherent in a particular construction (such as syntactic parameters), should be a target of consideration in the L2 learning. The definition of FTFL will be given, as shown in (1.8) and (1.9) below:

(1.8) FEATURE TRANSFER: The specification/value of the formal features (i.e., each of the φ-features (such as the *person-/gender-/number*-features)) within what we call *L1 feature inventory* should be *transferred* to transitional grammar.

(1.9) FEATURE LEARNING: The specification/value of each feature (such as the *person-/gender-/number*-features) in transitional grammar should be overwritten/replaced by the value of the corresponding feature in the relevant target item (i.e., *learned*), the mechanism of which is followed by the definition of *markedness* in learnability.

FTFL founds itself conceptually on the feature-based derivational syntax under the Minimalist framework (cf. Chomsky 1995 and its subsequent work). More specifically, FTFL stipulates that a formal feature within an L1 lexical item should be transferred to transitional grammar in the course of L2 learning, and a formal feature within a lexical item in a target language can or cannot be learned later in the course of the L2 learning, which is determined by *markedness* of the specification/value of the relevant features in terms of learnability.

Following, basically, the idea about the decomposition of φ-features proposed by Bouchard (1984) and Burzio (1991), a reflexive, if their φ-features are fully specified, is regarded as φ-complete; otherwise it counts as φ-defective. Employing FTFL, we will reveal in a deductive manner whether a reflexive in transitional grammar is φ-defective or not (i.e., φ-complete). For example, it will be revealed in Chapter 4 that the English reflexives in JLsE's transitional grammar are φ-defective.

CHAPTER 1   FRAMEWORK

Then, under the current minimalist assumptions of binding through *Agree* (see Heinat 2008, Quicolli 2008, Gallego 2010, Reuland 2011 ,and among others), we will give a theoretical explanation to the experimentally obtained fact, oft-reported in the literature on JLsE's learning of the English reflexives, the fact that JLsE are apt to allow a reflexive in their transitional grammar to be bound by an antecedent even when the binding dependency between them is separated by a non-tensed clause boundary (though disallowing the binding dependency between them when they are separated by a tensed clause boundary), and JLsE's reflexives in the transitional grammar show the subject orientation.

One of the theoretically important consequences of our theory proposed in this dissertation is that FTFL, if reinforced with the idea utilizing the φ-feature decomposition of reflexives, leads to a lucid solution of the theoretically interesting issue as to which one of the L1 anaphora, when L1 has more than one anaphoric expression, is to be selected as the source of consideration in the course of the L2 learning, because FTFL assumes that not lexical items but formal features within an L1 feature inventory are to be first transferred, and should or should not be overwritten later in the course of the L2 learning. FTFL is, therefore, perfectly pertinent to the current feature-based minimalist syntax, and is shown to be superior theoretically to major previous approaches not only because FTFL needs no additional stipulation pertaining to the syntactic parameters for the purpose of elucidating the syntactic mechanism for the English reflexives in JLsE's transitional grammar, but also because FTFL can give a consistent account to the syntactic mechanism for the Chinese reflexives in the transitional grammar of Japanese learners, for the Japanese reflexives in the transitional grammar of Chinese learners, for the German reflexives in the transitional grammar of Japanese learners, for the English reflexives in the transitional grammar of Chinese learners, and for the Japanese reflexives in the transitional grammar of English learners (as will be discussed in Chapter 5). In addition, we will show that FTFL is applicable coherently to the syntactic mechanism for multiple Specifiers in the transitional grammar of JLsE and ELsJ (as will be demonstrated in Chapter 7 and Chapter 8). Moreover, we will show that, if we apply FTFL to both the L2 learning of a reflexive item and the L2 learning of a functional head, the syntactic mechanism of the L2 learning of split binding is lucidly explained (as will be discussed in Chapter 9).

1.7.2. Empirical Aim

In order to achieve our goal, we will first report an empirically novel discovery concerning the specification of each φ-feature within the reflexive items in JLsE's transitional grammar: Through conducting several experimental surveys, we will first reconfirm the oft-reported facts: (a) The fact that the reflexive in JLsE's transitional grammar is locally bound when it is embedded in a tensed clause, whereas it can be bound by a long-distant antecedent over a clause boundary when it is embedded in a non-tensed clause; and (b) the fact that the reflexive in JLsE's transitional grammar shows the subject orientation. More significantly, we will reveal the following novel discoveries: (c) the reflexive in JLsE's transitional grammar does not have the *person*-neutral interpretation; (c') the reflexive in JLsE's transitional grammar does not have the *gender*-neutral interpretation; (c'') the reflexive in JLsE's transitional grammar does not have the *number*-neutral interpretation; and (d) even advanced JLsE are apt, mistakenly, to regard the English reflexives as having the distributive reading (as will be precisely reported in § 4.3). These facts (i.e., (c), (c'), (c''), and (d)) are very significant on empirical grounds, because each of the φ-features within a reflexive in transitional grammar (customarily called IL grammar) seldom been investigated in the literature on SLA.

The empirical aim of this dissertation is, therefore, to demonstrate that FTFL is applicable coherently to several crosslinguistic data concerning the L2 learning of the syntactic properties of reflexive binding (e.g., Japanese learners of the Chinese reflexives (JLsC), Chinese learners of the Japanese reflexives (CLsJ), Japanese learners of the German reflexives (JLsG), German learners of the Japanese reflexives (GLsJ), Chinese learners of the English reflexives (CLsE), German learners of the English reflexives (GLsE), and English learners of the Japanese reflexives (ELsJ)). Independent proposals on this issue, each of which was made so as to argue about an individual case, have been advanced in the literature and some of them seem to be descriptively adequate, but no theoretically coherent and explanatorily adequate account has been provided that is applicable simultaneously to cross-linguistic data on the L2 learning of all the syntactic properties of reflexive binding. The empirical purpose of this dissertation, therefore, is to give to the abovementioned problem an explanation that is adequate as a UG-based theory of L2 learning.

In addition to the syntactic mechanism for various reflexive binding in transitional grammar, predictions by FTFL are empirically consistent with our experimentally obtained data concerning the availability of multiple Specifiers in the transitional grammar of JLsE and ELsJ.

1.8. Theoretical Assumptions

1.8.1. Feature Binding through *Agree*

Abandoning the traditional binding theory developed in GB theory, we will adopt a new theory of binding under the minimalist assumptions, according to which the binding relation between an anaphoric expression and its antecedent is materialized not through c-commanding plus referential coindexing but through *Agree*. This approach has recently been developed and defended by not a few researchers (Heinat 2008, Quicoli 2008, Lee-Schoenfeld 2008, Hicks 2009, and Reuland 2011, *inter alia*). In recent studies on syntax of reflexive binding, it has often been proposed (see Reuland 2008, 2011, Uriagereka and Gallego 2006, and Gallego 2010) that a φ-defective reflexive/anaphor must become φ-complete at LF (Bouchard 1984, and Burzio 1991), where every element must be properly interpreted (Chomsky 1995). Consequently, the syntactic binding of (φ-defective) reflexives can be recast within the *Agree* theory under the current minimalist Probe-Goal framework (Chomsky 2001 and its subsequent work).

Following basically **Binding through Agree** (cf. Uriagereka and Gallego 2006, and Gallego 2010), we will make the following four assumptions: (I) First, a φ-defective reflexive, which counts as referentially deficient, must have its φ-features valued by a Probe with the whole φ-feature amalgam in order to become φ-complete for the purpose of its referenitial interpretation. (II) α binds β if they are Goals of the same Probe; otherwise, α and β are obviative. (III) We especially hypothesize, following Ishino and Ura (2011a), that T with the whole φ-feature amalgam supplies the φ-features through *Agree* to a φ-defective anaphor post Spell-Out, because referential interpretation is supposed to take place at LF; that is, a head with the whole φ-feature amalgam alone can serve as a Probe for a φ-defective anaphor.[9] (IV) The φ-completeness of an anaphoric expression is a requirement for interpretation (Bouchard 1984, and Burzio 1991); hence, the feature-binding through Agree takes place post Spell-Out (i.e., at LF). As a consequence, the notion of *Phase*, being a cycle for Spell-Out, no longer bears on the locality of feature-binding.

As stated above, the traditional notion of binding domain (and the parameter values for locality) can be reanalyzed as in the following way: Given the abovementioned assumptions, an ordinary binding relation between *zibun-zisin* at the object position of a tensed clause and the subject DP of the clause (such as (1.10a)) can be explained as shown in (1.10):

(1.10) a. John$_k$-ga   zibun-zisin$_k$-o   kirat-tei-ta   (koto).
            John-NOM   SELF-self-ACC   hate-PROG-PAST   (fact)
            Lit. '(the fact that) John$_k$ hated himself$_k$'

            ┌────────────Case────────────┐
     b. [$_{TP}$ John$_{[\text{NOM}, \varphi]}$-ga [$_{vP}$ *zibun-zisin*$_{[\varphi\text{-def}]}$-o V] T$_{[+\text{tense}] [\text{Case}, \varphi]}$]

            ┌────────────Case────────────┐
     c. [$_{TP}$ John$_{k[\text{NOM}, \varphi]}$-ga [$_{vP}$ *zibun-zisin*$_{k[\varphi]}$-o V] T$_{[+\text{tense}] [\text{Case}, \varphi]}$]
                         └──────────────φ──────────┘

T[+tense] agrees with the subject DP *John* to provide it with the nominative Case, as illustrated in (1.10b). We assume that T[+tense] always has the whole φ-feature amalgam and counts as a Probe for a φ-defective reflexive. Notice that whether T is [+tense] or [-tense] is not important here. Given that T[+tense] has the whole φ-feature amalgam, T[+tense] can agree with a φ-defective reflexive *zibun-zisin*$_{[\varphi\text{-def}]}$ in the same clause in order to supply it with φ-features, as shown in (1.10c). Then, the binding relation between the subject and the reflexive is successfully established through the mediation of T[+tense].[10]

Next, the clause-boundedness of *zibun-zisin* can be explained, as illustrated in (1.11) below:

(1.11) [$_{TP}$ DP-ga .... [$_{CP}$ [$_{TP}$ DP-ga [$_{vP}$ *zibun-zisin*-o V] **T$_{1[\varphi]}$**] C] T$_{2[\varphi]}$]

T_1[+tense] in the embedded CP has the whole φ-feature amalgam and T_1 in the embedded CP is the nearest Probe for *zibun-zisin*. The minimality condition prohibits the superordinate/matrix T_2 from agreeing with a φ-defective reflexive in the lower clause even though T_2[+tense] in the superordinate/matrix clause has the φ-features which enables it to agree with *zibun-zisin* in the embedded CP. Then, the agree relation can hold only between the DP$_h$ at the subject position of the embedded CP and *zibun-zisin* in the same single embedded clause, as illustrated in (1.12) below:

(1.12) [$_{TP}$ DP$_k$-ga ..... [$_{CP}$ [$_{TP}$ DP$_h$-ga [$_{vP}$ *zibun-zisin*$_{*k/h}$-o V] T$_{1[\varphi]}$] C] T$_{2[\varphi]}$]

As stated above, there is no need to invoke the notion of binding domain (which is also called *governing category* in the GB era). The notion of the binding domain can be reduced to a Probe-Goal dependency; that is, the locality on binding dependency can be fully captured by *Agree*.

With respect to the English reflexives, Gallego (2011) assumes that they are regarded as φ-defective, because they lack nominative counterparts (see Reinhart and Reuland 1993) and the *self* morpheme can move to T at LF. As a result, the *self* morpheme can be visible to the C-T Probe. Contrarily, we assume that the English reflexives are φ-complete according to the idea with the φ-feature composition to be defined hereinafter. Then, the binding relation between the English reflexives and their antecedents are materialized through co-argumenthood. If and only if it appears as one of the arguments of a predicate, the predicate must be interpreted reflexivity; whence, its strict locality follows (see Reinhart and Reuland 1993).

1.8.2. Range of FTFL

As previously stated in §1.5, anaphors can be divided into two morphological variations; namely, simplex anaphors and complex ones. It has occasionally been claimed (cf. Bennett and Progovac 1998) that the L1 acquisition of morphologically complex reflexives is more difficult for children than the L1 acquisition of morphologically simplex reflexives, which ordinarily allow long-distance binding. Given the observation that non-local binding manifests itself at an earlier stage of L1 acquisition, we would like to speculate that *zibun*, the morphologically simplex reflexive, is acquired at a stage earlier than the stage where PRONOUN+*zisin* is acquired, the speculation which conforms to the major consensus among some L2 researchers (Yusa 1998, and Shirahata 2007, among others), who claim that PRONOUN+*zisin* is the least common (i.e., marked) reflexive and most rarely used among the three reflexive forms in L1 Japanese. This leads us to the plausible hypothesis that the feature composition of *zibun(-zisin)*, which is a default element (i.e., unmarked), is recognized by JLsE as the target of FTFL when JLsE are learning the usage of the English reflexives (Notice here that *zibun-zisin* has the same φ-specification as *zibun*).

Given this hypothesis, we can naturally deduce the theoretical rationale as to why the φ-specification of *zibun(-zisin)* alone is included in the L1 feature inventory for JLsE. When we take the L2 learning of syntactic binding into consideration, it is very significant for FTFL that it is not all of the reflexive, but only the φ-defective reflexives (i.e., unmarked) that FTFL is to be applied to; for, we basically assume that feature-binding is applied only to φ-defective reflexives. Φ-complete reflexives need not feature binding through Agree because they are completely interpreted with respect to their φ-features. Consequently, the φ-specification of the φ-complete reflexives is not included in L2 learners' L1 feature inventory for their native anaphora. For examples, the L1 feature inventory of JLsE has the φ-specification of L1 *zibun(-zisin)* alone. The φ-specification of L1 *kare-zisin* is not included in JLsE's L1 feature inventory, because *kare-zisin* is φ-complete and needs no feature agreement. A special attention should be paid with respect to English learners. Φ-complete reflexives are regarded as marked, but L1 English has φ-complete reflexives alone for their native anaphora. The L1 feature inventory of ELsJ therefore includes the φ-specification of the φ-complete reflexives.

In this chapter, we have thus far introduced the conceptual/theoretical background of this dissertation and argued that the goal of this dissertation differs completely from the previous/existing L2 studies in terms of its perspectives and methodology. In Chapter 2, we will introduce the definition espoused in *Feature Transfer and Feature Learning Theory* and provide further details of its application.

Notes

1. Traditionally, parameters that describe superficial, binary variations in the realization of syntactic structures are called micro-parameters, contra so-called macro-parameters that distinguish entire groups of languages from others (Ayoun 2003: 12).
2. Parameters in UG are ordinarily assumed to have binary settings; for, language acquisition should be simplified, as indicated by the switch-setting analogy provided in Chomsky (1988) (cf. Radford 1997).
3. Governing Category (Chomsky 1981: 211): β is a governing category for α if and only if β is the minimal category containing α, a governor of α, and a SUBJECT accessible to α.
4. GCP (Wexler and Manzini 1987: 53) states that γ is a governing category for α iff γ is the minimal category which contains α and
    (a) has a subject, or
    (b) has an INFL, or
    (c) has a TNS, or
    (d) has an indicative TNS, or
    (e) has a root TNS.
5. We omit going into any detail about Null Subject Parameter, for which the reader is referred to the proposal presented in Seemi (1990) and Huang (1995).
6. Throughout this dissertation, the notation "$X_{j \otimes k}$" means that X is bound distributively by α_j and β_k; that is, if a conjoined antecedent [α_j and β_k] can bind a singular reflexive form, the reflexive is interpreted as being coreferential distributively with each of α_j and β_k distributively.

7   The binding domain of the Russian reflexive *sebja* is alleged to show the value (c) of GCP: It must be bound in a tensed clause, but it can allow the long-distance binding over a clause boundary when it is embedded in a non-tensed clause.

8   PRA (Wexler and Manzini 1987: 64) states that a proper antecedent for α is (a) a subject β; or (b) an element β whatsoever.

9   Gallego (2011) hypothesizes that v with the φ-features counts as a Probe for a φ-defective reflexive in English. We also consider the possibility that D counts as a Probe for a φ-defective reflexive in Japanese if D happens to have the φ-features which can agree with a φ-defective reflexive. Whether a head has some φ-features with the checking ability is important here. See § 5.2 for the relevant discussion about the checking ability of the φ-features in T.

10 Here it is basically assumed that when T[+tense]'s nominative Case-feature checks/values the nominative Case of the matrix subject DP, its nominative Case feature is deleted, as shown in (1.10b), because the nominative Case feature of the matrix subject DP is not necessary for interpretation and needs to be erased before Spell-Out (Chomsky 1995). Then, the φ-features of the matrix subject DP checks/values the φ-features in T[+tense] in narrow syntax (i.e., before Spell-Out), but its φ-features are necessary for interpretation at LF and are not erased in narrow syntax. The hypothesis for Binding through *Agree* states that the φ-feature checking between a reflexive and T[+tense] with the φ-features through *Agree* takes place at LF (i.e., after Spell-Out) and the φ-features in T[+tense] are remained (i.e., not erased) at LF although they are checked/valued in narrow syntax. The φ-feature checking ability of T[+tense] will be discussed in detail in § 5.2.

CHAPTER 2

Theory of Feature Transfer / Feature Learning

As stated in Chapter 1, the φ-feature specification of a lexical item plays the most significant role in our theory for the syntactic mechanism of reflexive binding in transitional grammar, so that it is essential for us to explicate the φ-feature specification of reflexive items. Before revealing the φ-feature specification within a reflexive, however, we will sketch out the criterion/ definition of the specification/value of syntactic formal features.

2.1. Three-Way Criterion of Φ-Feature Specification

First, we assume that feature specification can logically be classified into three types: (α) *underspecified*, (β) *strictly specified*, and (γ) *partially specified*. Our definition of the feature specification can be illustrated in Chart 1 below:[1]

CHART 1. Definition of Φ-Feature Specification

			markedness
(α) Underspecified		∅	*marked*
Specified	(β) Strictly	+	*unmarked*
	(γ) Partially	−	*unmarked*

We demarcate the three way distinction for the value of feature specification in precisely the same way as the logical/mathematical theory of relations.[2]

2.1.1. Underspecified Features

Now we define the following: (α) A feature F within a lexical item LI is **underspecified** iff every morphophonologically possible variation of F in a language L allows arbitrarily free (or neutral) interpretation; otherwise, F is **specified**.[3] For example, the Japanese reflexives *zibun* ('SELF') and *zibun-zisin* ('SELF-self') allow the *person-* and *gender-*neutral interpretations in the grammar of L1 Japanese, as shown in (2.1) below:

(2.1) a. Watasi$_k$-wa   kanojo$_h$-ni   *zibun(-zisin)*$_{k/h}$-o
        I-TOP   she-DAT   SELF(-self)-ACC
        rikais-ase-ta.
        understand-CAUSE-PAST
        Lit. 'I made her understand SELF(-self).'

     b. Anata$_k$-wa   kare$_h$-ni   *zibun(-zisin)*$_{k/h}$-o
        You-TOP   he-DAT   SELF(-self)-ACC
        rikais-ase-ta.
        understand-CAUSE-PAST
        Lit. 'You made him understand SELF(-self).'

     c. Sono otoko$_k$-wa ano   onna$_h$-ni   *zibun(-zisin)*$_{k/h}$-o
        the man-TOP   that   woman-DAT   SELF(-self)-ACC
        rikais-ase-ta.
        understand-CAUSE-PAST
        Lit. 'The man made that woman understand SELF(-self).'

Zibun(-zisin) in the grammar of L1 Japanese does not care whether it has a first-, second-, or third-person, masculine or feminine antecedent. To be precise, the well-formedness of the examples in (2.1a) and (2.1b) shows that arbitrarily free interpretation in *person* at all is allowed for *zibun* and

CHAPTER 2   THEORY OF FEATURE TRANSFER / FEATURE LEARNING

zibun-zisin; that is, the *person*-features within the L1 Japanese reflexives *zibun(-zisin)* are underspecified.

In a similar way, the well-formedness of the example in (2.1c) shows that arbitrarily free interpretation in *gender* at all is allowed for *zibun* and *zibun-zisin*; that is, the *gender*-features within the L1 Japanese reflexives *zibun(-zisin)* are underspecified.[4]

2.1.2. Strictly Specified Features

Next, we define the following: (β) A specified *F* is **strictly specified** iff each of *F*'s morphophonologically possible variations in *L* allows only one specific interpretation. For example, the reflexives in the grammar of L1 English are strictly specified with respect to their *person*-features, as shown in (2.2) below:

(2.2)   a. I criticized ^{ok}*myself* / *yourself / *himself / *herself / **itself.*
        b. You criticized *myself / ^{ok}*yourself* / *himself / *herself / **itself.*
        c. He criticized *myself / *yourself / ^{ok}*himself* / *herself / **itself.*
        d. She criticized *myself / *yourself / *himself / ^{ok}*herself* / **itself.*
        e. It criticized *myself / *yourself / *himself / *herself / ^{ok}*itself.*
        f. We criticized ^{ok}*ourselves* / *yourselves / **themselves.*
        g. You criticized *ourselves / ^{ok}*yourselves* / **themselves.*
        h. They criticized *ourselves / *yourselves / ^{ok}*themselves.*

The ill-formed examples in (2.2 a-e) show that, in the grammar of L1 English, (i) the first-person, singular reflexive *myself* cannot be bound either by the second-person pronoun (i.e., *you*) or by the third-person pronouns (i.e., *he/she/it*); (ii) the second-person, singular reflexive *yourself* cannot be bound either by the first-person pronoun (i.e., *I*) or by the third-person pronouns; and (iii) the third-person, singular reflexives *himself/herself/itself* cannot be bound either by the first-person pronoun or by the second-person pronoun. In a similar way, it is obvious from the ill-formed examples in (2.2 f-h) that (iv) the first-person, plural reflexive *ourselves* cannot be bound either by the second-person pronoun (i.e., *you*) or by the third-person pronoun (i.e., *they*); (v) the second-person, plural reflexive *yourselves* cannot be bound either by the first-person pronoun (i.e., *we*) or by the third-person pronoun; and (vi) the third-person, plural reflexive *themselves* cannot be bound either by the first-person pronoun or by the second-person pronoun. As can be seen from these facts, no arbitrarily free interpretation in terms of the *person*-feature is allowed for the L1 English reflexives. It follows that the *person*-feature of the L1 English reflexives is *not* underspecified. It is obvious from the ill-formed examples in (2.2) that the first-person reflexives disallow the second- or third-person interpretation, the second-person reflexives disallow the first- or third- person interpretation, and the third-person reflexives disallow the first- or second-person interpretation; that is, their interpretation in *person* is unarily fixed as each of their morphological variation shows, resulting in showing that all the L1 English reflexives are strictly specified in terms of their *person*-features.

2.1.3. Partially Specified Features

Lastly, we define the following: (γ) A specified F is **partially specified** iff F is neither underspecified nor strictly specified. To put it differently, if a feature F allows neither of an arbitrarily free interpretation nor a unarily fixed interpretation, F counts as partially specified. We will argue that some types of reflexives can be partially specified in terms of their *number*-feature. With respect to specific examples of the specification of a partially specified feature, we will explain them in detail later in § 3.2. Notice here again that the specification/value of formal features can be classified into the three types according to the following definitions: (α) A feature F within a lexical item LI is **underspecified** iff every morphophonologically possible variation of F in a language L allows arbitrarily free (or neutral) interpretation; otherwise, F is **specified**; (β) A specified F is **strictly specified** iff each of F's morphophonologically possible variations in L allows only one specific interpretation; and (γ) A specified F is **partially specified** iff F is neither underspecified nor strictly specified.

2.2. Markedness of Learnability

The rationale behind FTFL comes from the conception about the learnability of formal features with respect to their φ-feature specification. Consider the sets of underspecified features and specified features below:

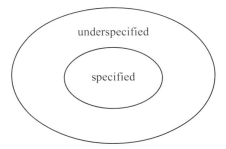

FIGURE 5. Subset Relation to Underspecified Features and Specified Features

Figure 5 depicts the subset relation to underspecified features and specified features. It is natural to presuppose that the set of underspecified features subsume the set of specified features. Of particular significance in our proposal is that we naturally assume that learners start to assume an unmarked value in the course of their language acquisition (cf. Chomsky 1981, and Gair 1988), as illustrated by Figure 6 below:

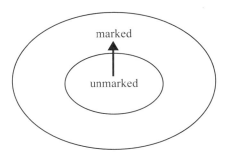

FIGURE 6. Markedness of Learnability

Figure 6 depicts rules of human languages, which are regarded as core or periphery: Core rules are regarded as unmarked, because they are held to be innate and governed by universal principles, whereas peripheral rules are regarded as marked and should be learned in the course of the language acquisition. To be more precise, unmarked features, unless provided sufficient positive evidence, are harder for learners to overwrite once they have been learned in the course of their L1 acquisition; as a result, we assume that an L1 feature, if it has an unmarked value, should be transferred to transitional grammar, and that marked features are easier to discard due to their perceptible transformation from the pristine state (unmarkedness), and very easy to reconvert to their unmarked state.

When we take it into consideration that specified features (irrespective of whether they are strictly specified or partially specified) are subsumed under underspecified ones as a subset, together with the assumption that the unmarked value is subsumed under the marked value as a subset, we are led to conclude that it is very plausible that features which are strictly or partially specified are naturally regarded as ***unmarked*** and underspecified ones are regarded as ***marked*** (see White 1986 for 'markedness' in SLA), under the subset principle (Berwick 1985, Wexler and Manzini 1987, and Gair 1988).

The feature specification is classified into the three types, as we have argued in the previous subsections. For the purpose of elucidating the syntactic mechanism for acquiring formal features, we argue that it is necessary to reduce the three-way classification of the feature specification to the generally-accepted theory of *markedness* in terms of learnability. We have hence classified the three types of the feature specification into two values according to markedness in SLA.

2.3. Feature Transfer and Feature Learning

FTFL demands that each feature among the *person-, gender-,* and *number*-features in L1 feature inventory, whether specified or not, should be ***transferred*** to transitional grammar in an earlier stage of the L2 learning,

CHAPTER 2   THEORY OF FEATURE TRANSFER / FEATURE LEARNING

but the markedness of the relevant transferred feature determines whether its specification is retained in transitional grammar or overwritten/replaced (*learned*) at a later stage by the corresponding target feature. The markedness of the feature specification therefore is regarded as the very significant notion in FTFL as much as it has been in traditional studies on the language acquisition.

In terms of markedness, we logically have four possible combinations of L1 and target feature specification; that is, (i) an L1 feature is marked and a target one is unmarked; (ii) an L1 feature is unmarked and a target one is marked; (iii) both an L1 feature and a target one are marked; and (iv) both an L1 feature and a target one are unmarked. In every possible pair of the feature specification, it is expected under FTFL that the relevant L1 feature should be transferred to transitional grammar in the early stage of the L2 learning thanks to *Feature Transfer*; however, depending on the combination of an L1 and a target feature specification, *Feature Learning* cannot take place even later in the course of the L2 learning. In the following subsections, we will give a full account of the application of FTFL in each and every case of the combination of an L1 and a target feature specification.

2.3.1.   Transferred and Overwritten

In this subsection, let us consider how to apply FTFL to the situation where an L1 feature is different from a target one with respect to the markedness of its feature specification. Consider the following: An L1 feature is marked and a target one is unmarked, as shown in (2.3) and (2.4) below (As previously noted in § 2.2, unmarked features are divided into two categories: A target feature is strictly specified, as shown in (2.3), or a target feature is partially specified, as shown in (2.4)):

(2.3) L1 *Marked* and Target *Unmarked* (strictly specified):
Transferred and overwritten

Stage in L2 Learning	L1 Feature Inventory	TG(Beginner/ Intermediate)	TG (Advanced)	Target Item
earlier	{Ø}⎯⎯⎯	⟶ Ø		
later		Ø ⇒	(+) ◂------	+

Notes.* FEATURE TRANSFER : (⎯⎯⎯⟶) FEATURE LEARNING : (◂--------)
TG=transitional grammar
The L1 value changes to the target value later in transitional grammar.

(2.4) L1 *Marked* and Target *Unmarked* (partially specified):
Transferred and overwritten

Stage in L2 Learning	L1 Feature Inventory	TG(Beginner/ Intermediate)	TG (Advanced)	Target Item
earlier	{Ø}⎯⎯⎯	⟶ Ø		
later		Ø ⇒	(−) ◂------	−

The L1 value changes to the target value later in transitional grammar.

First, how to read a chart in FTFL is explained in order: *L1 Feature Inventory* indicates what kind of feature specification of the relevant lexical item(s) an L2 learner has in the featural inventory as his/her L1 knowledge. Notice here that we try to indicate the L1 feature inventory for each syntactic formal feature utilizing the notion of the set (e.g., {Ø}). Under FTFL, which is conceptually based on the specification/value of syntactic formal features, any lexical item is not deemed to be a source of transfer. Next, *TG* means transitional grammar. *Beginner/Intermediate* learners are regarded as in the early stage in the course of the L2 learning, and *Advanced* learners are regarded as in the later stage in their L2 learning. The straight line from left to right (i.e., from the L1feature inventory to transitional grammar of beginner/intermediate) indicates *Feature Transfer*, which is assumed to take place in the early stage in transitional grammar. The dotted lines from right to left (i.e., from the target item to transitional grammar of advanced learners) indicate *Feature Learning*, which is assumed to take place in the

CHAPTER 2 THEORY OF FEATURE TRANSFER / FEATURE LEARNING

later stage in transitional grammar. Notice here that the transferred feature (i.e., in (2.3) and (2.4)) in transitional grammar of beginner/intermediate learners should be overwritten by the specification of the target item (i.e., Ø changes to + (as shown in (2.3)) or Ø changes to − (as shown in (2.4))) when Feature Learning takes place.

The rationale behind (2.3) and (2.4) is that, due to its perceptible transformation from the pristine state (unmarkedness), a marked feature in L1 is easier for learners to discard and reconvert to its unmarked state when the corresponding feature of the relevant item in the target item is unmarked.

Next, let us consider the following: An L1 feature is unmarked and a target one is marked, as shown in (2.5) and (2.6) below (Again notice that unmarked features are divided into two categories: An L1 feature is strictly specified, as shown in (2.5), or an L1 feature is partially specified, as shown in (2.6)):

(2.5) L1 *Unmarked* (strictly specified) and Target *Marked*:
       Transferred and overwritten

Stage in L2 Learning	L1 Feature Inventory	TG(Beginner/ Intermediate)	TG (Advanced)	Target Item
earlier	{+} ⟶	+		
later		+ ⟹ Ø	⟵------ Ø	

The L1 value changes to the target value later in transitional grammar.

(2.6) L1 *Unmarked* (partially specified) and Target *Marked*:
       Transferred and overwritten

Stage in L2 Learning	L1 Feature Inventory	TG(Beginner/ Intermediate)	TG (Advanced)	Target Item
earlier	{−} ⟶	−		
later		− ⟹ Ø	⟵------ Ø	

The L1 value changes to the target value later in transitional grammar.

In both cases in (2.5) and (2.6), FTFL stipulates that Feature Learning takes place later in transitional grammar of advanced learners, because L1 features (irrespective of whether it is strictly specified or partially specified) are different from the corresponding feature in the target item in terms of the markedness of their feature specification. As a result, the transferred feature (i.e., + (as shown in (2.5)) or − (as shown in (2.6))) in transitional grammar of beginner/intermediate learners should be overwritten to the specification of the target item (i.e., Ø) when Feature Learning takes place.

The rationale behind (2.5) and (2.6) is that an unmarked feature in L1 is easier for learners to overwrite/replace with a marked feature in a target item when they are provided sufficient positive evidence; for, we naturally assume that learners start to assume an unmarked value in the course of their first language acquisition (cf. Chomsky 1981, and Gair 1988).

2.3.2. Transferred and Retained

In the previous subsection, we have argued that Feature Learning takes place later in the learning when an L1 feature is distinct from a target feature in terms of the markedness of its specification. Let us consider the situations where L1 feature and a target feature are the same with respect to the markedness of their feature specification. Look at the following example: An L1 feature and a target feature are both marked (i.e., underspecified), it is naturally expected that the relevant feature in transitional grammar turns out to be underspecified (see (2.7) below):

(2.7)   L1 *Marked* and Target *Marked* : Transferred and retained

Stage in L2 Learning	L1 Feature Inventory	TG(Beginner/ Intermediate)	TG (Advanced)	Target Item
earlier	{Ø} ⟶	Ø		
later		Ø	Ø	Ø

FTFL therefore stipulates that Feature Learning does not take place in the case where an L1 feature and a target feature are the same in terms of the markedness of their specification: Consequently, an L1 feature which

CHAPTER 2   THEORY OF FEATURE TRANSFER / FEATURE LEARNING

is transferred to transitional grammar of beginner/intermediate learners should be retained in transitional grammar of advanced learners when both features are underspecified, as shown in (2.7) above.

In analogy with the case of marked features, as shown in (2.7), Feature Learning does not take place either in the case where both an L1 feature and a target feature are unmarked. For example, look at (2.8) and (2.9) below:

(2.8) L1 *Unmarked* (strictly specified) and Target *Unmarked* (strictly specified): Transferred and retained

Stage in L2 Learning	L1 Feature Inventory	TG(Beginner/ Intermediate)	TG (Advanced)	Target Item
earlier	{+}⟶	+		
later		+	+	+

No FEATURE LEARNING and the L1 value persists.

(2.9) L1 *Unmarked* (partially specified) and Target *Unmarked* (partially specified):
Transferred and retained

Stage in L2 Learning	L1 Feature Inventory	TG(Beginner/ Intermediate)	TG (Advanced)	Target Item
earlier	{−}⟶	−		
later		−	−	−

No FEATURE LEARNING and the L1 value persists.

Notice again that unmarked features are divided into two categories: An L1 feature and a target feature are both strictly specified, as shown in (2.8), or both are partially specified, as shown in (2.9). It is naturally expected that the relevant feature in transitional grammar turns out to be the same specification as the L1 and the target features.

Of particular interest here is: What will be theoretically predicted under FTFL when an L1 feature is the same as a target feature in terms of the markedness of its specification, whereas the L1 feature is distinct from the target feature in terms of its specification/value? To be more precise, look at the following examples, as shown in (2.10) and (2.11) below:

(2.10) L1 *Unmarked* (strictly specified) and Target *Unmarked* (partially specified): Transferred and retained

Stage in L2 Learning	L1 Feature Inventory	TG(Beginner/ Intermediate)	TG (Advanced)	Target Item
earlier	{+}⟶	+		
later		+	(+)	−

No FEATURE LEARNING and the L1 value persists.

(2.11) L1 *Unmarked* (partially specified) and Target *Unmarked* (strictly specified): Transferred and retained

Stage in L2 Learning	L1 Feature Inventory	TG(Beginner/ Intermediate)	TG (Advanced)	Target Item
earlier	{−}⟶	−		
later		−	(−)	+

No FEATURE LEARNING and the L1 value persists.

As previously noted, FTFL states that Feature Learning does not take place in the case where an L1 feature and a target feature are the same in terms of the markedness of their specification: Consequently, an L1 feature which is transferred to transitional grammar of beginner/intermediate learners should be retained in transitional grammar of advanced learners when both features are unmarked, though the L1 feature (i.e., +, as shown in (2.10) above) is distinct from the target one (i.e., −, as shown in (2.10) above) in terms of its specification/value. In the situation where even though the L1 feature (i.e., −, as shown in (2.11) above) is distinct from the target one (i.e., +, as shown in (2.11) above) in terms of its specification/value, both features are the same in terms of the markedness of their specification. As a result, FTFL predicts that there is no Feature Learning and the specification/value of the transferred L1 feature is expected to be retained persistently in transitional grammar of advanced learners.

The rationale behind (2.10) and (2.11) is that an unmarked feature is harder for learners to overwrite/replace with a target feature when the target feature is also unmarked but distinct from the L1 feature in terms of the specification/value; for, it is harder for learners to discern the specification of the L1 and the target values, even though they are provided sufficient positive evidence.

Finally, we will solve the aforementioned residual issue in the previous studies on SLA by giving a theoretically natural account in line with the widely-accepted learnability theory of markedness. As noted in Chapter 1, the biggest issue which remains to be unsolved in the literature is: Which one of L1 anaphora, when L1 has more than one anaphoric expression, is to be selected as the representative L1 anaphora in the course of the L2 learning? Under FTFL, utilizing the idea of the φ-feature (de)composition, it is of no use discussing which lexical item is selected, because FTFL stipulates that a syntactic formal feature in the L1 feature inventory is indeed the target of selection. Look at (2.12) and (2.13) below:

(2.12)

Stage in L2 Learning	L1 Feature Inventory	TG(Beginner/ Intermediate)	TG (Advanced)	Target Item
earlier	{∅, +} ──────▶	+		
later		+	+	−

No FEATURE LEARNING and the L1 value persists.

(2.13)

Stage in L2 Learning	L1 Feature Inventory	TG(Beginner/ Intermediate)	TG (Advanced)	Target Item
earlier	{∅, −} ──────▶	−		
later		−	−	+

No FEATURE LEARNING and the L1 value persists.

The examples in (2.12) and (2.13) show that Feature Learning does not take place when an L1 feature and a target feature are the same in terms of the markedness of their specification. Notice here that, as shown in (2.12) above, when the L1 feature inventory includes an underspecified feature and a strictly specified one, FTFL requires that the strictly specified feature should be transferred to transitional grammar because the strictly specified feature is regarded as unmarked. Moreover, when the L1 feature inventory includes both an underspecified feature and a partially specified one, as shown in (2.13), the unmarked feature should be selected to be a target of Feature Transfer under FTFL. As a result, the partially specified feature, but not the underspecified one, is transferred to transitional grammar. FTFL thus reduces the problem in terms of the selection of L1 lexical items to the markedness of the feature specification.

The markedness of an L1 and a target feature specifications, therefore, determines whether the transferred L1 feature is retained in transitional grammar or overwritten at the later stage in transitional grammar by the corresponding target feature. How to apply FTFL to specific examples of reflexive binding in transitional grammar will be discussed in greater detail in Chapter 4. Before demonstrating that FTFL empirically consists with experimental surveys on the syntactic behaviors of reflexives in JLsE's transitional grammar, in the next chapter, we will answer the question as to what about the specification/value of each of the φ-features in reflexives in the grammar of L1 Japanese and L1 English.

Notes

1 Throughout this dissertation, '+' stands for a strictly specified feature, '−' stands for a partially specified feature, and 'Ø' stands for an underspecified feature.

2 For example, the mathematical relation of reflexivity is defined ternarily: a relation R is either reflexive or non-reflexive, and a non-reflexive relation is irreflexive or not, as a consequence, R is necessarily either of reflexive, irreflexive, or non-reflexive, but not anything else (cf. Partee et al. 1990).

3 The term 'every morphophonologically possible variation' does not mean every variation in all human languages (i.e., universally). For example, some languages, such as German, have a morphologically three-way variation for the *gender*-feature (i.e.,

CHAPTER 2   THEORY OF FEATURE TRANSFER / FEATURE LEARNING

male/female/neuter distinction), whereas English has a morphophonologically two-way variation for the *gender*-feature. Hence, the existence/absence of the neuter interpretation for English reflexives is irrelevant, under our definition of φ-specification, for the purpose of discerning whether the *gender*-feature of English reflexives is underspecified or strictly/partially specified.

4 The well-formedness of (i) below indicates that *zibun(-zisin)* even allows the neuter interpretation. This fact also supports our observation that *zibun(-zisin)* is underspecified in terms of the *gender*-feature:

(i) ^{OK}Sono   table-wa   *zibun(-zisin)*-no   omomi-ni   taekaneta.
      the   table-TOP   SELF(-self)-GEN   weight-DAT   could not bear
      'The table could not bear its own weight.'

CHAPTER 3

Φ-Feature Specification of Reflexives

In this chapter, we will show the specification/value of each φ-feature (i.e., *person*-, *gender*-, and *number*-features) in reflexives and the compositional properties of the φ-features in reflexives. Some syntactic properties of a reflexive are determined by each specification of the φ-features in a reflexive. For example, acceptability of the person-neutral interpretation in a reflexive is determined by the specification of the *person*-feature in the reflexive. It can also safely be said that acceptability of the gender-neutral interpretation in a reflexive is determined by the specification of the *gender*-feature in the reflexive, and acceptability of the number-neutral interpretation in a reflexive is determined by the specification of the *number*-feature in the reflexive. More importantly, we will argue in the following sections whether the distributive reading of a reflexive is allowed or not is determined by the specification of the *number*-feature in the reflexive.

On the other hand, it should be noted that some syntactic properties of a reflexive are determined by the compositional properties of the φ-features in reflexives. For example, under the current Binding Theory through *Agree*, the syntactic properties of the locality on the binding dependency and the subject orientation of a reflexive are induced by the φ-defectiveness of a reflexive. In the following sections, we will explain the specification/value of each φ-feature and the compositional properties of the φ-features in reflexives in order.

3.1. Neutral Interpretation and Φ-Features

As we have introduced in § 2.1, the notion of underspecification states that a feature *F* within a lexical item *LI* is underspecified iff every morphologically possible variation of *F* in a language *L* allows neutral interpretation with respect to *F*. To put it differently, when *LI* does not allow neutral interpretation with respect to *F*, *F* is not underspecified (somehow specified). It is therefore presumed that the underspecified *person*-feature in a reflexive induces the person-neutral interpretation of the reflexive and the underspecified *gender*-feature in a reflexive induces its gender-neutral interpretation, and the underspecified *number*-feature in a reflexive induces its number-neutral interpretation.

3.2. Distributive Reading and *Number*-Feature

There are two morphological variants of the Japanese reflexives in terms of the *number*-feature (i.e., the singular form *zibun(-zisin)* and the plural form *zibun-tati(-zisin)*). Now we will consider the specification of the *number*-feature in the L1 Japanese reflexives. Let us look at (3.1):

(3.1) John$_j$-ga   *zibun(-*tati)$_j$/zibun(-*tati)-zisin$_j$*-o   seme-ta.
       John-NOM   SELF(-PL)/SELF(-PL)-self-ACC   blame-PAST
       Lit. 'John blamed John.'

The plural forms of the L1 Japanese reflexives (i.e., *zibun-tati* and *zibun-tati-zisin*) disallow the singular interpretation.[1] This fact leads us to conclude that the L1 Japanese plural reflexive *zibun-tati(-zisin)* is not underspecified in terms of the *number*-feature.

    Among the syntactic properties, the neutral interpretation for a certain feature *F* is directly linked to the underspecification of *F*. Another syntactic property, which is directly linked to the specification of *F* is the distributive reading of a reflexive. We will next discuss how the specification of the

CHAPTER 3 Φ-FEATURE SPECIFICATION OF REFLEXIVES

φ-features in a reflexive defines its availability of the distributive reading. It is natural to presume that, among the φ-features, the *number*-feature plays an important role in determining the distributive reading of a reflexive.

Let us look at (3.2) below:

(3.2) [John$_k$ to Mary$_j$]-wa   (sore-zore)   *zibun(-zisin)*$_{k \otimes j}$-o
John and Mary-TOP   (each)   SELF-self-ACC
hihansi-ta.
criticize-PAST
Lit. 'John criticized John, and Mary criticized Mary.'

Zibun(-zisin) regardless of whether the overt distributive operator *sorezore* 'each' is contained in its clause or not, as shown in (3.2) above, allow the distributive reading. The singular form can be bound distributively by the plural antecedents, here *[John to Bill]*, as shown in (3.2). This fact indicates that it is not the case that the singular reflexive form *zibun(-zisin)* allows only one specific interpretation in *number* (i.e., the singular interpretation).

According to Heim (2008), a bound pronominal/reflexive enters narrow syntax without φ-features, and the morphophonological realization of its φ-features is somehow materialized (at Spell-Out) by copying them from its syntactic antecedent (namely, the DP that binds (i.e., c-commands and is co-indexed with) it in narrow syntax). Given Heim's (2008) proposal, the fact observed in (3.2) indicates that *zibun(-zisin)* is *not* strictly specified in terms of its *number*-feature; for, the antecedent that c-commands it in (3.2) is the plural DP *[John to Bill]-ga*, so that it unavoidably inherits the plurality from its antecedent. Now that the singular form of *zibun(-zisin)* can be interpreted either as singular (as in (3.1)) or as plural (as in (3.2)), it follows that it allows arbitrary free interpretation; nevertheless, its plural form *zibun-tati(-zisin)* disallows its singular interpretation, as shown in (3.1). The conclusion is that all of the morphological variations of the Japanese reflexive *zibun(-zisin)* disallow arbitrary free interpretation nor strictly fixed interpretation; whence, we arrive at the conclusion, on the basis of our three way definition, that the *number*-feature of *zibun(-zisin)* is *partially specified*.

On the other hand, Heim, Lasnik, and May (1993) report that the singular reflexives in L1 English *himself/herself* cannot permit the distributive reading, regardless of whether the distributive operator *each* overtly exists or not, as exemplified in (3.3):[2]

(3.3)   a. *John$_k$ and Bill$_j$ (each) criticized *himself*$_{k\otimes j}$.
         b. *Mary$_k$ and Jane$_j$ (each) criticized *herself*$_{k\otimes j}$.

The ill-formedness of (3.3) indicates that *himself* and *herself* in (3.3) do not have the distributive reading; that is, it cannot be interpreted as "John criticized John, and Bill criticized Bill" even with the existence of the overt distributive operator (see Heim, Lasnik and May 1993 for syntactic/semantic discussion on the ill-formedness of (3.3)).[3]

Given Heim's (2008) hypothesis, this fact leads us to conclude that the *number*-feature of the reflexives in L1 English is strictly specified; for, the antecedent that c-commands the reflexive in (3.3) is the plural DP *[John and Bill]*; resulting in the ill-formedness of the singular reflexive in (3.3). The conclusion is that the fact shown in (3.3) indicates that the L1 English reflexives are strictly specified in their *number*-feature.

3.3. Φ-Defective *vs.* Φ-Complete

Before discussing the syntactic properties of a reflexive which are induced by the compositional property of the φ-features in a reflexive, we will frame a definition of *φ-completeness*. More importantly, we would like to reinterpret the afore-defined specification as identical to the φ-featural defectiveness proposed in Burzio (1991); that is, Burzio's (1991) φ-completeness requires the featurally complete specification of a given lexical item. According, fundamentally, to Burzio (1991), we define the following: An anaphor whose φ-features are all strictly specified is ***φ-complete***; otherwise it is ***φ-defective***. To put it differently, only a lexical item whose φ-features are specified as shown in the feature composition of {+, +, +} (i.e., It has the strictly specified *person*-feature, the strictly specified *gen-*

der-feature, and the strictly specified *number*-feature). Thus, when a lexical item is endowed with at least one feature which is not strictly specified, the relevant item counts as φ-defective. Given these definitions, we will, in the following sections, provide a piece of evidence to indicate how the φ-feature completeness of reflexive items in L1 English and L1 Japanese is identified through analyzing linguistic data.

3.4. Minimalist Account for Syntactic Binding of Φ-Defective Anaphora

Under the recent minimalist syntax, not a few researchers (cf. Heinat 2008, Quicolli 2008, Gallego 2010, Ishino and Ura 2011a, Reuland 2011, to mention only a few) have proposed that a φ-defective reflexive should have its φ-features checked in order for it to be properly interpreted at LF (cf. Bouchard 1984, and Burzio 1991).

The consequence of this proposal is that the syntactic binding of (φ-defective) reflexives should be recast within the *Agree* theory under the current minimalist Probe-Goal framework (Chomsky 2004 and its subsequent work): A φ-defective reflexive must have its φ-features valued by a Probe with the whole φ-feature amalgam in order to be properly interpreted at LF (the idea which we hereafter call **AGREE THEORY OF REFLEXIVE BINDING (ATRB)** (cf. Uriagereka and Gallego 2006, and Gallego 2010)). Under ATRB, it is assumed that α binds β if they are both Goals of a single relevant Probe; otherwise, α and β are obviative. Accordingly, the binding relation between a reflexive and a DP (i.e., its antecedent) is materialized not through c-command plus referential co-indexing, as the traditional binding theory assumes, but through *Agree*. To be concrete, when a single Probe with the whole φ-feature amalgam agrees with two Goals in terms of the φ-feature checking, such as a DP and a φ-defective reflexive, the binding relation between the DP and the reflexive is successfully materialized. (See Gallego 2010 for further applications of ATRB to empirically broad data.)

3.4.1. Subject Orientation

As a concrete instantiation of ATRB, take a brief look at the subject orientation of a reflexive, which is found abound in not a few languages in the world. It is a well-known fact that the Japanese reflexives *zibun* and *zibun-zisin* have the subject orientation (cf. Kuroda 1965, and Aikawa 1999). Given Ishino and Ura's (2011a) assumption that only T with the whole φ-feature amalgam, can serve as a Probe for φ-defective reflexives, ATRB leads to the prediction that a reflexive *R* shows the subject orientation if *R* is φ-defective. This is because T always bears a probe-goal relation with the subject DP of a clause to value the nominative Case of the DP; as a consequence, both the subject DP and a φ-defective reflexive are always mediated by T with the φ-features through *Agree*, resulting in the binding relation between the subject DP and the φ-defective reflexive; whence, the subject orientation of the φ-defective reflexive follows.[4]

Interestingly, PRONOUN+*zisin* in Japanese does not have the subject orientation and *zibun* and *zibun-zisin* show the subject orientation (see Nakamura 1987, and Aikawa 1999 for further discussion). As observed elsewhere in this dissertation, PRONOUN+*zisin* is a φ-complete reflexive and, hence, it needs no agreement with T, but *zibun* and *zibun-zisin* are both φ-defective. Therefore, we can predict under ATRB that *zibun* and *zibun-zisin*, but not PRONOUN+*zisin*, show the subject orientation, the prediction which is borne out empirically.

Taking the features of a reflexive into consideration, we assume the subject orientation of a reflexive is determined through the following condition. To be precise, (α) if a reflexive is φ-defective (such as *zibun(-zisin)* in L1 Japanese, *ziji* and *ta-ziji* in L1 Chinese, and *sich(-selbst)* in L1 German), it shows the subject orientation, because T[+tense], which agrees with the subject DP in the nominatice Case, also agrees with it in the φ-features; and (β) if a reflexive is φ-complete (such as *kare-zisin* in L1 Japanese, and *himself* in L1 English), it needs no agreement in the φ-features and does not show the subject orientation. The idea, following the minimalist spirit, that the set of features is the locus/motivation of syntactic derivations in human languages and their acquisition, enables us to explain syntactic properties of a reflexive item through (de)composing the features that the relevant item is endowed with. We can therefore derive the subject orientation of a given reflexive only from its φ-feature specification without using the syntactic parameters (such as Proper Antecedent Parameter, as initially proposed by Wexler and Manzini (1987)).

3.4.2. Locality on Binding Dependency

According to the Binding Theory under the GB framework (cf. Chomsky 1981, and Chomsky and Lasnik 1993), an anaphor must be bound in its syntactically local domain (what is called "binding domain"). In the grammar of L1 English, a reflexive cannot be bound astride a clause boundary, irrespective of whether the clause is tensed or non-tensed, as exemplified in (3.4) below:

(3.4) a. *John said [that the students praised *himself*].
　　　b. *John made [the students praise *himself*].

Let us try to explain the binding dependency of a φ-defective reflexive with ATRB. Take a look at the Japanese examples in (3.5) below:

(3.5) a. Taro$_j$-wa　[Jiro$_k$-ga *zibun$_{j/k}$/zibun-zisin$_{*j/k}$/kare-zisin$_{*j/k}$*-o
　　　　Taro-TOP　　Jiro-NOM　SELF/SELF-self/him-self-ACC
　　　　mi-ta　　to]　omot-ta.
　　　　see-PAST　C　　think-PAST
　　　　Lit. 'Taro thought that Jiro saw SELF/SELF-self/himself.'

　　　b. Taro$_j$-wa　[Jiro$_k$-ni　*zibun$_{j/k}$/zibun-zisin$_{j/k}$/kare-zisin$_{*j/k}$*-o
　　　　Taro-TOP　　Jiro-DAT　　SELF/SELF-self/him-self-ACC
　　　　mi]-sase]-ta.
　　　　see-CAUSE-PAST
　　　　Lit. 'Taro made Jiro see SELF/SELF-self/himself.'

The Japanese reflexive form *zibun-zisin* shows LC when it is embedded within a tensed clause (as the ill-formedness of (3.5a) shows),[5] but it shows LD when it is embedded within a non-tensed clause (as the well-formedness of (3.5b) shows),[6] the observation which was first reported in Kuroda (1965) but has long been neglected since then.[7] In contrast, the Japanese reflexive form, PRONOUN+*zisin* (such as *kare-zisin*), cannot be bound over a clause boundary, irrespective of whether it is tensed or non-tensed (namely, it shows LC everywhere), as shown by the ill-formedness of both (3.5a) and (3.5b).

Given that *zibun-zisin* is φ-defective but PRONOUN+*zisin* is φ-complete, the facts shown in (3.5) can be explained as in the following way: Following, basically, Kitagawa's (1986) idea about the Japanese causative clause, which is non-tensed, takes two types of clausal complement: One corresponds to vP without T, and the other corresponds to TP[-tense] with the whole φ-feature amalgam. When the causative clause is vP, a reflexive within the causative clause must have its φ-features checked by T[+tense] in the superordinate/matrix tensed clause, as shown in (3.6) below:

(3.6) Locality of Binding Dependency for a Φ-Defective (Complex) Reflexive in the vP-type Causative Clause

(linear order is irrelevant)

$[_{CP} [_{TP} DP_2 \quad T_{[+tense, \varphi]} \ldots [_{vP} DP_1 \ldots [V \ldots REF_{[\varphi\text{-def}]}]]]]$

As required, this results in the binding relation between the φ-defective reflexive $REF_{[\varphi\text{-def}]}$ in the embedded non-tensed causative clause and the subject DP_2 in the superordinate tensed clause, which has had its Case valued by T[+tense] in the tensed clause.[8]

When, on the other hand, the causative clause has T_1[-tense] with the whole φ-feature amalgam, the reflexive within the causative clause has its φ-features checked by the T_1[-tense] within the causative clause, because the T_1[-tense] within the causative clause is the nearest to the reflexive among the possible Probes for the φ-defective reflexive, as shown in (3.7) below:

CHAPTER 3 Φ-FEATURE SPECIFICATION OF REFLEXIVES

(3.7) Locality of Binding Dependency for a Φ-Defective (Complex) Reflexive in the TP-type Causative Clause

(linear order is irrelevant)

[$_{CP2}$ [$_{TP2}$ DP$_2$ T$_{2[+\text{tense}, \varphi]}$ ... [$_{TP1}$ DP$_1$ T$_{1[-\text{tense}, \varphi]}$ [$_{vP}$ [V ... REF$_{[\varphi\text{-def}]}$]]]]]]

Notice again that it is not always the case that every T, whether it is [+tense] or [-tense], can provide its φ-features to a φ-defective reflexive. Whether T has the φ-features with the checking ability (we call it *active* T with respect to its φ-features) or not (we call it *inactive* T with respect to its φ-features) is important. If T is active with respect to its φ-features, it can provide its φ-features to a φ-defective reflexive. On the other hand, if T is inactive with respect to its φ-features, it cannot provide the φ-features to a φ-defective reflexive. Throughout this dissertation, we presume that inactive T counts as a defective element that plays the role of invoking an intervention effect on the checking relation between the matrix T and a reflexive in the embedded CP. Accordingly, it blocks the agreement between the matrix T and a reflexive within the embedded clause. In the case where T is inactive and a relevant φ-defective reflexive is a complex form (such as *zibun-zisin*), the derivation crashes at LF, because the φ-defective reflexive cannot be properly interpreted at LF. If a φ-defective reflexive is a simplex form (such as *zibun*), we assume, following Katada (1991), that it can undergo LF movement. As a result, it can move up to the matrix T to get provided with the φ-features even when the embedded T structurally intervenes between the matrix T and the original/base-generated position of the reflexive within the embedded clause. With respect to active T, we will discuss, in detail, the φ-checking ability of T at a post Spell-Out level in § 5.2.

The well-formed schema in (3.7) depicts the binding relation between the φ-defective reflexive and the causee DP$_1$ within the non-tensed causative clause. The causee DP$_1$ has had its Case valued by T$_1$[-tense] within the non-tensed causative clause, because the T$_1$[-tense] within the non-tensed causative clause has the whole φ-feature amalgam and acts as the Probe for the causee's Case-valuation in the causative clause. We can, thus, explicate the ambiguity concerning the binder of *zibun-zisin* in (3.5b); that is, we can explain why *zibun-zisin* in (3.5b) can be bound either by the subject DP_2 in the superordinate tensed clause or by the causee DP_1 within the non-tensed causative clause. This explains the LD-property of *zibun-zisin* in a non-tensed clause.

On the other hand, when a φ-defective reflexive is embedded within a tensed clause, the reflexive always agrees with T_1[+tense] in the embedded tensed clause that includes the reflexive; for, T_1[+tense], which has the whole φ-feature amalgam, is the nearest to the φ-defective reflexive among any other possible T_2[+tense] within the whole sentence, as shown in (3.8) below:

(3.8) Locality of Binding Dependency for a Φ-Defective (Complex) Reflexive in a Tensed Clause

(linear order is irrelevant)

$[_{CP2} [_{TP2} DP_2 \ T_{2[+tense, \varphi]} \cdots [_{CP1} [_{TP1} DP_1 \ T_{1[+tense, \varphi]} [_{vP} [\ V \ \ldots \ REF_{[\varphi\text{-def}]}]]]]]]$

The minimality condition does not allow T_2[+tense] in the matrix clause to agree with the reflexive in the embedded CP. This explains the LC-property of *zibun-zisin* in a tensed clause.[9]

As for PRONOUN+*zisin*, which we already concluded to be φ-complete, it does not need to agree with T under ATRB. Following Aikawa (1993), we propose to assume that PRONOUN+*zisin* is a reflexivizer à la Reinhart and Reuland (1993) and the binding relation between PRONOUN+*zisin* and its antecedent is materialized through co-argumenthood. Given this, the LC-property of PRONOUN+*zisin* in any context follows naturally, just like the LC-property of the English reflexives in the grammar of L1 English (see Reinhart and Reuland 1993).[10]

To sum up, the locality on the binding domain is parametrically determined through the following two conditions; namely, (i) the φ-completeness of a reflexive and (ii) its morphological complexity. To be exact, (α) if a reflexive is φ-defective and morphologically simplex (such as the *zibun*-type), it can move at LF to cross over a tensed clause boundary. As a result, it can be bound by the superordinate/matrix subject DP even when it is in the embedded tensed clause; (β) if a reflexive is φ-defective and morphologically complex (such as the *zibun-zisin*-type), it must stay in situ and cannot cross over a tensed clause boundary; however, matrix T agrees with it when it is embedded in a non-tensed clause without T. As a result, it cannot be bound by the superordinate/matrix subject DP when it is in the embedded tensed clause, but it can be bound by a long-distant DP only when it is embedded in a non-tensed clause without T; and (γ) if a reflexive is φ-complete (such as the *kare-zisin*-type), it behaves like a reflexivizer and is always locally bound. Given that the locality on the binding dependency of a given reflexive can be explained through the locality of *Agree*, we can therefore derive the locality of a reflexive relying only on the feature specification of the given reflexive and its morphological complexity without use of the syntactic parameters, which we regard as conceptually unnecessary.

3.5. Summary on Φ-Feature Specification

3.5.1. L1 English Reflexives

As previously observed in § 2.1.2, the English reflexives are strictly specified in terms of their *person*-features. Moreover, the third-person singular reflexives in L1 English are strictly specified with respect to their *gender*-features, as shown in (3.9) below:

(3.9) a. The man$_k$ criticized ^{ok}*himself$_k$* / **herself$_k$*.
       b. The woman$_j$ criticized **himself$_j$* / ^{ok}*herself$_j$*.

The ill-formed examples in (3.9) show that, in the grammar of L1 English, (i) the third-person, singular, female reflexive *herself* cannot be bound by the third-person, singular, male antecedent; and (ii) the third-person, singular, male reflexive *himself* cannot be bound by the third-person singular female antecedent. From these facts, it can be said that no arbitrarily free interpretation in terms of the *gender*-feature is allowed for the L1

English third-person, singular reflexives. It follows that the *gender*-features of the L1 English third-person, singular reflexives are *not* underspecified. The ill-formed examples in (3.9) show that the third-person, singular, male reflexives only allow the male interpretation, and the third-person, singular, female reflexives only allow the female interpretation; that is, their interpretation in *gender* is unarily fixed as their morphological shapes demonstrate. Because the English reflexives have only two morphological variants in terms of the *gender*-features (i.e., *himself* and *herself*), the above fact that these third-person singular reflexives in L1 English allow a unarily fixed interpretation shows that the L1 English reflexives are strictly specified in terms of their *gender*-features. Thus, we conclude, from these observations, that the *person*-features and the *gender*-features within the L1 English reflexives are strictly specified; that is, they do not allow the *person*-neutral and *gender*-neutral interpretations.

The English third-person, singular reflexive *himself* does not permit the distributive reading, as observed in (3.3) above (repeated as (3.10) below):

(3.10) *[John$_j$ and Bill$_k$] criticized *himself*$_{j\otimes k}$.

The conclusion we have so far reached from the observation in (3.10) is that the English reflexive is strictly specified in terms of its *number*-feature.

To sum up, all of the φ-features in the English reflexives are strictly specified. The English reflexives hence count as φ-complete. As a result, they do not show the subject orientation, and they always show LC when they are embedded either in a tensed or a non-tensed clause. The specification of each φ-feature of the L1 English reflexives and their syntactic properties are summarized in (3.11) below:

(3.11) *L1 English*
    a. John$_j$ said that Bill$_k$ blamed *himself*$_{*j/k}$.
    b. John$_j$ told Bill$_k$ about *himself*$_{j/k}$.
    c. I$_i$ / You$_j$ / He$_k$ criticized *himself*$_{*i/*j/k}$.
    c'. He$_k$ / She$_h$ criticized *himself*$_{k/*h}$.

CHAPTER 3 Φ-FEATURE SPECIFICATION OF REFLEXIVES

   c". He_k / They_l criticized $\textit{himself}_{k/*l}$.
   d. *[John_j and Bill_k] criticized $\textit{himself}_{j \otimes k}$.   (Heim, Lasnik and May 1993)

L1 English	himself
(i) morphology	complex
(ii) φ-features	
person	+
gender	+
number	+
(iii) φ-completeness	φ-complete
(iv) syntactic properties	reflexivizer
Subject Orientation	no
Binding Dependency Tensed/Non-tensed	LC / LC
Distributive Reading	no

3.5.2. L1 Japanese Reflexives

As previously obserbed in § 2.1.1, the L1 Japanese reflexive *zibun(-zisin)* is underspecified in terms of the *person-/gender*-features. The *number*-feature of *zibun(-zisin)* is partially specified, however, as we have demonstrated in § 3.2. A comment on the other reflexive form in Japanese is in order: How about the featural specification of the φ-features within PRONOUN+*zisin* in the grammar of L1 Japanese? Its *person-* and *gender*-features are strictly specified; for, a pronominal prefix (e.g., *watasi* 'I', *anata* 'you', and *kare* 'he'), which has a fully specified featural morphology, is attached to *zisin* ('self'). With respect to its *number*-feature, PRONOUN+*zisin* (such as *kare-zisin*) is not tolerable with the distributive reading, as the ill-formedness of (3.12) shows:

  (3.12) *[John_k to Bill_h]-ga (sore-zore) $\textit{kare-zisin}_{k \otimes h}$-nituite katat-ta.
           John and Bill-NOM   each   himself   about   talk-PAST
           Lit. 'John talked about John, and Bill talked about Bill.'

The conclusion we have reached is that PRONOUN+*zisin* in L1 Japanese is strictly specified in terms of its *number*-feature; for, it disallows the distributive reading. From our observations that PRONOUN+*zisin* in L1 Japanese is strictly specified with respect to its *person*-, *gender*-, and *number*-features, it follows that PRONOUN+*zisin* in L1 Japanese is a φ-complete reflexive in the sense of Burzio (1991). PRONOUN+*zisin* in L1 Japanese hence counts as φ-complete. As a result, it does not show the subject orientation, and it always shows LC when it is embedded either in a tensed or a non-tensed clause. The specification of each φ-feature in the L1 Japanese reflexives and their syntactic properties are summarized in (3.13) below:

(3.13) *L1 Japanese*

    a. John$_j$-ga   [Bill$_k$-ga   *zibun$_{j/k}$/zibun-zisin$_{*j/k}$/kare-zisin$_{*j/k}$*-o
       John-NOM   Bill-NOM   SELF/SELF-self/he-self-ACC
       seme-ta   to]   it-ta.
       blame-PAST   C   say-PAST
       Lit. 'John said that Bill blamed SELF.'

    b. John$_j$-ga   Bill$_k$-ni   *zibun$_{j/*k}$/zibun-zisin$_{j/*k}$/kare-zisin$_{j/k}$*
       John-NOM   Bill-DAT   SELF/SELF-self/he-self
       nituite   hanashi-ta.
       about   tell-PAST
       Lit. 'John told Bill about SELF.'   (Aikawa 1999)

    c. [Watasi$_i$/Anata$_j$/Kare$_k$]-ga   *zibun(-zisin)$_{i/j/k}$/kare-zisin$_{*i/*j/k}$*-o
       I   /you   /he-NOM   SELF(-self)/he-self-ACC
       seme-ta.
       blame-PAST
       Lit. 'I/you/he blamed SELF.'

    c'. [Kare$_k$/Kanojo$_h$]-ga   *zibun(-zisin)$_{k/h}$/kare-zisin$_{k/*h}$*-o
       he   /she -NOM   SELF(-self)/he-self-ACC
       seme-ta.
       blame-PAST

CHAPTER 3   Φ-FEATURE SPECIFICATION OF REFLEXIVES

Lit. 'He/She blamed SELF.'

c". John$_j$-ga   zibun(-*tati)$_j$/zibun(-*tati)-zisin$_j$/kare(*ra)-zisin$_j$-o
John-NOM   SELF(-PL)/SELF(-PL)-self/he(-PL)-self -ACC
seme-ta.
blame-PAST
Lit. 'John blamed SELF.'[11]

d. [John$_j$ to Bill$_k$]-ga ^{OK}zibun$_{j\otimes k}$/^{OK}zibun-zisin$_{j\otimes k}$/*kare-zisin$_{j\otimes k}$-o
John and Bill-NOM   SELF/SELF-self/he-self-ACC
seme-ta.
blame-PAST
Lit. 'John blamed John, and Bill blamed Bill.'

(Katada 1991)

L1 Japanese	zibun	zibun-zisin	kare-zisin
(i) morphology	simplex	complex	complex
(ii) φ-features			
person	∅	∅	+
gender	∅	∅	+
number	−	−	+
(iii) φ-completeness	φ-defective	φ-defective	φ-complete
(iv) syntactic properties	syntactic binding	syntactic binding	reflexivizer
Subject Orientation	yes	yes	no
Binding Dependency[12] Tensed/Non-tensed	LD / LD	LC / LD	LC / LC
Distributive Reading	yes	yes	no

Recall here that, as previously mentioned in § 1.8.2, the L1 feature inventory of Japanese learners includes the featural composition of *zibun(-zisin)* (i.e., {∅, ∅, −}), but not the φ-composition of PRONOUN+*zisin* (i.e., {+, +,

+}); for, PRONOUN+*zisin* is a φ-complete reflexive and is irrelevant to the application of FTFL with respect to their learning of the English reflexives.

Notes

1. It is true that (3.1) is acceptable when *zibun* is used logophorically; namely, the *group reading* of *zibun* (i.e., 'John blamed the group of [John and someone else].') is available, but this dissertation aims to investigate the L2 learning of syntactic binding and the logophoric/emphatic use of a reflexive is neglected throughout this dissertation.
2. One might wonder whether the distributive operator has some influence on the contrast between (3.2) and (3.3); however, what is empirically significant here is the fact that the Japanese example allows the distributive reading without the distributive operator, whereas the English counterpart disallows it without the distributive operator. The conclusion we draw from these facts is that the existence of the distributive operator has nothing to do with the distributive reading for a reflexive, as we maintain in the text.
3. In fact, it seems that the following English sentence, entailing "John saw John, and Bill saw Bill," can be said to have the distributive reading:
    (i) ok[John and Bill] saw *themselves* in the mirror.
   But, as Langendoen (1978) and Langendoen and Magloire (2003) argue, this distributive reading can be generated as a logical implication from the reading "[John and Bill]$_I$ saw [John and Bill]$_I$," the reading which is brought out when the reflexive is bound by the conjoined plural DP *[John and Bill]* as a whole. In other words, the ostensibly distributive reading in (i) is attributed not to the defectiveness of the *number*-feature of the reflexive in (i), but to the reflexive's plurality (see Langendoen and Magloire 2003). It should be noted, here, that the Japanese sentence in (3.2), with which we claimed the truly distributive reading is concerned, does not have the plural reading (i.e., it does not mean "[John and Bill]$_I$ criticized [John and Bill]$_I$"); consequently, the distributive reading in (3.2) comes not from the reflexive's plurality, but from the defectiveness of the *number*-feature of the reflexive in (3.2).
4. We omit going into any detail about ATRB, for which the reader is referred to the extensive discussion presented in Gallego (2010).
5. 'LC' is used herein to mean the local binding where a reflexive and its antecedent are within a same clause.
6. 'LD' is used herein to mean the long-distant binding over a clause boundary.
7. It has widely been alleged in the literature on Japanese syntax that *zibun-zisin*, one of the morphologically complex reflexives in Japanese, shows the same binding dependency as PRONOUN+*zisin* does; namely, it shows LC in every context (cf. Nakamura 1987, and Katada 1991), though Kitagawa (1986) and Manning et al. (1999) endorsed

CHAPTER 3   Φ-FEATURE SPECIFICATION OF REFLEXIVES

Kuroda's (1965) observation. Through polling more than 200 native Japanese speakers, including more than 20 linguistic professionals, Ishino and Ura (2009) revealed (i) that more than 90% of them judge that (3.5a) is strictly unacceptable, and (ii) that 75% of those who judge (3.5a) as unacceptable judge that *zibun-zisin* in (3.5b) is far better than (3.5a) though *kare-zisin* in (3.5b) is as bad as (3.5a). For much extensive discussion, see Ishino and Ura (2009).

8   As we argued above, it is because φ-defective reflexives must be interpreted properly at LF that they must be provided with the full specification of φ-features through Agree by T. Here, we assume that Agree between a φ-defective reflexive and T is executed at LF, where Spell-Out has already been executed. Thus, a phase, which is the domain of Spell-Out, is irrelevant to Agree between a φ-defective reflexive and T.

9   We assume that *zibun*, another φ-defective reflexive in Japanese, shows the same locality as *zibun-zisin* shows; however, *zibun*, which is a simplex form, can move at LF due to its morphological property (cf. Katada 1991). Thanks to the morphological simplicity of *zibun*, it can undergo a long-distant LF movement over a tensed clause boundary. As a result, even when it is embedded in a tensed clause, it can be bound by the subject DP in the superordinate clause. On the other hand, *zibun-zisin* cannot move because of its lexical integrity. As a result, it shows LC in a tensed clause. We will discuss in detail the movement property of the morphologically simplex reflexive *zibun* in L1 Japanese and that of *sich* in L1 German in § 5.2.

10   We purposely neglect the logophoric use of reflexives throughout this dissertation.

11   (3.14c'') is acceptable when *zibun* is used logophorically in that the *group reading* of *zibun* (i.e., 'John blamed the group of [John and someone else].') is available, but this dissertation aims to investigate the L2 acquisition of syntactic binding and the logophoric/emphatic use of a reflexive is neglected throughout this dissertation.

12   The difference between *zibun* and *zibun-zisin* in their binding dependencies comes not from their featural properties, but exclusively from their morphological complexities (see Faltz 1977, Katada 1991, and Ishino and Ura 2011a for further discussion). See footnote 9 above.

CHAPTER 4

Φ-Feature Specification of TG Reflexives: Prediction by FTFL and Experimental Results

For our theory of FTFL, it is important to clarify the specification of the reflexives in JLsE's transitional grammar; nevertheless, no experimental/empirical data for our purpose of explicating it have been reported in the literature. Accordingly, we have conducted experimental surveys for this purpose, with which we will deal minutely in this chapter. Before revealing the syntactic properties of the English reflexives in the transitional grammar of JLsE, we will deductively demonstrate the specification of the φ-features in the English reflexives in the transitional grammar of JLsE through FTFL.[1]

4.1. Prediction of the L2 Learning of the English Reflexives by Japanese Learners of English (JLsE)

Look at (4.1) below:

(4.1)

(i) level		L1 Japanese	TG *himself*		Target English *himself*
			Beginner/ Intermediate	(High-intermediate) / Advanced	
(ii)	φ-features				
	person	{Ø} ⟶	Ø ⟹	+ ⟵ -----	+
	gender	{Ø} ⟶	Ø ⟹	+ ⟵ -----	+
	number	{−} ⟶	−	(−)	+
(iii)	φ-completeness		φ-defective (*a*)	φ-defective (*b*)	φ-complete
(iv)	syntactic properties		syntactic binding	syntactic binding	reflexivizer
	Subject Orientation		yes (*c*)	yes (*d*)	no
	Binding Dependency tensed/non-tensed		LC / LD (*e*)	LC / LD (*f*)	LC / LC
	Distributive Reading		yes (*g*)	yes (*h*)	no

It should be noticed here that, in the case of JLsE, their L1 feature inventory consists of the *person*-feature which is underspecified, as indicated by the set of {Ø} in (4.1), the *gender*-feature which is also underspecified, as indicated by the set of {Ø} in (4.1), and the *number*-feature which is partially specified, as indicated by the set of {−} in (4.1). Notice again that the feature specification of the marked reflexive in L1 Japanese, such as PRONOUN+*zisin*, is not at all involved in their L1 feature inventory. As we have discussed in § 3.3, it is stipulated, according, fundamentally, to Burzio (1991), that a reflexive whose φ-features are all strictly specified counts as a reflexivizer because of its φ-completeness. Accordingly, the Japanese reflexive PRONOUN+*zisin* is not a φ-defective anaphor whose syntactic properties are determined by the feature binding through *Agree* by T. To put it differently, the feature specification of a φ-defective anaphor is the only source of our consideration.

CHAPTER 4 Φ-FEATURE SPECIFICATION OF TG REFLEXIVES

4.1.1. *Person*-Neutral Interpretation

Next, let us consider how to apply FTFL to the English reflexives in the transitional grammar of JLsE. First, with respect to the *person*-feature, an L1 feature is different from a target one in terms of the markedness of its feature specification; that is, the L1 feature which is underspecified is marked, but the target feature which is strictly specified is unmarked, as previously indicated in (2.3) (repeated as (4.2) below):

(4.2) L1 *Marked* and Target *Unmarked* (strictly specified):
Transferred and overwritten

Stage in L2 Learning	L1 Feature Inventory	TG (Beginner/ Intermediate)	TG (Advanced)	Target Item
earlier	{Ø} ⟶	Ø		
later		Ø	⟹ (+) ⬅------	+

Notes. *FEATURE TRANSFER: (⟶) FEATURE LEARNING: (⬅------)
The L1 value changes to the target value later in transitional grammar.

FTFL therefore demands that the *person*-feature in the English reflexives in the transitional grammar of beginner/intermediate JLsE be underspecified due to Feature Transfer, but that of the English reflexives in the transitional grammar of advanced JLsE turns out to be strictly specified thanks to Feature Learning, which stipulates that the L1 feature should be overwritten/replaced by the target feature when the L1 feature is distinct from the target one in terms of its markedness, and, thus, it is expected that advanced JLsE do not regard the English reflexives as having the *person*-neutral interpretation.

4.1.2. *Gender*-Neutral Interpretation

The *gender*-feature in the L1 feature inventory of JLsE is also different from a target one in terms of the markedness of its feature specification; that is, the L1 feature which is underspecified is marked, but the target feature which is strictly specified is unmarked. It is also predicted under FTFL that the *gender*-feature in the English reflexives in the transitional grammar of beginner/intermediate JLsE is underspecified due to Feature Transfer, but that of the English reflexives in the transitional grammar of advanced JLsE turns out to be strictly specified thanks to Feature Learning. Therefore, it is expected that advanced JLsE do not regard the English reflexives as having the *gender*-neutral interpretation.

4.1.3. *Number*-Neutral Interpretation

Next, let us consider the *number*-feature. In the case of the *number*-feature in the English reflexives in the transitional grammar of JLsE, the L1 feature is the same as the target feature in terms of the markedness of its specification, whereas the L1 feature is distinct from the target feature in terms of its specification. FTFL stipulates that Feature Learning does not take place when both of the L1 features and the target one are unmarked, as previously indicated in (2.11) (repeated as (4.3) below):

(4.3) L1 *Unmarked* (partially specified) and Target *Unmarked* (strictly specified): Transferred and retained

Stage in L2 Learning	L1 Feature Inventory	TG (Beginner/ Intermediate)	TG (Advanced)	Target Item
earlier	{−} ⟶	−		
later		−	(−)	+

No FEATURE LEARNING and the L1 value persists.

Consequently, an L1 feature which is transferred to transitional grammar of beginner/intermediate learners should be retained in transitional grammar of advanced learners when the L1 feature (i.e., −, as shown in (4.3) above) is distinct from the target one (i.e., +, as shown in (4.3) above) in terms of its specification, whereas both features are the same in terms of the markedness of their specifications. Therefore, it is expected that advanced JLsE do not regard the English reflexives as having the *number*-neutral interpretation.

Of particular importance here is: As a consequence of FTFL, the feature specification of the English reflexives in the transitional grammar of advanced JLsE is expected to be the feature composition of {+,+,−},

CHAPTER 4 Φ-FEATURE SPECIFICATION OF TG REFLEXIVES

which means that the English reflexives in their transitional grammar have the strictly specified *person*-feature, the strictly specified *gender*-feature, and the partially specified *number*-feature. Insofar as FTFL is theoretically correct, moreover, we reach the conclusion that the English reflexives in their transitional grammar are *φ-defective* due to the partially specified *number*-feature.

Our conclusion that JLsE's transitional reflexives are φ-defective brings theoretically important consequences, which we will discuss in what follows. From this conclusion, what else is predictable concerning the syntactic behaviors of JLsE's TG reflexives?

4.1.4. Locality on Binding Dependency

As we have argued in § 3.4.2, under ATRB, the locality on the binding dependency of a φ-defective anaphor is determined through *Agree* by T with the whole φ-feature amalgam. That is, if a relevant reflexive is φ-defective, it needs to be supplied with the φ-features to be properly interpreted. ATRB states that a φ-defective anaphor can be bound by a matrix subject DP through *Agree* by a matrix T[+tense] with the whole φ-feature amalgam only when the relevant anaphor is located in the embedded non-tensed clause (such as, a causative clause), whereas a φ-defective anaphor cannot be bound by a matrix subject DP when it is located in the embedded tensed clause due to the minimality effect.

In the previous subsections, it is demonstrated under FTFL that the English reflexives in the transitional grammar of JLsE are expected to be φ-defective, as shown in (*a*) and (*b*) in (4.1). FTFL therefore predicts that the English reflexives in the transitional grammar of JLsE are expected to be locally bound when they are embedded in a tensed clause, whereas they are expected to be able to be bound by a long-distant antecedent over a clause boundary when they are embedded in a non-tensed clause, as shown in (*e*) and (*f*) in (4.1).

FTFL predicts the set of the φ-feature specification, so that the feature compoisition of *himself* in the transitional grammar is {Ø,Ø,−} for beginner/intermediate JLsE and the feature compoisition of *himself* is {+,+,−} for (high-intermediate)/advanced JLsE. Note that their specifications indicate that both of them are φ-defective through applying the idea utilizing the φ-feature composition in FTFL. Given that *himself* in the transitional grammar of JLsE is φ-defective, one might conjecture that *himself* in the transitional grammar of JLsE behaves like *zibun*, which also has the feature compoisition of {∅,∅,−} and is φ-defective. Recall here, as we have argued in § 3.4.2, that the morphological complexity of a φ-defective reflexive is another essential condition in determining its locality on the binding dependency. To be concrete, it is assumed that a φ-defective and complex reflexive cannot move like *zibun*, which is a φ-defective simplex reflexive. The morphological complexity of a given reflexive (whether it is complex or simplex) can be easily detected for learners. Insofar as JLsE can detect the morphological complexity of the English reflexive *himself*, *himself* in their transitional grammar cannot move at LF and stays in situ. It follows that it shows LC in a tensed clause but LD in a non-tensed clause.

4.1.5. Subject Orientation

Another significant consequence of ATRB is the subject orientation; for, T with the whole φ-feature amalgam agrees not only with a φ-defective reflexive but also obligatorily with a subject of the relevant clause where T is merged for the Case reason. To put it differently, if a reflexive is φ-defective, it shows the subject orientation. For example, φ-defective reflexives, such as *zibun(-zisin)* in L1 Japanese and *ziji* and *ta-ziji* in L1 Chinese are subject oriented. On the other hand, φ-complete reflexives, such as *kare-zisin* in L1 Japanese and *himself* in L1 English do not show the subject orientation. FTFL therefore predicts that the English reflexives in the transitional grammar of JLsE are expected to show the subject orientation, as shown in (*c) and (*d) in (4.1).

4.1.6. Distributive Reading

In the previous § 4.1.3, we have demonstrated that FTFL predicts that the English reflexives in the transitional grammar of JLsE are initially expected to be partially specified in terms of the *number*-feature due to Feature Transfer from the L1 feature inventory. FTFL also predicts that the English reflexives in the transitional grammar of advanced JLsE are persistently expected to have the *number*-feature which is partially specified; for, the target feature in L1 *himself* is strictly specified and also unmarked.

Given that a reflexive allows the distributive reading only when its *number*-feature is not strictly specified, as we have argued in § 3.2, it is predicted under FTFL that advanced JLsE are persistently expected to allow the English reflexives in the transitional grammar to have the distributive reading, as shown in (*g) and (*h) in (4.1).

In what follows, it will be demonstrated that either of the previous approaches (PRA nor LTA) fails to predict all the significant syntactic properties of the English reflexives in the transitional grammar of JLsE that FTFL can precisely predicts.

4.2. Empirical Problems in Predictions by Previous Studies (PRA and LTA)

According to the advocates for PRA, the reason why it is rather hard for JLsE to acquire the correct parameter value for the English reflexives stems from the fact that the Japanese value includes the English one as a proper subset; the instance which is, according to the Subset Principle, rather hard for learners to acquire only with positive evidence. There also remains a crucial methodological problem of PRA; namely, the parameter value for the representative L1 reflexive *zibun*. Now we argue that any micro-parameter resetting approach cannot coherently explain the syntactic mechanism observed in the course of the L2 learning of reflexives. The proponents of PRA follow the idea that language L is individually assigned its distinctive parameter value under GCP. It should be noted here that Wexler and Manzini (1987) originally propose a lexical parameterization hypothesis: All anaphors in language L are not assigned the same parameter value, where the language L has more than one anaphor. The proponents of PRA found their theoretical rationale upon the notion of GCP with the misconception that GCP is one of the micro-parameters (i.e., language-specific parameters). Moreover, under GCP, the parameter value for the locality on the binding dependency of L1 *zibun* is the most unmarked value among the parameters of GCP. If L1 *zibun* is selected by JLsE and regarded as the parameter value for the binding domain of the representative L1 reflexivs (i.e., the value (e) of GCP), which is the most unmarked one among the five possible parameter values, the parameter value for the binding domain of the target English reflexives (i.e., the value (a) of GCP) turns out to be the least restrictive one. We should notice that the problem here is that it can be said that all possible experimental data about the parameter value for the binding domain of the reflexives in transitional grammar are concluded to lie between the parameter value for the binding domain of their L1 and the value for that of their target language: Consequently, it is predicted that every experimental result is expected to show that JLsE reset their L1 parameter value intermediate between the value for their L1 and that for their target language. If a given hypothesis can explain all experimental results, we see it as having a methodological problem even though it is true that the explanation with PRA is pertinent to the oft-reported observation concerning the locality on binding dependency of JLsE's IL reflexives.

In addition, PRA is not consistent with explanations to other syntactic properties (such as interpretation in *person*, *gender*, or *number* and the distributive reading): Obviously, GCP is not only irrelevant to interpretation in *person*, *gender*, or *number* of a given reflexive but also irrelevant to the distributive reading of a given reflexive, and it seems highly implausible to speculate that there exists some parameters for interpretation in *person*, *gender*, or *number* and also a parameter for the distributive reading in UG. If this kind of speculation were approved, then UG would admit extremely many syntactic parameters, the number of which equates to the number of all the possible interpretations observable in UG, resulting in the collapse of the generative enterprise. To conclude, PRA cannot give a consistent account to all the syntactic properties of reflexive binding in transitional grammar. This indicates that PRA is insufficient on empirical grounds.

On the other hand, if LTA is on the right track, it is predicted that there must be a reflexive form in L1 Japanese that syntactically behaves the same as the English reflexives in the transitional grammar of JLsE; for, LTA postulates that all of the syntactic properties of the selected reflexive form in L1 are transferred and materialized in learners' IL grammar. In Chart 2 below, we make a comparison between the syntactic properties of each reflexive form in L1 Japanese, L1 English and the English reflexives in the transitional grammar of JLsE.

CHART 2. The Syntactic Properties of L1 *Japanese*/ TG / L1 *English* Reflexives

Syntactic Properties	L1 Japanese			TG	L1 English
	zibun	zibun-zisin	kare-zisin	himself	himself
(A) Locality Tensed/Non-tensed	LD/LD	LC/LD	LC/LC	LC/LD	LC/LC
(B) Subject Orientation	yes	yes	no	yes	no
(C) Neutral Interpretation					
(i) *person*-neutral	yes	yes	no	no	no
(ii) *gender*-neutral	yes	yes	no	no	no
(iii) *number*-neutral	no	no	no	no	no
(D) Distributive Reading	yes	yes	no	yes	no

Here we will briefly provide our empirical observation concerning the syntactic properties of the English reflexives in the transitional grammar of JLsE; that is, it will be revealed that (A) the English reflexives in the transitional grammar of JLsE are locally-bound within a tensed clause, but able to be bound by a long-distant antecedent over a non-tensed clause boundary; (B) they show the subject orientation; (C) they do not have the *person-/gender-/number*-neutral interpretation; and (D) they allow the distributive reading. More detailed analyses on our experimental surveys into JLsE will be provided and discussed in the next section.

Contrary to the prediction by LTA, none of the Japanese reflexive forms accords behaviorally with the English reflexives in the transitional grammar of JLsE, as can be seen in Chart 2. Therefore, this counts as an empirically serious problem for LTA, because previous proposals on the L2 acquisition of reflexive binding mostly consider the syntactic properties of a reflexive, such as the locality on the binding dependency and the subject orientation. To conclude, LTA cannot give a consistent account to all of the syntactic properties of the English reflexives in the transitional grammar of JLsE. This indicates that LTA, too, is insufficient on empirical grounds.

In addition to some conceptual problems immanent in PRA and LTA, as we have discussed in § 1.6, in this section we have so far pointed out some empirical problems immanent in both approaches respectively, each of which is too troublesome for PRA or LTA to be maintained as a plausible theory about JLsE's learning of reflexive binding. In what follows, we will demonstrate that our experimental data are all coherently explainable under our theory of the feature (de)composition of reflexives.

4.3. Experimental Results on JLsE's TG Reflexives

4.3.1. Subjects of Experiments

We first set out the following four surveying tests in order to examine (i) whether reflexives in the transitional grammar of JLsE can have the *person*-neutral interpretation (Test 1.1), (ii) whether they can have the *gender*-neutral interpretation (Test 1.2), (iii) whether they can have the *number*-neutral interpretation (Test 1.3), and (iv) whether they have the distributive reading (Test 1.4), to all of which have scarcely been paid attention in the L2 literature. Then, we next set out two follow-up tests to examine (v) whether reflexives in the transitional grammar of JLsE are subject oriented (Test 1.5) and to reconfirm (vi) the locality on their binding dependency (Test 1.6), both of which are extensively investigated in the L2 literature, as previously noted in Chapter 3.

59 university students (26 male students and 33 female students) participated in Test 1.1 to 1.3. Then, we found it necessary to disclose the *number* interpretation of the reflexives in the transitional grammar of JLsE. We therefore set out Test 1.4 to 154 university students (69 male students and 85 female students), including the abovementioned 59 students in Test 1.1 to 1.3. With respect to the follow-up tests, we set out Test 1.5 to 369 university students (208 male students and 161 female students) and Test 1.6 to 288 university students (152 male students and 136 female students), including the abovementioned 154 students in Test 1.4. All of our

CHAPTER 4   Φ-FEATURE SPECIFICATION OF TG REFLEXIVES

experimental subjects were native Japanese and had studied English as a second language for more than seven years, but none of them had lived in English-speaking countries for a short or long period of time. At the time of our experiments, they were all in the freshman year in the university and registered for a couse in linguistics. Their average age was 18.7. Their average score of TOEFL(P) (TOEFL Paper-based Test) is approximately 505. A preliminary survey conducted at the beginning of their linguistic class indicates that they have the correct capability both to discern the matrix/embedded clausal distinction and to recognize that the subject is structurally higher than the object in an active, declarative clause (that is, the subject asymmetrically c-commands the object in an ordinary clause). We therefore regard them as being at the high-intermediate level in their L2 English learning stage. In addition, we had a control group consisting of 20 native speakers of English, all of whom stayed in Japan as exchange students (they were all undergraduate students at college and their average age was 18.9).

4.3.2. Procedures of Experiments

At the time of our experimental survey, the participants were told about the aim of the experiments and their anonymity. They were given a sheet of questionnaire and were informed that their anonymous answers would be used in a linguistic research. Some couple of test sentences with a few control sentences were presented. At the top of the questionnaire, the following directions were given in Japanese: "Do it yourself without consulting with anyone," and "Answer each question within a minute, and do not hesitate and do not take time to think about." All questions were presented in the way that is called *Grammatical Judgment Test*. The following direction was given in Japanese: "If you regard each sentence as grammatical/acceptable, fill in the blank with a circle; otherwise (that is, if you regard it as ungrammatical/unacceptable), fill in the blank with a cross," Even when our experimental subjects could not determine the acceptability of a sentence, they were required to answer by intuition. Our experimental subjects were not allowed to change their answers once they filled a blank in the questionnaire.

4.3.3. Test 1.1: *Person*-Neutral Interpretation

In order to discern whether JLsE consider the *person*-feature of the English reflexives to be specified or underspecified in their transitional grammar, we presented our experimental subjects with the following test sentences, both of which are ill-formed in L1 English, as shown in (4.4) below:[2]

(4.4) a. *Bill and I hit *yourselves*.
b. *Bill likes *yourself*.

If JLE subjects regard (4.4) as acceptable, the English reflexives in the transitional grammar of JLsE are concluded to be underspecified in terms of the *person*-feature; otherwise, they are specified in terms of the *person*-feature. The result of this survey is delineated in Table 1.1:

TABLE 1.1. Acceptability of the *Person*-Neutral Interpretation

(%)	JLsE[a]	Control[b]
acceptable	*0.0*	*0.0*
unacceptable	*100.0*	*100.0*

[a]n=59. [b]n=20.

As Table 1.1 shows, 100% of our 59 JLE subjects correctly interpreted the test sentences in (4.4) as unacceptable. That is to say, none of the JLE subjects mistakenly judged that the English reflexives in their transitional grammar have the *person*-neutral interpretation, which indicates that they are either strictly or partially specified in terms of the *person*-feature. Our experimental survey further revealed that all of the experimental subjects can never interpret all of the eight variant forms (i.e., *myself, ourselves, yourself, yourselves, himself, herself, itself,* and *themselves*) as referring to any other person than the person the morphology of the respective form designates. This indicates that the English reflexives in the transitional grammar of JLsE allow only one specific interpretation (i.e., they allow a unarily fixed interpretation); therefrom, it is concluded that the *person*-feature of JLsE's TG reflexives is strictly specified.

4.3.4. Test 1.2: *Gender*-Neutral Interpretation

Next, in order to discern whether JLsE consider the *gender*-feature of the English reflexives in their transitional grammar to be specified or underspecified, we presented our experimental subjects with the test sentences in (4.5), both of which are ill-formed in the grammar of L1 English:

(4.5) a. *The girl criticized *himself.*
       b. *The boy criticized *herself.*

We intended these test sentences to make it clear whether our JLE subjects can interpret *himself* in (4.5a), for example, as being coreferential with *the girl*: If a subject can accept this interpretation, he/she regards the sentence as acceptable and the English reflexives in their transitional grammar is concluded to be underspecified in terms of the *gender*-feature; otherwise, they are specified in terms of the *gender*-feature. The result of this survey is delineated in Table 1.2:

TABLE 1.2. Acceptability of the *Gender*-Neutral Interpretation

(%)	JLsE[a]	Control[b]
acceptable	0.0	0.0
unacceptable	100.0	100.0

[a]$n=59$. [b]$n=20$.

As Table 1.2 shows, 100% of our 59 JLE subjects correctly interpreted the test sentences in (4.5) as unacceptable. That is to say, none of the JLE subjects mistakenly judged that the English reflexives in the transitional grammar have the *gender*-neutral interpretation, which indicates that they are either strictly or partially specified in terms of the *gender*-features. Our experimental survey further revealed that all of the experimental subjects can never interpret the third-person, non-neuter, singular reflexives (i.e., *himself* and *herself*) as referring to the opposite gender. This indicates that their TG reflexives allow only one specific interpretation (i.e., they allow a unarily fixed interpretation); therefrom, it is concluded that the *gender*-feature of the English reflexives in the transitional grammar of JLsE are strictly specified.

4.3.5. Test 1.3: *Number*-Neutral Interpretation and Distributive Reading

Now, in order to discern whether JLsE consider the *number*-feature of the English reflexives in their transitional grammar to be specified or underspecified, we presented our experimental subjects with the test sentences in (4.6), both of which are ill-formed in the grammar of L1 English:

(4.6) a. *Bill likes *themselves*.
       b. *We like *myself*.

If JLE subjects regard the sentences as acceptable, the English reflexives in their transitional grammar are concluded to be underspecified in terms of the *number*-feature, because underspecification in terms of the *number*-feature leads to arbitrarily any interpretation in *number*. The result of this survey is delineated in Table 1.3:

TABLE 1.3. Acceptability of the *Number*-Neutral Interpretation

(%)	JLsE[a]	Control[b]
acceptable	1.7	0.0
unacceptable	**98.3**	100.0

[a]$n=59$. [b]$n=20$.

As Table 1.3 shows, only 1.7% of our 59 JLE subjects regarded the sentences in (4.6) as acceptable; therefrom, we infer that the *number*-feature within JLsE's TG reflexives is either strictly or partially specified.

Now we also contrived another test in order to reveal one of the yet unknown properties of the English reflexives in the transitional grammar of JLsE. In order to make it clear whether JLsE consider the English reflexives to allow the distributive reading in their transitional grammar, we adopted the test sentence in (4.7), which is unacceptable in L1 English:

(4.7) *Mary and Sue saw *herself* in the mirror.

The subjects in our experiments were asked whether (4.7) has the interpretation "Mary saw Mary, and Sue saw Sue," (which is regarded as the distributive reading). We intended this test to make it clear whether the English singular reflexive in JLsE's transitional grammar is tolerable with the distributive reading without the overt distributive operator *each*. If a subject cannot accept this reading, he/she regards the sentence as unacceptable and the *number*-feature of the English reflexives in the transitional grammar of JLsE are concluded to be strictly specified, as argued in § 3.2. The result is shown in Table 1.4:

TABLE 1.4. Acceptability of the Distributive Reading

(%)	JLsE[a]	Control[b]
acceptable	62.2	0.0
unacceptable	37.8	100.0

[a]n=154. [b]n=20. *Notes.* There is a statistically significant difference between the JLE group and the control group: t=6.59, p<.01.

Of great importance on empirical grounds is the result that 62.2% of the total JLE subjects mistakenly regarded their TG singular reflexives as allowing the distributive reading without the overt distributive operator. It follows that it is not the case that the *number*-feature of the English reflexives in the transitional grammar of JLsE allow a unarily fixed interpretation; as a result, they are ***not*** strictly specified in terms of the *number*-feature.

Taking into consideration this result together with the result reported in Table 1.3 (which we have interpreted as indicating that the *number*-feature of JLsE's TG reflexives is not underspecified), we have now arrived at the conclusion that the *number*-feature within the English reflexives in the transitional grammar of JLsE is *partially specified*.

4.3.6. Interim Summary of Our Experimental Surveys

In the preceding subsections we reported that the English reflexives in the transitional grammar of JLsE have the strictly specified *person*-feature (as shown in Table 1.1), the strictly specified *gender*-feature (as shown in Table 1.2), and the partially specified *number*-feature (as shown in Table 1.3 and Table 1.4). From the discussion we made through these subsections, we now would like to draw the conclusion that the φ-feature composition of the

English reflexives in the transitional grammar of JLsE is schematized in Chart 3 below:

Chart 3. Φ-Feature Composition of TG Reflexives for JLsE

φ-feature composition	*Transitional Grammar*
person	+
gender	+
number	−

Given our proposal (made in § 3.3 above) that our definition of defectiveness should be identified with the featural defectiveness in the sense of Burzio (1991), it follows that the English reflexives in the transitional grammar of JLsE turn out to be *φ-defective*; for, their φ-features include a feature which is not strictly specified (i.e., their *number*-feature turns out, through our experiments, to be partially specified). Following, essentially, Burzio's (1991) insight, we assume that a lexical item counts as φ-defective unless all of its φ-features are featurally complete.

4.3.7. Test 1.4: Subject Orientation

More importantly, our conclusion that the English reflexives in the transitional grammar of JLsE are φ-defective leads us to the prediction that they show the subject orientation despite the fact that the reflexives in L1 English do not show the subject orientation, as we have argued in § 4.1.5. By conducting an experimental survey, we ascertained that this prediction is indeed borne out. In order to examine whether the English reflexives in the transitional grammar of JLsE show the subject orientation or not, we utilized the English test sentences in (4.8) and (4.9):

(4.8) ^{OK}The boy told these girls about *himself.*
(4.9) ^{OK}These girls told the boy about *himself.*

If an experimental subject cannot accept the interpretation under which the reflexive in (4.9) is coreferential grammatically with the object, he/she is alleged to regard their TG reflexives as showing the subject orientation. The results of the above tests are shown in Table 1.5:

TABLE 1.5. **Acceptability of Object Antecedents**

(%)	JLsE[a]		Control[b]	
	SUB	OBJ	SUB	OBJ
acceptable	91.8	22.2	100.0	70.0
unacceptable	8.2	77.8	0.0	30.0

[a]n=369. [b]n=20. *Notes.* There are statistically significant differences: between the reflexive which is bound by the subject (as shown in (4.8)) for the JLE group and the reflexive which is bound by the object (as shown in (4.9)) for the JLE group (t=-19.6, p<.01.): between the reflexive which is bound by the object (as shown in (4.9)) for the JLE group and that for the control group (t=-4.57, p<.01.)

It should be noted that 77.8% of the total JLE subjects mistakenly interpreted *himself* as being unable to be bound by the object; that is, the English reflexives in their transitional grammar show the subject orientation. This is exactly what FTFL predicts, and hence it proves the validity of FTFL.

4.3.8. Test 1.5: Locality on Binding Dependency

Given our conclusion that the English reflexives in the transitional grammar of JLsE are φ-defective, ATRB leads us to predict that their locality on the binding dependency is LC in a tensed clause and LD in a non-tensed clause. In what follows, we will show that this prediction is, indeed, borne out and perfectly pertinent to experimental results.

For the purpose of discerning the precise binding domain of the English reflexives in the transitional grammar of JLsE, the subjects in our experiments were asked whether various types of LD-bound reflexives are acceptable or not. We have utilized test sentences in which an English reflexive is contained either within an embedded tensed clause (as in (4.10)), or within a causative clause (as in (4.11)):

(4.10) *The boy believes [that the girl loves *himself*].
(4.11) *The boy made [the girl understand *himself*].

Note that these English test sentences are ill-formed in the grammar of L1 English, because there is no proper antecedent for each of the reflexives within the embedded clause, irrespective of whether the clause is tensed or non-tensed. If a subject judges (4.10) as acceptable, he/she is alleged to interpret the reflexive as being bound astride a tensed clause boundary; namely, he/she regards a reflexive within a tensed clause as showing LD. If a subject judges (4.10) as unacceptable, he/she is alleged to interpret the reflexive as not being bound astride a tensed clause boundary; namely, he/she regards a reflexive within a tensed clause as showing LC. Moreover, we examined the binding dependency of JLsE's TG reflexives within a non-tensed clause: Those who judge (4.11) as acceptable regard a reflexive within a non-tensed clause as showing LD. The results of our experimental tests are shown in Table 1.6:

TABLE 1.6. **Locality on the Binding Dependency**

(%)	JLsE[a]		Control[b]	
	Tensed	Non-tensed	Tensed	Non-tensed
LC	**64.6**	24.9	90.0	95.0
LD	35.4	**75.1**	10.0	5.0

[a]n=288. [b]n=20. *Notes.* There are statistically significant differences: between the reflexive which is contained in the tensed clause (as shown in (4.10)) for the JLE group and the reflexive which is contained in the non-tensed clause (as shown in (4.11)) for the JLE group (t=7.01, p<.01.): between the reflexive which is contained in the non-tensed clause for the JLE group and that for the control group (t=12.71, p<.01.)

As the bold numbers (i.e., 64.6% and 75.1%) in Table 1.6 show, the result of our experimental survey has reconfirmed the well-known observation (see, among many others, Hirakawa 1990, Thomas 1995, and Watanabe et al. 2008) that many JLsE in their transitional grammar regard an English reflexive within a tensed clause as showing LC and one within a non-tensed clause as showing LD.

Of great importance is the fact that these experimental results (as well as the results of many former experiments in the same vein) are what we predict with FTFL. This, in turn, lends strong support, on both empirical and theoretical grounds, to our claim that FTFL is a more adequate theory for the L2 learning of reflexive binding.

We have so far explained our empirical/experimental data about the various syntactic properties of reflexive binding in the transitional grammar of JLsE: Given that the English reflexives in the transitional grammar of JLsE are φ-defective, FTFL, if reinforced with ATRB, enables us to provide a coherent account to the following observations obtained from our experimental survey: (i) The English reflexives in the transitional grammar of JLsE show the subject orientation; and (ii) the locality of the binding domain shows LC in a tensed clause and LD in a non-tensed clause.

4.4. Experiments to Beginner JLsE

FTFL predicts that the specification of the *person-/gender*-features of the English reflexives in the transitional grammar of beginner JLsE are underspecified and their *number*-feature is partially specified due to Feature Transfer. In order to investigate (i) whether reflexives in the transitional grammar of beginner JLsE can have the person-neutral interpretation (Test 1.7), (ii) whether they can have the gender-neutral interpretation (Test 1.8), (iii) whether they can have the number-neutral interpretation (Test 1.9), and (iv) whether they can have the distributive reading (Test 1.10), we set out the following experiments to beginner JLsE.

55 junior high school students in the ninth grade, all of whom were in the advanced English course, and 32 freshmen in high school participated in our follow-up surveys. All of them were native Japanese and had studied English as a second language for about three years. At the time of our experiment, less than half year has passed since they had learned the usage of the English reflexives. We regard them as being at a very early stage in the L2 learning of English. In order to reveal the φ-specification of the English reflexives in the transitional grammar of beginner JLsE, we gave the same test sentences (as shown from (4.4) to (4.6)) to our beginner JLE subjects. The experiments showed the similar results to the ones to our high-intermediate JLE subjects, which were reported in Table 1.1 to Table 1.3. This

does not comply with the prediction by FTFL, because FTFL demands that the English reflexives in the transitional grammar of beginner JLsE have the feature composition of $\{\emptyset,\emptyset,-\}$ due to Feature Transfer. However, we would like to insist, here, that FTFL correctly predicts the syntactic properties of the English reflexives in the transitional grammar of beginner JLsE, notwithstanding this result. Now, in order to demonstrate clearly whether or not beginner JLsE indeed understand the structure of a given test sentence, we try to eliminate the influence of the context and set out the following preliminary test to our experimental subjects, as shown in (4.12) below:

(4.12) a. ^{OK}John$_k$ loved himself$_k$.
       b. Mary$_j$ loved her$_{*j/h}$.
       c. John$_k$'s daughters loved him$_{k/h}$.

The given sentence in (4.12a) is acceptable in L1 Enlgish, but (4.12b) is unacceptable when *Mary* and *her* are co-indexed, because *her* is c-commanded by its antecedent *Mary*. (4.12c) is acceptable when *him* is coreferential with *John*. If our beginner JLE subject correctly regards (4.12a) as acceptable when *himself* is coreferential with *John*, we can say that he/she correctly understands Principle A, which states that an anphor must be bound in its local domain. If our beginner JLE subject correctly regards (4.12b) as unacceptable when *her* is coreferential with *Mary*, we can say that he/she correctly understands Principle B, which states that a pronominal is free in its local domain. If our beginner JLE subject correctly regards (4.12c) as acceptable where *John* and *him* are coreferential, we can say that he/she correctly understands that the genitive DP *John* in the subject DP *John's daughters* does not c-command the object DP *him*. There were 64 beginner JLE subjects who answered correctly to all of the above three preliminary tests.

     In order to discern whether beginner JLsE consider the English reflexives to allow the *person*-neutral interpretation in their transitional grammar, we presented abovementioned 64 experimental subjects with the following test sentence, which is unacceptable in the grammar of L1 English, as shown in (4.13) below:

(4.13) *Our dauthers loved *ourselves.*

If beginner JLE subjects regard (4.13) as acceptable, the English reflexives in the transitional grammar of beginner JLsE are concluded to be underspecified in terms of the *person*-feature. The result of this survey is delineated in Table 1.7:

TABLE 1.7. **Acceptability of the *Person*-Neutral Interpretation**

(%)	Beginner JLsE[a]	Control[b]
acceptable	**67.2**	*0.0*
unacceptable	*32.8*	*100.0*

[a]$n=64$. [b]$n=20$.

As Table 1.7 shows, 67.2% of our 64 JLE subjects mistakenly interpreted the test sentence in (4.13) as acceptable; therefrom, it is concluded that the *person*-feature of beginner JLsE's transitional reflexives is underspecified.

With respect to the *gender*-feature, we have revealed that beginner JLsE consider the English reflexives to allow the *gender*-neutral interpretation in their transitional grammar. We presented our experimental subjects with the following test sentence, which is unacceptable in L1 English, as shown in (4.14) below:

(4.14) *Every mother's son loved *herself.*

If beginner JLE subjects regard (4.14) as acceptable, the English reflexives in the transitional grammar of beginner JLsE are concluded to be underspecified in terms of the *gender*-feature. The result of this survey is delineated in Table 1.8:

TABLE 1.8. Acceptability of the *Gender*-Neutral Interpretation

(%)	Beginner JLsE[a]	Control[b]
acceptable	**89.1**	*0.0*
unacceptable	*10.9*	*100.0*

[a]$n=64$. [b]$n=20$.

As Table 1.8 shows, 89.1% of our 64 JLE subjects mistakenly interpreted the test sentence in (4.14) as acceptable; therefrom, it is concluded that the *gender*-feature of beginner JLsE's transitional reflexives is underspecified.

Next, in order to discern whether beginner JLsE consider the English reflexives to allow the *number*-neutral interpretation in their transitional grammar, we set out the following test. The given test sentence in (4.15) is unacceptable in L1 English:

(4.15) *We love *myself.*

If beginner JLE subjects regard (4.15) as acceptable, the English reflexives in the transitional grammar of beginner JLsE are concluded to be underspecified in terms of the *number*-feature. The result of this survey is delineated in Table 1.9:

TABLE 1.9. Acceptability of the *Number*-Neutral Interpretation

(%)	Beginner JLsE[a]	Control[b]
acceptable	*17.8*	*0.0*
unacceptable	**82.2**	*100.0*

[a]$n=73$. [b]$n=20$.

As Table 1.9 shows, 82.2% of our JLE subjects correctly rejected the test sentence in (4.15). We can conclude that the *number*-feature of beginner JLsE's TG reflexives is *not* underspecified.

Finally, in order to make it clear whether the *number*-feature of the English reflexives in the transitional grammar of beginner JLsE is strictly specified or partially specified, we adopted the test sentence in (4.16), which is unacceptable in L1 English:

CHAPTER 4 Φ-FEATURE SPECIFICATION OF TG REFLEXIVES

(4.16) *Mary and Sue saw *herself* in the mirror.

If beginner JLE subjects regard (4.16) as acceptable, the English reflexives in the transitional grammar of beginner JLsE are concluded to be partially specified in terms of the *number*-feature. The result of this survey is delineated in Table 1.10:

TABLE 1.10. **Acceptability of the Distributive Reading**

(%)	Beginner JLsE[a]	Control[b]
acceptable	**61.6**	*0.0*
unacceptable	*38.4*	*100.0*

[a]$n=73$. [b]$n=20$.

61.6% of our JLE subjects mistakenly regarded the English singular reflexive as allowing the distributive reading. It can be concluded that the *number*-feature of beginner JLsE's TG reflexives is *partially specified*.

We have so far observed that the English reflexives in the transitional grammar of beginner JLsE have the underspecified *person*-feature (as shown in Table 1.7), the underspecified *gender*-feature (as shown in Table 1.8), and the partially specified *number*-feature (as shown in Table 1.9 and Table 1.10). Now it can be safely said that the φ-feature composition of the English reflexives in the transitional grammar of beginner JLsE is schematized as in Chart 4 below:

CHART 4. **Φ-Feature Composition of TG Reflexives for Beginner JLsE**

φ-feature composition	*Transitional Grammar*
person	Ø
gender	Ø
number	–

4.5. Follow-up Experiments to High-Intermediate JLsE

An empirically significant question soon arises: Do we not need to clearly demonstrate that high-intermediate JLsE indeed understand the structure of a given test sentence? Accordingly, we gave the same follow-up surveys (as shown in (4.13) and (4.14)) to 37 high-intermediate JLsE to ensure that they correctly understand the structure of the given test sentences, as shown in Table 1.11 and Table 1.12 below:

TABLE 1.11. **Acceptability of the *Person*-Neutral Interpretation**

(%)	High-intermediatr JLsE[a]	Control[b]
acceptable	*10.8*	*0.0*
unacceptable	**89.2**	*100.0*

[a]$n=37$. [b]$n=20$.

TABLE 1.12. **Acceptability of the *Gender*-Neutral Interpretation**

(%)	High-intermediatr JLsE[a]	Control[b]
acceptable	*24.3*	*0.0*
unacceptable	**75.7**	*100.0*

[a]$n=37$. [b]$n=20$.

As shown in Table 1.11, 89.2% of the high-intermediate JLE subjects correctly regarded the test sentence in (4.13) as unacceptable. Notice that 67.2% of our beginner JLE subjects mistakenly interpreted it as acceptable, as shown in Table 1.7 above; therefrom, it is concluded that the *person*-feature of high-intermediate JLsE's TG reflexives is indeed strictly specified. Next, as shown in Table 1.12, 75.7% of the high-intermediate JLE subjects correctly regarded the test sentence in (4.14) as unacceptable. Notice again that 89.1% of our beginner JLE subjects mistakenly interpreted it as acceptable, as shown in Table 1.8 above; therefrom, it is confirmed that the gender-feature of high-intermediate JLsE's TG reflexives is indeed strictly specified.

FTFL predicts that *himself* in the transitional grammar of beginner JLsE has the feature compoisition of {Ø,Ø,−}, because FEATURE TRANSFER takes place with respect to every φ-feature in the L1 feature inventory. It is also predicted that *himself* in the transitional grammar of (high-intermedaite) /advanced JLsE has the feature composition of {+,+,−}, because at their later stage of the L2 learning of the English reflexives, FEATURE LEARNING takes place with respect to the *person-* and *gender-*features. (Incidentally, Feature Learning does not take place with respect to the *number-*feature due to the markedness of the feature specification.) Our experimental results reported in this section (as shown in Chart 3 and 4) are therefore on par with the prediction by FTFL.

In this chapter, we explored FTFL under the more general theory of L2 learning through considering how our feature-(de)composition analysis of reflexives can be implemented under FTFL, and demonstrated that FTFL is an adequate theory for JLsE's L2 learning of reflexive binding on conceptual and empirical grounds. In order to show that the theory to be proposed in this dissertation is theoretically superior to the previous approaches to the SLA of reflexives, we will, in the next chapter, explore some implication of our theory within the UG-based approach to SLA.

NOTES

1   Portions of this chapter were reported in Ishino (2012).
2   Additional test sentences were indeed given in our survey, the number of which seems to be adequate to ensure that our experimental results reflect the transitional grammar of JLsE.

CHAPTER 5

Crosslinguistic Investigations on TG Reflexives

In this chapter, we will demonstrate that FTFL is theoretically applicable to the syntactic properties of other reflexives in transitional grammar. In what follows, first let us take for instance the Chinese reflexives in the transitional grammar of Japanese learners of Chinese (JLsC) and the Japanese reflexives in the transitional grammar of Chinese learners of Japanese (CLsJ).[1]

5.1. Chinese *Ziji* and *Ta-ziji* and Feature Specification

Let us first consider the syntactic properties of reflexives in the grammar of L1 Chinese, as exemplified in (5.1) below:

(5.1) *L1 Chinese*
    a. Zhangsan$_i$ renwei [Lisi$_j$ zhidao [Wangwu$_k$ xihuan
       Zhangsan think   Lisi know   Wangwu like
       ziji$_{i/j/k}$/ta-ziji$_{*i/*j/k}$].
       SELF/he-self
       Lit. 'Zhangsan thinks that Lisi knows that Wangwu likes SELF.'
                                                  (Cole et al. 1990)

b. Zhangsan$_i$ song Lisi$_j$ yizhang ziji$_{i/*j}$ de xiangpian.
   Zhangsan give Lisi one-CLA SELF DE picture
   Lit. 'Zhangsan gave Lisi a picture of SELF.'
   (Huang 1982, and Huang and Tang 1991)

b'. Zhangsan$_i$ shuo Lisi$_j$ song gei Wangwu$_k$ yizhang
    Zhangsan say Lisi give to Wangsu one-CLA
    ta-ziji$_{*i/j/*k}$ de zhaopian.
    he-self DE picture
    Lit. 'Zhangsan said Lisi gave Wangwu a picture of he-SELF.'
    (Xue 1991)

c. wo$_i$ danxin Zhangsan$_j$ hui piping ziji$_{i/j}$.
   I worry Zhangsan will criticize SELF
   Lit. 'I am worried that Zhangsan will criticize himself/me.'
   ni$_i$ danxin Zhangsan$_j$ hui piping ziji$_{i/j}$ ma?
   you worry Zhangsan will criticize SELF Q
   Lit. 'Are you worried that Zhangsan will criticize himself/you?'
   (Huang, Li, and Li 2009)

c'. Zhangsan shuo ta qipian-le ziji.
    Zhangsan say he/she cheat-LE SELF
    Lit. 'Zhangsan said that he/she cheated himself/herself.'
    (Huang, Li, and Li 2009)

c". Zhangsan$_i$ juede tamen$_j$ lao piping ziji$_{i/j}$.
    Zhangsan feel they incessantly criticize SELF
    Lit. 'Zhangsan felt that they criticized themselves/him
    all the time.' (Huang, Li, and Li 2009)

d. [Zhangsan$_i$ he Lisi$_j$] zai piping ^{OK}ziji$_{i\otimes j}$/*ta-ziji$_{i\otimes j}$.
   Zhangsan and Lisi at criticize SELF/he-SELF
   Lit. 'Zhangsan is criticizing Zhangsan, and Lisi is
   criticizing Lisi.' (Huang 2001)

CHAPTER 5   CROSSLINGUISTIC INVESTIGATIONS ON TG REFLEXIVES

As shown in (5.1c) and (5.1c') above, the L1 Chinese simplex reflexive *ziji* is underspecified in terms of its *person-/gender*-features, whereas the complex form *ta-ziji* in L1 Chinese is strictly specified in *person* and underspecified in *gender*, because it cannot be interpreted as first-/second-person, but can be interpreted as either masculine or feminine. *Ziji* in L1 Chinese, having no plural forms, allows free interpretation in *number*, as exemplified in (5.1c"), but the complex form *ta-ziji* (and its plural form *tamen-ziji*) disallow any free interpretation in *number*. Thus, the *number*-feature of *ziji* is defined as underspecified and the one for *ta-ziji* is not defined as underspecified. We conclude, from these observations, that *ziji* allows the *person*-neutral, *gender*-neutral and *number*-neutral interpretations, but *ta-ziji* only allows the *gender*-neutral interpretation.

Given our observation that *ziji* is underspecified in terms of its *number*-feature and *ta-ziji* is not, it is expected that L1 *ziji* permits the distributive reading, while L1 *ta-ziji* does not, as observed in (5.1d) above (repeated as (5.2) below):

(5.2)   [Zhangsan$_i$ he Lisi$_j$]   zai   piping $^{OK}ziji_{i\otimes j}$/*ta-$ziji_{i\otimes j}$.
        Zhangsan and Lisi   at   criticize   SELF/he-SELF
        Lit. 'Zhangsan is criticizing Zhangsan, and Lisi is criticizing Lisi.'

We conclude therefore that L1 *ta-ziji* is strictly specified in terms of the *number*-feature, as we have concluded, from their inavailability of the distributive reading, that the *number*-feature of *himself* in L1 English and that of *kare-zisin* in L1 Japanese are strictly specified.

To sum up, both of the L1 Chinese reflexives *ziji* and *ta-ziji* hence count as φ-defective; for, none of the φ-features in *ziji* is strictly specified and among the φ-features in *ta-ziji*, the *gender*-feature is not strictly specified. As a result, they show the subject orientation, as shown in (5.1b), and the locality on their binding dependency shows LD when they are embedded in a non-tensed clause, but shows LC when they are embedded in a tensed clause. In analogy with the locality on the binding dependency of L1 *zibun*, the Japanese morphologically simple reflexive, L1 *ziji* can move at LF to be bound by a superordinate subject DP due to its morphological simplicity, resulting in its wider locality than that of the complex form (that is, *ziji* shows LD in a tensed clause). The specification of each φ-feature in the L1 Chinese reflexives and their syntactic properties are summarized in (5.3) below:

(5.3)

	L1 *Chinese*	*ziji*	*ta-ziji*
(i)	morphology	simplex	complex
(ii)	φ-features		
	person	∅	+
	gender	∅	∅
	number	∅	+
(iii)	φ-completeness	φ-defective	φ-defective
(iv)	syntactic properties	syntactic binding	syntactic binding
	Subject Orientation	yes	yes
	Binding Dependency Tensed/Non-tensed	LD / LD	LC / LD
	Distributive Reading	yes	no

5.1.1. Prediction by Previous Studies (PRA and LTA)

As was mentioned initially in Chapter 1, we have addressed the theoretically significant issue in the previous researches into L2 learning of reflexive binding conducted under the generative framework. It is obvious that the abovementioned various syntactic properties are not regarded as language-specific, but rather as lexical specific. It is necessary for the previous proposals (PRA and LTA) to presuppose that a certain L1 anaphora is to be selected as the source of their consideration when L1 has more than one anaphoric expression (as in Japanese and Chinese). In the case of JLsC and CLsJ, not only their L1 anaphora but also their target languages have more than one reflexive form.

CHAPTER 5   CROSSLINGUISTIC INVESTIGATIONS ON TG REFLEXIVES

PRA is founded conceptually upon Governing Category Parameter (GCP). Advocates for PRA (Hirakawa 1990, *inter alia*) hold that JLsE reset their L1 parameter value (i.e., the value (e) of GCP); for, they take *zibun*, which has the value (e), to be representative of the Japanese reflexive forms, ignoring the other reflexive forms. Specifically, they argue that JLsE tend to adopt an intermediate parameter value (i.e., the value (c)) between the value for L1 *zibun* and the value for the English reflexive (i.e., the value (a)), concluding that JLsE adopt the value (c), the Russian type of binding dependency. It is very important, here, to notice that PRA has only managed to describe one of the possibilities of the parametric value for the binding domain of reflexives in the transitional grammar of JLsE.

Now, if we take *zibun* to be representative of the Japanese reflexive forms for JLsC, as presupposed in PRA, it is predicted that JLsC correctly utilize the parameter value for *ziji* (i.e., the value (e)). Moreover, with respect to the parameter value for *ta-ziji* (i.e., the value (c)), it is predicted that JLsC mistakenly regard its parameter value as the value (b), which lies between their L1 value and the target value.

On the other hand, LTA (Yuan 1994, *inter alia*) states that L2 learners select, from among their L1 reflexives, the one that corresponds to the target reflexive in terms of its morphological complexity (without any recourse to φ-completeness), and they transfer the syntactic features of the selected reflexive to their transitional grammar. Thus, LTA correctly predicts that *ziji* in JLsC's transitional grammar shows the same locality on the binding dependency as the one of *zibun,* because they are both morphologically simplex. LTA, if it presupposes that PRONOUN+*zisin* is selected as the source of the transfer, predicts that *ta-ziji* always shows LC, and, if it presupposes that *zibun-zisin* is selected as the source of the transfer, LTA predicts that *ta-ziji* shows LC in a tensed clause and shows LD in a non-tensed clause. In the grammar of L1 Japanese *zibun-zisin* is distinct from PRONOUN+*zisin* in other respects as well as the locality on the binding domain. It is important to notice here that all of the syntactic properties of the selected item, whether *zibun-zisin* or PRONOUN+*zisin*, are unexceptionally transferred and materialized in transitional grammar.

5.1.2. Prediction by FTFL

As repeated previously, FTFL demands that each feature in a lexical item should be the source of consideration, and it is stipulated that each φ-feature in an L1 feature inventory should be first transferred to transitional grammar and then it is determined by the markedness of the relevant feature whether it should (or should not) be replaced by the equivalent feature in a target item. Accordingly, FTFL is theoretically more pertinent to the current theory of syntax under the minimalist framework (Chomsky 1995), because the feature-based mechanics of Chomsky's minimalism is appositely encoded under FTFL.

FTFL cannot only therefore predict the specification of each φ-feature in a reflexive in transitional grammar no matter how many anaphoric expressions an L1 (and also a target language) has, but also can predict how a reflexive in transitional grammar syntactically behaves, because it is precisely predicted under FTFL that the relevant reflexive is φ-defective or φ-complete. Let us apply FTFL to the case of the Chinese reflexives of Japanese learners and first consider the properties of *ziji* in the transitional grammar of beginner/intermediate and advanced JLsC.

CHAPTER 5   CROSSLINGUISTIC INVESTIGATIONS ON TG REFLEXIVES

(5.4)   Prediction of the properties of *ziji* in the transitional grammar of beginner/intermediate and advanced JLsC:

(i)	level	L1 *Japanese*[2]	TG *ziji* Beginner/ Intermediate	TG *ziji* Advanced	Target *Chinese ziji*
(ii)	φ-features				
	person	{∅} ⟶	∅	∅	∅
	gender	{∅} ⟶	∅	∅	∅
	number	{−} ⟶	− (α) ⟹	∅ (β) ⟵	∅
(iii)	φ-completeness		φ-defective(*a)	φ-defective(*b)	φ-defective
(iv)	syntactic properties		syntactic binding	syntactic binding	syntactic binding
	Subject Orientation		yes (*A)	yes (*B)	yes
	Binding Dependency Tensed/Non-tensed		LD / LD	LD / LD	LD / LD
	Distributive Reading		yes (*c)	yes (*d)	yes
	Number-neutral interpretation		no (*e)	yes (*f)	yes

First, with respect to the *person-/gender-*features, L1 features are the same as the target ones in terms of their feature specification; that is, both of the L1 features and the target ones are underspecified, as previously indicated in (2.7) (repeated as (5.5) below):

(5.5)   L1 *Marked* and Target *Marked* : Transferred and retained

Stage in L2 Learning	L1 Feature Inventory	TG (Beginner/ Intermediate)	TG (Advanced)	Target Item
earlier	{∅} ⟶	∅		
later		∅	∅	∅

FTFL therefore demands that the *person-/gender-*features in *ziji* in the transitional grammar of beginner/intermediate JLsC be underspecified due to

Feature Transfer, and those in the transitional grammar of advanced JLsC are the same as those for beginner/intermediate JLsC. Thus, it is expected that beginner/intermediate and advanced JLsC correctly regard *ziji* as having the *person-/gender*-neutral interpretation.

Next, with respect to the *number*-feature in *ziji* in the transitional grammar of JLsC, the L1 feature is distinct from the target one in terms of the markedness of its specification; that is, the L1 feature is partially specified and unmarked, and the target one is underspecified, but marked. FTFL therefore demands that the *number*-feature in *ziji* in the transitional grammar of beginner/intermediate JLsC be partially specified due to Feature Transfer, but later it is predicted that the *number*-feature of *ziji* in the transitional grammar of advanced JLsC turns out to be underspecified thanks to Feature Learning, which stipulates that the L1 feature should be overwritten by the target one when the L1 feature is distinct from the target one in terms of its markedness, as previously indicated in (2.6) (repeated as (5.6) below):

(5.6)   L1 *Unmarked* (partially specified) and Target *Marked*:
Transferred and overwritten

Stage in L2 Learning	L1 Feature Inventory	TG (Beginner/ Intermediate)	TG (Advanced)	Target Item
earlier	{−} ⟶	−		
later		− ⟹ Ø	Ø ⟵	Ø

The L1 value changes to the target value later in transitional grammar.

Therefore, it is expected that advanced JLsC correctly regard *ziji* as having the *number*-neutral interpretation.

As a consequence of FTFL, *ziji* in the transitional grammar of beginner/intermediate JLsC is expected to be in the feature compoisition of {Ø,Ø,−}, and it is expected to become the feature composition of {Ø,Ø,Ø} for advanced JLsC. Now the conclusion we reach is that *ziji* in their transitional grammar are φ-defective, as shown in (*a*) and (*b*) in (5.4). From this conclusion, it is also predicted that *ziji* in the transitional grammar of JLsC is expected to show LD in a non-tensed clause and also expected to

CHAPTER 5 CROSSLINGUISTIC INVESTIGATIONS ON TG REFLEXIVES

show the subject orientation.[3] With respect to the distributive reading, *ziji* in the transitional grammar of JLsC allows it, because its *number*-feature is not strictly specified, as shown in (*c*) and (*d*) in (5.4). More importantly, its *number*-feature in the transitional grammar of beginner/intermediate JLsC is partially specified, but that for advanced JLsC is underspecified thanks to Feature Learning. As a result, *ziji* in the transitional grammar of beginner/intermediate JLsC cannot have the number-neutral interpretation, as shown in (*e*) in (5.4), but *ziji* for advanced JLsC has the *number*-neutral interpretation, as shown in (*f*) in (5.4).

Next, let us consider the properties of *ta-ziji* in the transitional grammar of beginner/intermediate and advanced JLsC, as shown in (5.7) below:

(5.7) Prediction of the properties of *ta-ziji* in the transitional grammar of beginner/intermediate and advanced JLsC:

		L1 *Japanese*	TG *ta-ziji* Beginner/Intermediate	TG *ta-ziji* Advanced	Target *Chinese ta-ziji*
(i)	level				
(ii)	φ-features				
	person	{Ø}	Ø	+	+
	gender	{Ø}	Ø (α)	Ø	Ø
	number	{−}	− (β)	−(γ)	+
(iii)	φ-completeness		φ-defective(*a*)	φ-defective(*b*)	φ-defective
(iv)	syntactic properties		syntactic binding	syntactic binding	syntactic binding
	Subject Orientation		yes (*A)	yes (*B)	yes
	Binding Dependency Tensed/Non-tensed		LC / LD	LC / LD	LC / LD
	Distributive Reading		yes (*c*)	**yes (*d*)**	no

With respect to the *person*-feature, the L1 feature is different from the target one in terms of the markedness of its feature specification; that is, the L1 feature which is underspecified is marked, but the target one which is strictly specified is unmarked. FTFL therefore demands that the *person*-feature in *ta-ziji* in the transitional grammar of beginner/intermediate JLsC be underspecified due to Feature Transfer, but the *person*-feature of *ta-ziji* in the transitional grammar of advanced JLsC turns out to be strictly specified thanks to Feature Learning. It is thus expected that advanced JLsC do not regard *ta-ziji* as having the *person*-neutral interpretation. With respect to the *gender*-feature, the L1 feature is the same as the target one in terms of its feature specification; that is, both of the L1 feature and the target one are underspecified. FTFL therefore demands that the *gender*-feature in *ta-ziji* in the transitional grammar of advanced JLsC be the same as the one in the transitional grammar of beginner/intermediate JLsC. Thus, it is expected that JLsC correctly regard *ta-ziji* as having the *gender*-neutral interpretation. In the case of the *number*-feature in *ta-ziji* in the transitional grammar of JLsC, the L1 feature is the same as the target feature in terms of the markedness of its specification, whereas the L1 feature is distinct from the target one in terms of its specification. FTFL stipulates that Feature Learning does not take place when both of the L1 feature and the target one are unmarked, as previously indicated in (2.11) (repeated as (5.8) below):

(5.8) L1 *Unmarked* (partially specified) and Target *Unmarked* (strictly specified): Transferred and retained

Stage in L2 Learning	L1 Feature Inventory	TG (Beginner/ Intermediate)	TG (Advanced)	Target Item
earlier	{−} ⟶	−		
later		−	(−)	+

No FEATURE LEARNING and the L1 value persists.

Consequently, it is expected that advanced JLsC do not regard *ta-ziji* as having the *number*-neutral interpretation.

As a consequence of FTFL, *ta-ziji* in the transitional grammar of beginner/intermediate JLsC is expected to be in the feature compoisition of {Ø,Ø,−}, and it is expected to become the feature compoisition of {+,Ø,−} for advanced JLsC. It leads us to conclude that *ta-ziji* in the transitional

CHAPTER 5 CROSSLINGUISTIC INVESTIGATIONS ON TG REFLEXIVES

grammar of JLsC is φ-defective, as shown in (*a) and (*b) in (5.7). Now we also predict that *ta-ziji* in the transitional grammar of JLsC is expected to show LC/LD as the locality on the binding dependency and it shows the subject orientation. Notice here that even highly advanced JLsC are mistakenly apt to regard *ta-ziji* in their transitional grammar as allowing the distributive reading, because Feature Learning does not take place and its *number*-feature is partially specified (i.e., not strictly specified), as shown in (*c) and (*d) in (5.7).

Needless to say, FTFL can be applied to the case of the properties of the Japanese reflexives in the transitional grammar of beginner/intermediate and advanced CLsJ.

(5.9) Prediction of the properties of *zibun(-zisin)* in the transitional grammar of beginner/intermediate and advanced CLsJ:

		L1 Chinese	TG *zibun(-zisin)*		Target *Japanese zibun(-zisin)*
(i)	level		Beginner/ Intermediate	Advanced	
(ii)	φ-features				
	person	{∅,(+)} (*a)	→ + ▫▫ ⇒	∅ ◄--------	∅
	gender	{∅} (*b)	→ ∅	∅	∅
	number	{∅,(+)} (*c)	→ + (α)	(+)(β)	–
(iii)	φ-completeness		φ-defective (*d)	φ-defective (*e)	φ-defective
(iv)	syntactic properties		syntactic binding	syntactic binding	syntactic binding
	Subject Orientation		yes	yes	yes
	Binding Dependency Tensed/Non-tensed		LD/LD (*zibun*) LC/LD (*zibun-zisin*)	LD/LD (*zibun*) LC/LD (*zibun-zisin*)	LD/LD (*zibun*) LC/LD (*zibun-zisin*)
	Distributive Reading		no (*f)	no (*g)	yes

First, it should be noticed here that both the feature specification of *ziji* and that of *ta-ziji* are included in the list of the L1 feature inventory of Chinese learners, whereas the feature specification of *kare-zisin* is excluded from the L1 feature inventory of Japanese learners; for, *kare-zisin* is regarded as a reflexivizer because of its φ-completeness. For Chinese learners, *ziji* and *ta-ziji* are both recognized as φ-defective anaphors in syntax (i.e., they are not reflexivizers in the sense of Reinhart and Reurland 1993).

One of the theoretically significant implications derived from FTFL is that it does no longer become a controversial issue as to which one of L1 anaphora is to be selected as the source of consideration. To put it differently, FTFL stipulates that the specification of each feature is to be selected as the only source of consideration. To be precise, (I) in terms of the *person*-feature in the L1 feature inventory of Chinese learners, they have two specifications/values; namely, *underspecified* (which is materialized in *ziji*) and *strictly specified* (which is materialized in *ta-ziji*), as shown in the feature set of {Ø,+}(*a) in (5.9); (II) in terms of the *gender*-feature in the L1 feature inventory, Chinese learners only have one specification/ value; namely, *underspecified* (which is materialized both in *ziji* and *ta-ziji*), as shown in the feature set of {Ø}(*b) in (5.9); and (III) in terms of the *number*-feature in the L1 feature inventory, Chinese learners have two specifications/values; namely, *underspecified* (which is materialized in *ziji*) and *strictly specified* (which is materialized in *ta-ziji*), as shown in the feature set of {Ø,+}(*c) in (5.9). It follows that FTFL can predict each feature specification of reflexives in transitional grammar no matter how may reflexive forms learners' L1 has.

Notice also here that when a certain feature in the L1 feature inventory includes more than one specification (such as the *person-/number*-features in the L1 inventory of Chinese learners), an unmarked feature is supposed to be transferred to transitional grammar under FTFL, which is based on the general guideline for the learnability of markedness.[4]

Then, let us apply FTFL to each feature of the Japanese reflexives in the transitional grammar of CLsJ. First, with respect to the *person*-feature in *zibun(-zisin)* in the transitional grammar of CLsJ, the *person*-feature in their L1 inventory includes an underspecified feature and a strictly specified

CHAPTER 5 CROSSLINGUISTIC INVESTIGATIONS ON TG REFLEXIVES

feature. Feature Transfer demands that the strictly specified *person*-feature be initially transferred to the transitional grammar of beginner/intermediate CLsJ, because the relevant feature is unmarked, as previously indicated in (2.3) (repeated as (5.10) below):

(5.10) L1 *Unmarked* (strictly specified) and Target *Marked*:
Transferred and overwritten

Stage in L2 Learning	L1 Feature Inventory	TG (Beginner/ Intermediate)	TG (Advanced)	Target Item
earlier	{+} ⟶	+		
later		+ ⟹	Ø ◀	Ø

The L1 value changes to the target value later in transitional grammar.

The transferred L1 feature is distinct from the target one in terms of the markedness of its specification: Consequently, later in their L2 learning, it is predicted that the *person*-feature of *zibun(-zisin)* in the transitional grammar of advanced CLsJ turns out to be underspecified thanks to Feature Learning, which stipulates that the L1 feature should be overwritten by the target one when the L1 feature is distinct from the target one in terms of its markedness. Therefore, it is expected that advanced CLsJ correctly regard *zibun(-zisin)* as having the *person*-neutral interpretation. With respect to the *gender*-feature, the L1 feature is the same as the target one in terms of its feature specification; that is, both of them are underspecified. FTFL therefore explains that the *gender*-feature in *zibun(-zisin)* in the transitional grammar of CLsJ is underspecified.

Finally, with respect to the *number*-feature in *zibun(-zisin)* in the transitional grammar of CLsJ, the *number*-feature in their L1 inventory includes an underspecified feature and a strictly specified one. Feature Transfer demands that the strictly specified *number*-feature be initially transferred to the transitional grammar of beginner/intermediate CLsJ, because the relevant feature is assumed to be unmarked, and what is more, the transferred L1 feature is the same as the target one in terms of the markedness of its specification, even though the transferred L1 feature is distinct from the target one in terms of its specification. According to FTFL, Feature Learning does not take place when the L1 feature and the target one are both unmarked, as previously indicated in (2.12) (repeated as (5.11) below):

(5.11) L1 *Unmarked* (strictly specified) and Target *Unmarked* (partially specified): Transferred and retained

Stage in L2 Learning	L1 Feature Inventory	TG (Beginner/ Intermediate)	TG (Advanced)	Target Item
earlier	{+} ⟶	+		
later		+	(+)	–

No FEATURE LEARNING and the L1 value persists.

As a result, it is expected that the *number*-feature in *zibun(-zisin)* is strictly specified even for highly advanced CLsJ.

Now we conclude that *zibun(-zisin)* in the transitional grammar of beginner/intermediate CLsJ is expected to be in the feature compoisition of {+,Ø,+}, and it is expected to become the feature compoisition of {Ø,Ø,+} for advanced CLsJ. Therefore, *zibun(-zisin)* in their transitional grammar are φ-defective, as shown in (*d*) and (*e*) in (5.9). It should be noted here that even advanced CLsJ persistently regard *zibun(-zisin)* as disallowing the distributive reading, because Feature Learning does not take place and its *number*-feature is strictly specified, as shown in (*f*) and (*g*) in (5.9).

Finally, let us take a look at the properties of *kare-zisin* in the transitional grammar of beginner/intermediate and advanced CLsJ:

CHAPTER 5   CROSSLINGUISTIC INVESTIGATIONS ON TG REFLEXIVES

(5.12) Prediction of the properties of *kare-zisin* in the transitional grammar of beginner/intermediate and advanced CLsJ:

		L1 *Chinese*	TG *kare-zisin*		Target *Japanese kare-zisin*
			Beginner/ Intermediate	Advanced	
(i)	level				
(ii)	φ-features				
	person	{Ø(+)} ⟶	+	+	+
	gender	{Ø} ⟶	Ø (A) ⟹	+ (B) ⟵-----	+
	number	{Ø(+)} ⟶	+ (α)	+ (β)	+
(iii)	φ-completeness		φ-defective (*a)	φ-complete (*b)	φ-complete
(iv)	syntactic properties		syntactic binding	reflexivizer (*c)	reflexivizer
	Subject Orientation		yes (*d)	no (*e)	no
	Binding Dependency Tensed/Non-tensed		LC / LD	LC / LC	LC / LC
	Distributive Reading		no (*f)	no (*g)	no

First, with respect to the *person*-feature in *kare-zisin* in the transitional grammar of CLsJ, as previously argued, the *person-/number*-features in their L1 inventory includes underspecified features and strictly specified ones, and the strictly specified ones should be transferred to the transitional grammar of beginner/intermediate CLsJ. Therefore, it is expected that CLsJ correctly regard *kare-zisin* as disallowing the *person-/number*-neutral interpretation. With respect to the *gender*-feature, an L1 feature is different from a target one in terms of the markedness of its feature specification; that is, the L1 feature which is underspecified is marked, but the target one which is strictly specified is unmarked, as previously indicated in (2.3) (repeated as (5.13) below):

(5.13) L1 *Marked* and Target *Unmarked* (strictly specified):
Transferred and overwritten

Stage in L2 Learning	L1 Feature Inventory	TG (Beginner/ Intermediate)	TG (Advanced)	Target Item
earlier	{Ø} ⟶	Ø		
later		Ø ⟹	(+) ⟵---	+

The L1 value changes to the target value later in transitional grammar.

The *gender*-feature in *kare-zisin* in the transitional grammar of beginner/ intermediate CLsJ is initially underspecified due to Feature Transfer, but later in their transitional grammar, the *gender*-feature of *kare-zisin* turns out to be strictly specified thanks to Feature Learning. To put it differently, *kare-zisin* in the transitional grammar of beginner/intermediate CLsJ is expected to be in the feature composition of {+,Ø,+}, but it is expected to become the feature compoisition of {+,+,+} for advanced CLsJ.

In addition to the prediction that advanced CLsJ do not regard *kare-zisin* as disallowing the *gender*-neutral interpretation, change of the specification for the *gender*-feature in their transitional grammar leads us to a theoretically very significant consequence; that is, *kare-zisin* in the transitional grammar of beginner/intermediate CLsJ is φ-defective (as shown in (*a*) in (5.12)), because it includes the *gender*-feature, which is underspecified, but *kare-zisin* in the transitional grammar of advanced CLsJ becomes φ-complete (as shown in (*b*) in (5.12)) because its *gender*-feature turns out to be strictly specified. The specification indicates that *kare-zisin* in the transitional grammar of advanced CLsJ is regarded as a reflexivizer, as shown in (*c*) in (5.12). This leads us to predict that beginner/intermediate CLsJ mistakenly regard *kare-zisin* as showing the subject orientation, but advanced CLsJ correctly reject its subject orientation (as shown in (*d*) and (*e*) in (5.12)) because a reflexivizer does not necessarily show the subject orientation. Finally, it is also predicted that CLsJ correctly regard *kare-zisin* as disallowing the distributive reading because its *number*-feature is strictly specified, as shown in (*f*) and (*g*) in (5.12).

CHAPTER 5 CROSSLINGUISTIC INVESTIGATIONS ON TG REFLEXIVES

5.1.3. Experiments

Exploiting FTFL, we have so far demonstrated in a deductive manner how each φ-feature in the Chinese/Japanese reflexives are specified at every stage/level of the transitional grammar of JLsC/CLsJ and the syntactic properties of the relevant reflexives in their transitional grammar. In what follows, a piece of supporting evidence will be provided to ensure that our experimental data are coherently explainable under our theory of the feature composition of reflexives.

Beginner/intermediate JLsC who participated in our experimental surveys were divided into three groups consisting of 41 (25 male students and 16 female students), 16 (2 male students and 14 female students), and 12 (1 male students and 11 female students). All of our experimental subjects were native Japanese and at the time of our experiment, they had studied Chinese at university for one to four years and none of them had lived in Chinese-speaking countries. Their average age was 19.4. Advanced JLsC who participated in our experimental surveys were Japanese teachers who had taught Chinese to undergraduate students at university. We had also a control group consisting of 12 native speakers of Chinese, all of whom stayed in Japan as exchange students (they were all undergraduate students at college).

The group of beginner/intermediate CLsJ who participated in our experimental surveys consisted of 15 university students (7 male students and 8 female students), all of whom were native Chinese and stayed in Japan as exchange students. At the time of our experiment, they had studied Japanese at university for two to three years. Their average age was 20.1. Advanced CLsJ who participated in our experimental surveys were Chinese teachers who had taught Chinese to undergraduate students at university in Japan. All of the advanced CLsJ had lived in Japan for more than ten years. We had a control group consisting of 12 native speakers of Japanese, all of whom were undergraduate students at college.

Let us first examine whether beginner/intermediate JLsC consider the *gender*-feature of *ta-ziji* in their transitional grammar to be specified or underspecified. We presented our experimental subjects with the test sentences in (5.14), both of which are acceptable in the L1 grammar of Chinese:[5]

(5.14) a. ᴼᴷ张三　　告訴　　公安　　有關　　他自己
　　　　　Zhangsan　gaosu　gongan　youguan　tā-zijǐ
　　　　　Mr. Zhang　tell　　police　about　　SELF
　　　　　Lit. 'Mr. Zhang tells the police about himself.'

　　　b. ᴼᴷ李小姐　　批评　　她自己
　　　　　Li xiaojie　piping　tā-zijǐ
　　　　　Miss Li　　criticize　SELF
　　　　　Lit. 'Miss Li criticizes herself.'

We intended these test sentences to make it clear whether beginner/intermediate JLC subjects in our experimental surveys can interpret *ta-ziji* in (5.14a) as being coreferential with the male antecedent *Zhangsan*, what is more, we should make it clear whether they can interpret *ta-ziji* in (5.14b) as being coreferential with the female antecedent *Li xiaojie*: If a subject can accept both of these interpretations, *ta-ziji* in the transitional grammar of beginner/intermediate JLsC is concluded to be underspecified in terms of the *gender*-feature; otherwise, it is specified in terms of the *gender*-feature. The result of this survey is delineated in Table 2.1:

TABLE 2.1. **Acceptability of the *Gender*-Neutral Interpretation**

(%)	Beginner/Intermediate JLsC[a]		Control[b]	
(*antecedent*)	(*male*)	(*female*)	(*male*)	(*female*)
acceptable	**95.1**	**78.0**	*100.0*	*100.0*
unacceptable	*4.9*	*22.0*	*0.0*	*0.0*

[a]*n*=41.　[b]*n*=12.

As Table 2.1 shows, 95.1% of our 41 JLC subjects correctly interpreted the test sentences in (5.14a) as acceptable. On the other hand, 78.0% of our 41 JLC subjects correctly interpreted the test sentences in (5.14b) as acceptable. These results in Table 2.1 show that *ta-ziji* in the transitional grammar of beginner/intermediate JLsC can be bound either by a male antecedent or by a female antecedent. That is to say, the *gender*-neutral interpretation of

CHAPTER 5 CROSSLINGUISTIC INVESTIGATIONS ON TG REFLEXIVES

ta-ziji in their transitional grammar indicates that *ta-ziji* in their transitional grammar is underspecified in terms of the *gender*-feature. FTFL predicts that JLsC correctly regard the *gender*-feature in *ta-ziji* as underspecified, as shown in (α) in (5.7), and our experimental result is consistent with the prediction by FTFL.

Next, in order to discern whether JLsC consider the *number*-feature of *ziji* in their transitional grammar to be specified or underspecified, we presented both of the beginner/intermediate JLC group and the advanced JLC group in our experimental surveys with the test sentence in (5.15), which is acceptable in the grammar of L1 Chinese:

(5.15) OK[张三   和   李四]*ᵢ*   批评   自己*ᵢ*
        Zhangsan   he   Lisi   piping   *ziji*
        Mr. Zhang   and   Mr. Li   criticize SELF
        Lit. '[Mr. Zhang and Mr. Li] criticize [Mr. Zhang and Mr. Li.]'
                                       (*group reading*)

Ziji in the grammar of L1 Chinese can be bound by the plural antecedent, [*Zhangsan he Lisi*] because *ziji* is underspecified in terms of the *number*-feature. It is therefore acceptable that the sentence in (5.15) means '(the group of) Mr. Zhang and Mr. Li criticize (the group of) Mr. Zhang and Mr. Li,' which we call *group reading*. If JLC subjects regard the sentence as acceptable, we conclude that *ziji* in their transitional grammar is underspecified in terms of the *number*-feature because underspecification in terms of the *number*-feature leads to arbitrarily any interpretation in *number*. The result of this survey is delineated in Table 2.2:

TABLE 2.2. **Acceptability of the *Number*-Neutral Interpretation**

(%)	Beginner/Intermediate JLsC[a]	Advanced JLsC[b]
acceptable	45.0	**100.0**
unacceptable	**55.0**	0.0

[a]*n*=40. [b]*n*=4.

As Table 2.2 shows, 55.0% of our 40 JLC subjects regarded the sentences in (5.15) as unacceptable; therefrom, we infer that the *number*-feature within *ziji* in the transitional grammar of beginner/intermediate JLsC is not underspecified. Of empirically interesting point here is that 100% of our advanced JLC subjects regarded the sentence in (5.15) as acceptable. We conclude from the results shown in Table 2.2 that the *number*-feature of *ziji* in the transitional grammar of advanced JLsC turns out to be underspecified. FTFL predicts that the *number*-feature in *ziji* in the transitional grammar of beginner/intermediate JLsC is (partially) specified (though it has not yet been revealed from our experiment in Table 2.2 that it is partially specified, so that we need a follow-up experiment to ensure it is indeed partially specified) due to Feature Transfer but that of *ziji* for advanced JLsC is overwritten by the target feature and becomes underspecified due to Feature Learning, as shown in (α) and (β) in (5.4). As a consequence of FTFL, it is predicted that beginner/intermediate JLsC mistakenly regard *ziji* as disallowing the *number*-neutral interpretation, but later in their transitional grammar, advanced JLsC correctly regard it as allowing the *number*-neutral interpretation, as shown in (*e) and (*f) in (5.4), and our experimental results are consistent with the prediction by FTFL.

Now we have to investigate precisely whether *ziji* and *ta-ziji* in the transitional grammar of beginner/intermediate/advanced JLsC are strictly specified, partially specified or underspecified in terms of their *number*-features. Then, we adopted the test sentences in (5.16) below:

(5.16) a. ^{OK}[张三$_k$ 和 李四$_j$] 批评 自己$_{k\otimes j}$
Zhangsan he Lisi piping *ziji*
Lit. 'Mr. Zhang criticized Mr. Zhang, and Mr. Li criticized Mr. Li.'

b. *[张三$_k$ 和 李四$_j$] 批评 他自己$_{k\otimes j}$
Zhangsan he Lisi piping *ta-ziji*
Lit. 'Mr. Zhang criticized Mr. Zhang, and Mr. Li criticized Mr. Li.'

(5.17) *[张三 和 李四]*ᵢ* 批评 他自己*ᵢ*
Zhangsan he Lisi piping *ta-ziji*
Lit. '(The group of) Mr. Zhang and Mr. Li criticized(the group of) Mr. Zhang and Mr. Li.'

Ziji in the grammar of L1 Chinese allows the distributive reading, as shown in (5.16a), because its *number*-feature is not strictly specified, whereas, *ta-ziji* in the grammar of L1 Chinese disallows the distributive reading because of its *number*-feature, which is strictly specified, as shown in (5.16b). It is obvious, as exemplified in (5.17) above, that *ta-ziji* in the L1 Chinese disallows the group reading because its *number*-feature is strictly specified and disallows the neutral interpretation in terms of the relevant feature.

The subjects in our experiments were asked whether the sentences in (5.16) have the interpretation "Mr. Zhang criticized Mr. Zhang, and Mr. Li criticized Mr. Li." We intended this test to make it clear whether *ziji* and *ta-ziji* in JLsC's transitional grammar are tolerable with the distributive reading. If a subject cannot accept this reading, it can be safely concluded that the *number*-features of *ziji* and *ta-ziji* in their transitional grammar are strictly specified. Their results are shown in Table 2.3 and Table 2.4:

TABLE 2.3. **Acceptability of the Distributive Reading (*Ziji*)**

(%)	Beginner/Intermediate JLsC[a]	Control[b]
acceptable	**81.2**	**58.3**
unacceptable	18.8	41.7

[a]$n=16$. [b]$n=12$. *Notes*. There is not a statistically significant difference between the JLC group and the control group: $p>.05$.

TABLE 2.4. **Acceptability of the Distributive Reading (*Ta-ziji*)**

(%)	Beginner/Intermediate JLsC[a]	Advanced JLsC[b]	Control[c]
acceptable	**43.8**	**75.0**	*16.7*
unacceptable	*56.2*	*25.0*	**83.3**

[a]$n=16$. [b]$n=4$. [c]$n=12$. *Notes.* There is a statistically significant difference between the beginner/intermediate JLC group and the control group: $t=-4.112, p<.001$.

As shown in Table 2.3, 81.2% of our 16 JLC subjects, all of whom are beginners to intermediate learners, regarded the sentence in (5.16a) as acceptable; for, there is not a statistically significant difference between the JLC group and the control group. That is to say, *ziji* in their transitional grammar is ***not strictly specified*** in terms of its *number*-feature. As we have inferred from the results in Table 2.2, the *number*-feature in *ziji* in their transitional grammar is ***not underspecified*** either. The *number*-feature of *ziji* in the transitional grammar of beginner/intermediate JLsC is logically concluded from the results in Table 2.3 together with the results in Table 2.2 to be ***partially specified***.

Of great importance on empirical grounds is the result shown in Table 2.4 that 75.0% of even advanced JLC subjects mistakenly regarded *ta-ziji* as allowing the distributive reading. It follows that it is not the case that the *number*-feature of *ta-ziji* in their transitional grammar allow a unarily fixed interpretation; as a result, they are ***not strictly specified*** in terms of the *number*-feature. One may wonder whether *ta-ziji* for advanced JLsC is underspecified in terms of the *number*-feature. We have also presented the advanced JLC subjects with the sentence in (5.17) in order to examine whether they mistakenly allow the *number*-neutral interpretation for *ta-ziji*. As a result, 75% of them correctly disallowed it. The result of our follow-up test shows that *ta-ziji* in the transitional grammar of advanced JLsC is ***not underspecified*** either. Taking into consideration this result together with the result reported in Table 2.4, we have now arrived at the conclusion that the

CHAPTER 5 CROSSLINGUISTIC INVESTIGATIONS ON TG REFLEXIVES

number-feature within *ta-ziji* in the transitional grammar of advanced JLsC is ***partially specified***.

According to FTFL, the *number*-feature in *ziji* in the transitional grammar of beginner/intermediate JLsC is partially specified due to Feature Transfer but that of *ziji* for advanced JLsC is underspecified due to Feature Learning, as shown in (α) and (β) in (5.4). Moreover, the *number*-feature in *ta-ziji* in the transitional grammar of beginner/intermediate JLsC is partially specified due to Feature Transfer but that of *ta-ziji* for advanced JLsC is still partially specified because Feature Learning does not take place, as shown in (β) and (γ) in (5.7). Our experimental results, which are consistent with the prediction by FTFL, therefore provide a piece of strong supporting evidence to show the validity of FTFL.

Our empirical/experimental observation that *ziji* and *ta-ziji* in the transitional grammar of JLsC have more than one feature that is not strictly specified leads us to conclude that both of them count as φ-defective as the same as *ziji* and *ta-ziji* in the grammar of L1 Chinese. More importantly, from our conclusion that both of *ziji* and *ta-ziji* in the transitional grammar of JLsC at any stage in their L2 learning are φ-defective, we predict that they show the subject orientation, as shown in (*A) and (*B) in (5.4) and (5.7). By conducting an experimental survey, we ascertained that this prediction is indeed borne out. In order to examine whether *ziji* and *ta-ziji* in the transitional grammar of JLsC show the subject orientation or not, we utilized the Chinese test sentences in (5.18) and (5.19) below:

(5.18) *公安　　告訴　　张三　　　有關　　自己
　　　 gongan　gaosu　Zhangsan　youguan　*ziji*
　　　 police　 tell　 Mr.Zhang　 about　 SELF
　　　 Lit. 'The police tell Mr. Zhang about himself.'

(5.19) *他们　　告訴　　李小姐　　 有關　　她自己
　　　 tamen　 gaosu　 Li Xiaojie　youguan　*ta-ziji*
　　　 they　　tell　　 Miss. Li　　about　　her-self
　　　 Lit. 'They tell Miss Li about herself.'

Both of the sentences in (5.18) and (5.19) are ill-formed in the grammar of L1 Chinese because *ziji* in (5.18) is bound by the object *Zhangsan*, and *ta-ziji* in (5.19) is also bound by the object *Li Xiaojie*. If our JLC subject cannot accept the interpretation under which the reflexives in (5.18) and (5.19) are coreferential grammatically with the objects, he/she is alleged to regard their TG reflexives as showing the subject orientation. The results of the above tests are shown in Table 2.5 and Table 2.6:

TABLE 2.5. Acceptability of Object Antecedents (*Ziji*)

(%)	Beginner/Intermediate JLsC[a]	Advanced JLsC[b]
acceptable	25.0	0.0
unacceptable	**75.0**	*100.0*

[a]$n=12$. [b]$n=4$.

TABLE 2.6. Acceptability of Object Antecedents (*Ta-ziji*)

(%)	Beginner/Intermediate JLsC[a]	Advanced JLsC[b]
acceptable	0.0	0.0
unacceptable	**100.0**	*100.0*

[a]$n=12$. [b]$n=4$.

It should be noted that none of the total advanced JLC subjects mistakenly interpreted *ziji* nor *ta-ziji* as being able to be bound by the object; that is, *ziji* and *ta-ziji* in their transitional grammar show the subject orientation. This is exactly what FTFL predicts, and hence it also proves the validity of FTFL.

Next, in what follows let us examine the syntactic properties of the Japanese reflexives in the transitional grammar of CLsJ. According to FTFL, CLsJ are mistakenly apt to regard *zibun(-zisin)* as disallowing the distributive reading, because Feature Learning does not take place and the *number*-feature, which is strictly specified, in their L1 inventory should not be replaced by the target feature, as shown in (α) and (β) in (5.9). On the one hand, CLsJ correctly regard *kare-zisin* as disallowing the distributive reading, because the strictly specified *number*-feature in their L1 inventory should be transferred to their transitional grammar as shown in (α) and (β) in (5.12).

Then, we have to confirm whether *zibun(-zisin)* and *kare-zisin* in the transitional grammar of CLsJ are strictly specified in terms of their *number*-features. We adopted the test sentences in (5.20) and (5.21) below:

(5.20) OKJohn to Bill-wa   *zibun(-zisin)*-o   home-ta.
        John and Bill-TOP   SELF(-self)-ACC   praise-PAST
        Lit. 'John praised John, and Bill praised Bill.'

(5.21) *John to Bill-wa   *kare-zisin*-o   home-ta.
        John and Bill-TOP   him-self-ACC   praise-PAST
        Lit. 'John praised John, and Bill praised Bill.'

Zibun(-zisin) in the grammar of L1 Japanese allows the distributive reading, as shown in (5.20) above, because its *number*-feature is not strictly specified, whereas *kare-zisin* in the grammar of L1 Japanese disallows it because of its *number*-feature, which is strictly specified, as shown in (5.21). The CLJ subjects in our experiments were asked whether (5.20) and (5.21) have the interpretation "John praised John, and Bill praised Bill." If a subject cannot accept this interpretation, we conclude that the *number*-feature of *zibun(-zisin)* or *kare-zisin* in their transitional grammar is strictly specified. Their results are shown in Table 2.7 and Table 2.8:

TABLE 2.7. **Acceptability of the Distributive Reading (*Zibun(-zisin)*)**

(%)	Beginner/Intermediate	
	CLsJ[a]	Control[b]
acceptable	26.7	**100.0**
unacceptable	73.3	0.0

[a]n=15. [b]n=12.

TABLE 2.8. Acceptability of the Distributive Reading (*Kare-zisin*)

(%)	Beginner/Intermediate CLsJ[a]	Control[b]
acceptable	26.7	**0.0**
unacceptable	**73.3**	100.0

[a]$n=15$. [b]$n=12$.

As shown in Table 2.7, 73.3% of our 15 CLJ subjects mistakenly regard the sentence in (5.20) as unacceptable. That is to say, *zibun(-zisin)* in their transitional grammar is **strictly specified** in terms of its *number*-feature. In addition to the results in Table 2.7, the *number*-feature of *kare-zisin* in their transitional grammar is concluded to be strictly specified; for, 73.3% of our CLJ subjects reject the distributive reading of *kare-zisin*, as indicated in Table 2.8. FTFL explains that with respect to the *number*-feature of the reflexives in the transitional grammar of CLsJ, their L1 inventory includes an underspecified feature and a strictly specified one, and the strictly specified one should be transferred to their transitional grammar under the general guideline for the learnability of markedness. It is predicted therefore that CLsJ mistakenly regard *zibun(-zisin)* as disallowing the distributive reading, whereas they correctly regard *kare-zisin* as disallowing it, as shown in (*f*) and (*g*) in (5.9) and (5.12). Thus, our experimental results are also consistent with the prediction by FTFL in this respect.

Finally, let us confirm the theoretically significant consequence of FTFL: We have to confirm whether *zibun(-zisin)* and *kare-zisin* in the transitional grammar of CLsJ show the subject orientation or not. We utilized the Japanese test sentences in (5.22) and (5.23) below:

(5.22) *Iinkai-wa   John-ni   *zibun(-zisin)*
         The committee-TOP John-DAT   SELF(-self)
         nituite   hanashi-ta.
         about   tell-PAST
         Lit. 'The committee told John about himself.'

Chapter 5 Crosslinguistic Investigations on TG Reflexives

(5.23) ᴼᴷIinkai-wa   John-ni   *kare-zisin*
       The committee-TOP John-DAT   him-self
       nituite   hanashi-ta.
       about   tell-PAST
       Lit. 'The committee told John about himself.'

The sentences in (5.22) is unacceptable in the grammar of L1 Japanese, because *zibun(-zisin)*, which is always subject oriented, is bound by the object *John* in (5.22). On the other hand, the sentence in (5.23) is acceptable in the grammar of L1 Japanese, because *kare-zisin* does not show the subject orientation. L1 *kare-zisin* is a φ-complete reflexive and it is not necessary for L1 *kare-zisin* to be supplied with the φ-features through *Agree* by T. Accordingly, *kare-zisin* is not necessarily bound by a subject. If our CLJ subject cannot accept the interpretation under which the reflexives in (5.22) and (5.23) are coreferential grammatically with the objects, he/she is alleged to regard their TG reflexives as showing the subject orientation. The results of the above tests are shown in Table 2.9 and Table 2.10:

TABLE 2.9. **Acceptability of Object Antecedents (*Zibun(-zisin)*)**

(%)	Beginner/Intermediate CLsJ[a]	Advanced CLsJ[b]
acceptable	26.7	0.0
unacceptable	**73.3**	*100.0*

[a]n=15. [b]n=3.

TABLE 2.10. **Acceptability of Object Antecedents (*Kare-zisin*)**

(%)	Beginner/Intermediate CLsJ[a]	Advanced CLsJ[b]
acceptable	40.0	*100.0*
unacceptable	**60.0**	0.0

[a]n=15. [b]n=3.

Notice that none of the advanced CLJ subjects mistakenly interpreted *kare-zisin* as disallowing to be bound by the object, whereas 60.0% of the beginner/intermediate CLJ subjects in our experiment mistakenly regard *kare-zisin* as showing the subject orientation. That is to say, *kare-zisin* in the transitional grammar of beginner/intermediate CLsJ is φ-defective and shows the subject orientation, but *kare-zisin* for advanced CLsJ is φ-complete and lacks the subject orientation, as shown in (*d*) and (*e*) in (5.12), because FTFL predicts that the *gender*-feature of *kare-zisin* turns out to be strictly specified due to Feature Learning, as shown in (A) and (B) in (5.12). It hence also proves the validity of FTFL.

In this section, we have so far demonstrated that FTFL is theoretically applicable to the syntactic properties of the Chinese reflexives in the transitional grammar of JLsC and the Japanese reflexives in the transitional grammar of CLsJ. Next in what follows, we will apply FTFL to the syntactic properties of the German reflexives in the transitional grammar of Japanese learners of German (JLsG).

5.2. German *Sich* and *Sich selbst* and Feature Specification

Let us next consider the syntactic properties of the German morphologically simplex reflexive *sich* and the German morphologically complex one *sich selbst* as shown in (5.24) below:

(5.24) *L1 German*
    a. Max$_k$ weiß, [$_{CP}$ daß Maria$_i$ sich*$_{k/i}$/sich selbst*$_{k/i}$ mag].
        Max knows that Maria SELF/SELF-self likes
        Lit.'Max$_k$ knows that Maria$_i$ likes SELF/SELF-self.'

(Fischer 2004)

a'. Hans$_k$ ließ [$_{VP}$ Otto$_i$ sich$_{k/i}$/sich selbst$_{*k/i}$ rasieren].
Hans   let   Otto SELF/SELF-self   shave
Lit.'Hans$_k$ let Otto$_i$ shave SELF/SELF-self.'

(Gallmann 2009)

b. *Die Leute schlagen den Fragenden *sich* als Vorhandlungsführer vor.
Lit. 'The people proposed the questioner SELF as the principal negotiator.' (Everaert 1986)

b' *Das Ausschuß erzählt Johann etwas über *sich/sich selbst*.
Lit. 'The committee told John something about SELF.'

(Ishino and Ura 2011c)

c. Ich habe *mich* verletzt.
I   have me   hurt
Lit. 'I've hurt myself.'

c'. Eine Dame/Ein Herr   washt/washst   *sich*.
A lady/A gentleman   washes   SELF
Lit. 'A lady washes herself./A gentleman washes himself.'

c".i. Die Kinder   bewunderten   *sich*.
the children   admired   SELF
Lit. 'The children admired themselves.'

c".ii. Wir hassen   *uns*.
We hate   us
Lit. 'We hate ourselves.'

d. [Hans$_i$ und Maria$_j$] lichen über   *sich*$_{i \otimes j}$.
John   and   Mary   laugh at/about   SELF
Lit. 'John laughs at John, and Mary laughs at Mary.'

(Gast and Haas 2008)

According to Reuland (2011), we see *sich*, which only occurs in 3rd person, as the German reflexive; for 1st and 2nd person are realized in a pronominal form with singular/plural contrast (e.g., *mich* 'myself' in (5.24c) and *uns* 'ourselves' in (5.24c".ii)). As a result, L1 *sich* is strictly specified in terms of the *person*-feature because it cannot be interpreted as first-/second-person, whereas its *gender*-feature is underspecified because it can be interpreted either as masculine or as feminine, as exemplified in (5.24c'). *Sich* in the grammar of L1 German, having no plural form, allows free interpretation in *number*, as exemplified in (5.24c".i). Thus, the *number*-feature of L1 *sich* is defined as underspecified. These observations lead us to conclude that *sich* allows the *gender*-neutral and *number*-neutral interpretations, but it does not have the *person*-neutral interpretation.

Given that the *number*-feature of *sich* is underspecified, it is expected that it permits the distributive reading, as observed in (5.24d) above. The compositional property of *sich* shows that it is φ-defective in the sense of Burzio (1991), because its *gender-/number*-features are concluded to be underspecified. Applying ATRB to the German reflexive, it can be safely said that L1 *sich* is always subject oriented, as shown in (5.24b). (5.24a) and (5.24a') above illustrate the locality on its binding dependency (cf. Lee-Shoenfeld 2008, and Gallmann 2009). L1 *sich* shows LD when it is embedded in a non-tensed clause, but it shows LC when it is embedded in a tensed clause.[6] *Sich* therefore shows the different locality on the binding dependency from the Japanese morphologically simplex reflexive *zibun* in that *zibun* can move at LF and shows LD in a tensed clause.

A number of studies, following Pica's (1987) analysis, have advocated for a movement analysis for simplex reflexives, such as *sich* in L1 German (*inter alia*, Reinhart and Reuland 1991), *zibun* in L1 Japanese (*inter alia*, Katada 1991) and *ziji* in L1 Chinese (*inter alia*, Cole, Hermon and Sung 1990, Cole and Sung 1994, and Huang and Tang 1991). It has been extensively argued (Reinhart and Reuland 1991) that in verb raising languages simplex anaphors first adjoin to their governing V. Then, V with the adjoined anaphor moves up to T, and the V-T complex next moves up to a higher V, then to a higher T. In another raising analysis (e.g., Lee-Shoenfeld 2008), it is proposed that a landing site of *sich* for its covert movement is a phase edge, such as a Spec of *v*P in the case of causative constructions. It is assumed that a reflexive has what she calls *reflexive feature*, which should be probed by a matching feature on the embedded *v*P phase edge. As a result, such covert movement can pass a specified subject (namely, a causee of a causative construction) in order to be bound by a matrix/superordinate subject DP (namely, a causer of a causative construction). Therefore it is stipulated that a reflexive has the reflexive feature and its matching feature is on the embedded *v*P edge. When a reflexive is bound by a specified subject in an embedded clause (i.e., when it is locally bound), by what kind of matching feature a reflexive can be probed, though?

We therefore reject the idea that the LD-property of *sich* in a non-tensed clause is brought by its LF movement property. In Reuland (2001), one of the most recent influential studies on anaphora, *sich* does not move; rather, the relations which reflect dependencies between a subject DP, T, V, and an anaphor can be composed to connect a feature chain, which he calls *composite dependency*. We see a feature chain proposed in Reuland (2011) as basically the same as the dependency of the syntactic binding that is proposed in ATRB.

According to Ishino and Ura (2011a) endorsing ATRB, following Faltz's (1977) typological classification, it is assumed that morphologically simplex reflexives, such as *zibun* in L1 Japanese, can move at LF to adjoin to the matrix subject DP_1 (as shown in (5.25)), whereas a complex one in L1 Japanese *zibun-zisin* cannot move because of its lexical integrity (as shown in (5.26)).

(5.25) Locality of Binding Dependency for a Φ-Defective Simplex Reflexive (the *zibun*-type) in a Tensed Clause

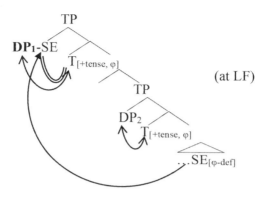

(5.26) Locality of Binding Dependency for a Φ-Defective Complex Reflexive (the *zibun-zisin*-type) in a Tensed Clause

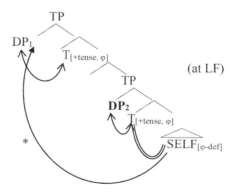

Given that a morphologically simplex reflexive can undergo a covert movement up to the matrix clause, as shown in (5.25), *sich* in L1 German, which is also morphologically simple, is supposed to behave as such. *Sich* is expected to be bound by the subject DP_1, but it is not borne out. *Sich* is locally bound when it is embedded in a tensed clause, as observed in (5.24a). Contrary to L1 *zibun* (as shown in (5.25)) *sich* in L1 German cannot be bound by the matrix subject DP_1 over a tensed clause boundary. Look at (5.27) below:

(5.27) Locality of Binding Dependency for a Φ-Defective Simplex Reflexive (the *sich*-type) in a Tensed Clause

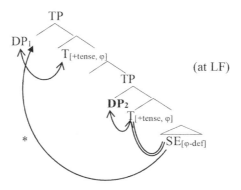

(at LF)

Sich is morphologically simplex, so that it is natural to assume that *sich* can move at LF. As depicted in (5.27), however, *sich* cannot move at LF to adjoin to the matrix subject DP_1 due to the φ-feature checking ability of T[+tense] in L1 German. To put it differently, the difference between the locality on the binding dependency of *sich* and that of *zibun* (as well as *ziji*) can be accounted for as follows: All of them are φ-defective simplex anaphors and it is uniformly explained under ATRB that all of them need to be supplied with the φ-features at LF by T with the whole φ-feature amalgam to be properly interpreted. We assume that the φ-feature checking property of T in L1 German is different from that of L1 Japanese (and L1 Chinese) in terms of the activeness in the feature checking ability at LF. Under the *Agree* Theory (cf. Chomsky 2000) uninterpretable features of a probe α and a goal β are checked/deleted and erased before Spell-Out, because they are not necessary for interpretation at LF. It has widely been acknowledged, for example, that the nominative Case feature of DP should be erased before Spell-Out, because it is not necessary for interpretation, but the φ-features of DP should not be erased, because it is necessary for interpretation at LF (i.e., it is only checked at narrow syntax). When the φ-features of DP matches the φ-features of T[+tense] in terms of the feature identity, they are checked/deleted in narrow syntax, but the φ-features of T are necessary for interpretation at LF and should not be erased in narrow syntax. Given that the φ-features in T[+tense] are checked in narrow syntax but not erased before LF, the φ-feature checking between a φ-defective reflexive and T[+tense] can take place at LF, as assumed in Binding through *Agree*. This is schematized in (5.28) below:

(5.28) The φ-feature checking ability of T
    a. Case feature checking
        [DP$_{uCase, \varphi1}$ T$_{\varphi1}$ [vp .... SELF$_{\varphi\text{-def}}$ ....]]
            └─AGREE─┘   (before Spell-Out)

    b. φ-feature checking
        [DP$_{uCase, \varphi1}$ T$_{\sqrt{\varphi1}}$ [vp .... SELF$_{\varphi1}$ .....]]
            └─AGREE─┘ └──AGREE──┘   (at LF)

As indicated in (5.28b) above, the φ-feature of T becomes $\sqrt{\varphi}$ at LF (that is, T retains the ability of entering into the checking relation in the φ-features at LF) after it is checked/deleted before Spell-Out under the structural relation of the Case feature checking, as shown in (5.28a). Then, we stipulate that $\sqrt{\varphi}$ can count as *active* Probe or *inactive* Probe for agreement with a φ-defective reflexive *SELF$_{\varphi\text{-def}}$*. Only active $\sqrt{\varphi}$ can agree with *SELF$_{\varphi\text{-def}}$* in order to supply the relevant reflexive with its φ-features; otherwise, the given structure cannot be properly interpreted because a φ-defective reflexive cannot be interpreted due to its referential deficiency.

As we have stated previously, we assume that the φ-feature checking property of T in L1 German is different from that of L1 Japanese in terms of the activeness in the φ-feature checking ability at LF. More precisely, the φ-feature checking property of an active $\sqrt{\varphi}$ determines the presence/absence of the multiple checking property of $\sqrt{\varphi}$ in T. There is a two-way distinction in the number of the checking ability of $\sqrt{\varphi}$ in T; that is, (i) inactive $\sqrt{\varphi}$ does not agree with a φ-defective reflexive, and (ii) active $\sqrt{\varphi}$ can agree with a φ-defective reflexive once or more than once. Notice here that only active $\sqrt{\varphi}$ has the ability to agree with a refleIxive in the φ-features; however, both of active $\sqrt{\varphi}$ and inactive $\sqrt{\varphi}$ counts as defective elements and may block the agreement between a φ-defective reflexive and another Probe which

CHAPTER 5 CROSSLINGUISTIC INVESTIGATIONS ON TG REFLEXIVES

is located at the structurally higher position. If a situation rises where the embedded T has inactive $\sqrt{\varphi}$, a φ-defective simplex reflexive (such as *zibun*) moves up to the matrix T in order to become φ-complete through *Agree*. Then the long-distant binding of *zibun* in a tensed clause is successfully established. On the other hand, in the same situation where the embedded T has inactive $\sqrt{\varphi}$, a φ-defective complex reflexive (such as *zibun-zisin*) cannot be provided with the φ-features by inactive $\sqrt{\varphi}$ because a reflexive cannot move at LF. As a result, a φ-defective complex reflexive cannot be properly interpreted and the derivation crashes at LF. When the embedded T has active $\sqrt{\varphi}$, the embedded T counts as a Probe for *zibun-zisin*. Then it can be explained that *zibun-zisin* in a tensed clause always shows LC.

Returning to the locality of binding dependency for simplex reflexives, we make the following hypothesis: (i) $\sqrt{\varphi}$ of T[+tense] in L1 German is always active and can agree with a goal only once; that is, $\sqrt{\varphi}$ of T[+tense] in L1 German obligatorily agrees with *sich* in the φ-features if there is *sich* in the same clause, so that the embedded T[+tense] unexceptionally agrees with *sich* in situ in the same embedded clause, as shown in (5.27). The economy condition prevents *sich* from moving up to the matrix clause, because it has already been supplied with the φ-features by the embedded T[+tense]. It follows that *sich* always shows LC in a tensed clause; on the other hand, (ii) $\sqrt{\varphi}$ of T[+tense] in L1 Japanese can be active or inactive. Moreover, when it is active, it can agree with multiple goals. When $\sqrt{\varphi}$ of T in L1 Japanese is active, the locality is the same as that of L1 *sich*. As a result, $\sqrt{\varphi}$ in the embedded T must agree with *zibun* in situ and *zibun* does not need to move up into the matrix clause. Then, *zibun* shows LC in a tensed clause. On the other hand, when $\sqrt{\varphi}$ of T in L1 Japanese is inactive, it cannot provide the φ-features to *zibun*. Accordingly, *zibun* moves up into the matrix clause and feature binding between the matrix T and *zibun* can be established. Then, *zibun* shows LD in a tensed clause. As a result, *zibun* optionally shows LD in a tensed clause thanks to the checking ability of $\sqrt{\varphi}$ in T.[7]

German has the complex reflexive form *sich selbst*, which is morphologically made of a simplex reflexive *sich* 'SELF' and a focalizing particle *-selbst* '-self.' The specification of each φ-feature in the German reflexives and their syntactic properties are summarized in (5.29) below:

(5.29)

L1 *German*	*sich*	*sich selbst*
(i) morphology	simplex	complex
(ii) φ-features		
person	+	+
gender	∅	∅
number	∅	∅
(iii) φ-completeness	φ-defective	φ-defective
(iv) syntactic properties	syntactic binding	syntactic binding
Subject Orientation	yes	yes
Binding Dependency Tensed/Non-tensed	LC / LD	LC / LC
Distributive Reading	yes	yes

The feature composition of *sich selbst* is the same as that of *sich* (that is, the strictly specified *person*-feature and the underspecified *gender*-/*number*-features). Their feature composition indicates that *sich* and *sich selbst* count as φ-defective under FTFL.

Then, an important question soon arises: Why is it that *sich selbst*, which is assumed to be φ-defective under FTFL, shows the different locality from other φ-defective complex reflexives (e.g., *zibun-zisin* shows LC in a tensed clause, but LD in a non-tensed clause). L1 *sich selbst* always shows LC although it requires the syntactic binding due to its property of the φ-feature deficiency. We assume that an embedded causative clause in L1 German has T[-tense] with the whole φ-feature amalgam. As we have discussed in § 3.4.2, we assume that the Japanese causative clause takes two types of clausal complement: One corresponds to *v*P without T, and the other corresponds to TP[-tense] with the whole φ-feature amalgam. Then, we assume that the German causative clause takes one type of clausal complement; namely, TP[-tense] with the whole φ-feature amalgam. As a result, the local binding relation between a φ-defective reflexive and the causee within the non-tensed causative clause emerges through the mediation by T[-tense]. It is expected that *sich selbst* is always locally bound. More importantly, *sich selbst* stays in situ because of its lexical integrity and it becomes φ-complete only when it is provided with the φ-features through *Agree* mediated by T. Returning to the assumption in ATRB that the subject orientation of a φ-defective reflexive is induced by *Agree* mediated by T, we can explain it straightforwardly that *sich selbst* shows the subject orientation.

5.2.1. Prediction by Previous Studies (PRA and LTA)

In analogy with the theoretical problems immanent in the prediction by PRA and LTA with respect to the syntactic properties of the Chinese reflexives in the transitional grammar of JLsC, their approaches require to presuppose that a certain L1 anaphora is to be selected as the source of their consideration because both of the L1 and the target language of JLsG have more than one reflexive form.

If we take *zibun* to be representative of the Japanese reflexive forms for JLsG, as presupposed in PRA, it is predicted that JLsG mistakenly regard the parameter value for *sich* (i.e., the value (c)) as the value (b), which lies between their L1 value and the target value, what is more, it is also predicted that JLsG mistakenly regard the parameter value for *sich selbst* (i.e., the value (a)) as the value (c).

On the other hand, LTA predicts that *sich* in the transitional grammar of JLsG shows the same locality on binding dependency as the one of L1 *zibun* because they are both morphologically simplex. With respect to *sich selbst* in the transitional grammar of JLsG, LTA predicts (*inter alia*, Ishino and Ura 2010) that JLsG are very apt to misconceive the locality on the binding dependency of *sich selbst*; that is, the locality on the binding dependency of *sich selbst* in the transitional grammar of JLsG show LD in a non-tensed clause and LC in a tensed clause (i.e., the value (c)). It is very important here again to notice that LTA should stipulate an additional reason other than the morphological complexity (such as the φ-completeness (cf. Ishino and Ura 2009)) for the selection of the L1 representative reflexive; for, advocates for LTA, if they only take the morphological complexity into consideration, cannot determine which one of the L1 complex reflexives *zibun-zisin* or *kare-zisin* syntactically behaves on a par with *sich selbst* in the transitional grammar of JLsG because both of them are equivalent to each other in terms of the morphological complexity.

5.2.2. Prediction by FTFL

Let us first apply FTFL to the German reflexives in the transitional grammar of JLsG, as shown in (5.30) below:

(5.30) Prediction of the properties of *sich* and *sich selbst* in the transitional grammar of beginner/intermediate and advanced JLsG:

(i) level		L1 Japanese	TG *sich*		Target German *sich* / *sich selbst*
			Beginner/ Intermediate	Advanced	
(ii)	φ-features				
	person	{∅} ⟶ ∅ ⟹		+ ⟵------	+
	gender	{∅} ⟶ ∅		∅	∅
	number	{−} ⟶ −(α) ⟹		∅ (β) ⟵------	∅
(iii)	φ-completeness		φ-defective(*a)	φ-defective	φ-defective
(iv)	syntactic properties		syntactic binding	syntactic binding	syntactic binding
	Subject Orientation		yes (*b)	yes (*c)	yes
	Binding Dependency Tensed/Non-tensed		LD/LD (*sich*) LC/LD (*sich selbst*)	LC/LD (*sich*) LC/LC (*sich selbst*)	LC/LD (*sich*) LC/LC (*sich selbst*)
	Distributive Reading		yes (*d)	yes (*e)	yes
	Number-neutral interpretation		no (*f)	yes (*g)	yes

With respect to the *person*-feature in *sich* and *sich selbst* in the transitional grammar of JLsG, Feature Transfer demands that the *person*-feature, which is underspecified, in their L1 feature inventory be initially transferred to the transitional grammar of beginner/intermediate JLsG. Then, the transferred L1 feature is distinct from the target one in terms of the markedness of its specification. As a result, it is predicted that the *person*-feature of *sich* and *sich selbst* in the later stage of the transitional grammar of advanced JLsG should become strictly specified thanks to Feature Learning, as previously indicated in (2.3) (repeated as (5.31) below):

(5.31) L1 *Marked* and Target *Unmarked* (strictly specified):
Transferred and overwritten

Stage in L2 Learning	L1 Feature Inventory	TG (Beginner/ Intermediate)	TG (Advanced)	Target Item
earlier	{Ø} ⟶	Ø		
later		Ø ⟹	(+) ◄------	+

The L1 value changes to the target value later in transitional grammar.

It is therefore expected that beginner/intermediate JLsG are mistakenly apt to regard *sich* and *sich selbst* as having the *person*-neutral interpretation; however, advanced JLsG correctly regard them as not having the *person*-neutral interpretation. With respect to the *gender*-feature, an L1 feature inventory includes the same specification as the target one does; that is, both of them are underspecified. Under FTFL, it is explained that the *gender*-feature in *sich* and *sich selbst* in the transitional grammar of JLsG is underspecified.

Next, with respect to the *number*-feature in *sich* in the transitional grammar of JLsG, the L1 feature is distinct from the target one in terms of the markedness of its specification; that is, the L1 feature is partially specified and unmarked, and the target one is underspecified and marked. FTFL predicts that the *number*-feature in *sich* in the transitional grammar of beginner/intermediate JLsG is partially specified due to Feature Transfer, but it is also predicted that the *number*-feature of *sich* for advanced JLsG is replaced by the target feature, which is underspecified, thanks to Feature Learning, as previously indicated in (2.6) (repeated as (5.32) below):

(5.32) L1 *Unmarked* (partially specified) and Target *Marked*: Transferred and overwritten

Stage in L2 Learning	L1 Feature Inventory	TG (Beginner/ Intermediate)	TG (Advanced)	Target Item
earlier	{−} ⟶	−		
later		− ⟹	Ø	⟵ Ø

The L1 value changes to the target value later in transitional grammar.

We can infer from the prediction by FTFL that beginner/intermediate JLsG mistakenly regard *sich* as not having the *number*-neutral interpretation, but advanced JLsG correctly consider *sich* as allowing it, as shown in (*f*) and (*g*) in (5.30). With respect to the distributive interpretation, the German reflexives in the transitional grammar of JLsG correctly permit it, as shown in (*d*) and (*e*) in (5.30); for they are not strictly specified in terms of the *number*-feature. Applying FTFL to the transitional grammar of JLsG, we can conclude that *sich* and *sich selbst* in their transitional grammar are φ-defective and show the subject orientation, as shown in (*b*) and (*c*) in (5.30).

Given that *sich* in the transitional grammar of beginner/intermediate JLsG is φ-defective and morphologically simplex, we can predict its locality on the binding dependency through ATRB; that is, it is predicted that *sich* in the transitional grammar of JLsG shows LD both in a tensed and a non-tensed clause. Note again that we need a special discussion on the locality of L1 *sich*. Whether beginner/intermediate JLsG misconceive its locality on the binding dependency or not depends on the activeness and the φ-feature checking ability of $\sqrt{\varphi}$ in T in their transitional grammar. If $\sqrt{\varphi}$ in T[+tense] in their transitional grammar is active and obligatorily agrees with a single φ-defective reflexive in the φ-features, *sich* in their transitional grammar shows LD in a non-tensed clause, but shows LC in a tensed clause because *sich* in situ is always provided with the φ-features by the nearest T[+tense]. Then, there is no possibility for *sich* to move at LF. The economy condition does not permit such unmotivated movement. On the other hand, if $\sqrt{\varphi}$ in T[+tense] in their transitional grammar is inactive and is allowed to agree with no goal, it does not count as a defective element. It is necessary for *sich* in their transitional grammar to move up to a higher T passing a lower T with the inactive φ-features, resulting in its wider locality (that is, *sich* shows LD in a tensed clause). Its morphological simplicity allows *sich* in the transitional grammar of JLsG to move to the matrix T, when $\sqrt{\varphi}$ in embedded T[+tense] is inactive. It follows that T[+tense]'s activeness and its checking ability determine the locality on the binding dependency of *sich* in JLsG's transitional grammar.

Under ATRB, the locality on the binding dependency of *sich selbst* in the transitional grammar of beginner/intermediate JLsG is expected to show LC in a tensed clause and LD in a non-tensed clause. As we have argued in § 5.2, *sich selbst* is a φ-defective anaphor in line with the definition embraced in FTFL. Consequently, FTFL predicts that beginner/intermediate JLsG mistakenly regard *sich selbst* as showing LD in a non-tensed clause and LC in a tensed clause, the locality which φ-defective complex reflexives show. In addition, we stipulate that once they correctly regard $\sqrt{\varphi}$ in T[+tense] in L1 German can agree one and only goal, *sich selbst* in advanced JLsG's transitional grammar shows LC both in a tensed and a non-tensed clause. To put it differently, we assume that a trigger which changes the LD-property of *sich selbst* in a non-tensed clause to the LC-property is the checking property of $\sqrt{\varphi}$ in T, so that it is not explained straightforwardly from the application of FTFL.

In what follows let us apply FTFL to the Japanese reflexives in the transitional grammar of German learners of Japanese (GLsJ), as shown in (5.33) below:

(5.33) Prediction of the properties of *zibun(-zisin)* in the transitional grammar of beginner/intermediate and advanced GLsJ:

(i) level	L1 German	TG *zibun(-zisin)* Beginner/ Intermediate	TG *zibun(-zisin)* Advanced	Target Japanese *zibun(-zisin)*
(ii) φ-features				
person	{+} ⟶ +	⟹ Ø	⟵ Ø	
gender	{Ø} ⟶ Ø	Ø	Ø	
number	{Ø} ⟶ Ø	⟹ –	⟵ –	
(iii) φ-completeness		φ-defective(*a)	φ-defective	φ-defective
(iv) syntactic properties		syntactic binding	syntactic binding	syntactic binding
Subject Orientation		yes (*b)	yes (*c)	yes
Binding Dependency Tensed/Non-tensed		LD/LD (*zibun*) LC/LC (*zibun-zisin*)	LD/LD (*zibun*) LC/LC (*zibun-zisin*)	LD/LD (*zibun*) LC/LC (*zibun-zisin*)
Distributive Reading		yes (*d)	yes (*e)	yes
Number-neutral interpretation		yes (*f)	no (*g)	no

First, with respect to the *person*-feature, the strictly specified one in the L1 inventory of GLsJ should be transferred to their transitional grammar. Then, the transferred L1 feature is distinct from the target one in terms of the markedness of its specification. It is predicted that the *person*-feature of *zibun(-zisin)* in the transitional grammar of advanced GLsJ should be replaced by the target feature, which is underspecified, thanks to Feature Learning, as previously indicated in (2.5) (repeated as (5.34) below):

CHAPTER 5 CROSSLINGUISTIC INVESTIGATIONS ON TG REFLEXIVES

(5.34) L1 *Unmarked* (strictly specified) and Target *Marked*:
Transferred and overwritten

Stage in L2 Learning	L1 Feature Inventory	TG (Beginner/ Intermediate)	TG (Advanced)	Target Item
earlier	{+} ⟶	+		
later		+ ⟹	Ⓞ	⟵------ Ø

The L1 value changes to the target value later in transitional grammar.

We predict that advanced GLsJ correctly regard *zibun(-zisin)* as having the *person*-neutral interpretation. With respect to the *gender*-feature, the L1 feature is the same as the target one in terms of its specification; that is, both of them are underspecified. The *gender*-feature in *zibun(-zisin)* in the transitional grammar of GLsJ is expected to be underspecified.

Finally, with respect to the *number*-feature, the marked feature in the L1 feature inventory of GLsJ should be transferred to their transitional grammar. Then, the transferred L1 feature is distinct from the target one in terms of the markedness of its specification. As a result, Feature Learning predicts that the *number*-feature of *zibun(-zisin)* in the transitional grammar of advanced GLsJ should be replaced by the target one, which is partially specified, as previously shown in (2.4) (repeated as (5.35) below):

(5.35) L1 *Marked* and Target *Unmarked* (partially specified):
Transferred and overwritten

Stage in L2 Learning	L1 Feature Inventory	TG (Beginner/ Intermediate)	TG (Advanced)	Target Item
earlier	{Ø} ⟶	Ø		
later		Ø ⟹	(−)	⟵------ −

The L1 value changes to the target value later in transitional grammar.

Accordingly, FTFL predicts that beginner/intermediate GLsJ mistakenly regard *zibun(-zisin)* as allowing the *number*-neutral interpretation, but advanced GLsJ correctly consider *zibun(-zisin)* as disallowing it, as shown

134

in (*f) and (*g) in (5.33). Moreover, it is predicted that *zibun(-zisin)* in the transitional grammar of GLsJ permits the distributive reading, as shown in (*d) and (*e) in (5.33); for, their *number*-feature is not strictly specified. Now the conclusion we have reached is that *zibun(-zisin)* in the transitional grammar of GLsJ is φ-defective and shows the subject orientation, as shown in (*b) and (*c) in (5.33).[8]

Next, we will apply FTFL to *kare-zisin* in their transitional grammar, as shown in (5.36) below:

(5.36) Prediction of the properties of *kare-zisin* in the transitional grammar of beginner/intermediate and advanced GLsJ:

		L1 German	TG *kare-zisin*		Target Japanese *kare-zisin*
(i)	level		Beginner/ Intermediate	Advanced	
(ii)	φ-features				
	person	{+} →	+	+	+
	gender	{Ø} →	Ø ⇒	+	+
	number	{Ø} →	Ø ⇒	+ ← ----	+
(iii)	φ-completeness		φ-defective (*a)	φ-complete (*b)	φ-complete
(iv)	syntactic properties		syntactic binding	reflexivizer	reflexivizer
	Subject Orientation		yes (*c)	no (*d)	no
	Binding Dependency Tensed/Non-tensed		LD / LC	LC / LC	LC / LC
	Distributive Reading		yes (*e)	no (*f)	no
	Number-neutral interpretation		no	no	no

With respect to the *person*-feature, the strictly specified feature in the L1 feature inventory of GLsJ should be transferred to their transitional grammar. It is therefore expected that GLsJ correctly regard *kare-zisin* as

CHAPTER 5 CROSSLINGUISTIC INVESTIGATIONS ON TG REFLEXIVES

disallowing the *person*-neutral interpretation. With respect to the *gender-/number*-features, their L1 features are different from the target ones in terms of the markedness of the feature specification, as indicated in (2.3) (repeated as (5.37) below):

(5.37) L1 *Marked* and Target *Unmarked* (strictly specified):
Transferred and overwritten

Stage in L2 Learning	L1 Feature Inventory	TG (Beginner/ Intermediate)	TG (Advanced)	Target Item
earlier	{Ø} ⟶	Ø		
later		Ø ⟹	(+) ◀------	+

The L1 value changes to the target value later in transitional grammar.

Notice here that *kare-zisin* in the transitional grammar of GLsJ is expected to be in the feature compoisition of {+,Ø,Ø} at the early stage of their L2 learning, but at the later stage of their transitional grammar, it is expected to become the feature composition of {+,+,+}: Consequently, *kare-zisin* in the transitional grammar of beginner/intermediate GLsJ is φ-defective (as shown in (*a*) in (5.36)) because it includes the *gender-/number*-features which are deemed to be underspecified, but *kare-zisin* in the transitional grammar of advanced GLsJ becomes φ-complete (as shown in (*b*) in (5.36)) because its *gender-/number*-features turn out to be strictly specified due to Feature Learning. This lead us to conclude that *kare-zisin* in the transitional grammar of advanced GLsJ is regarded as a reflexivizer according to its φ-completeness. As a significant consequence of FTFL, beginner/intermediate GLsJ are mistakenly apt to regard *kare-zisin* as showing the subject orientation because *kare-zisin* in their transitional grammar is φ-defective, but advanced GLsJ correctly reject its subject orientation because *kare-zisin* in their transitional grammar is φ-complete (as shown in (*c*) and (*d*) in (5.36)). Finally, it is also predicted that beginner/intermediate GLsJ mistakenly regard *kare-zisin* as allowing the distributive reading, but advanced GLsJ correctly regard *kare-zisin* as disallowing it because its *number*-feature is strictly specified, as shown in (*e*) and (*f*) in (5.36).

5.2.3. Experiments

In the previous subsection, we have so far demonstrated the application of FTFL to the specification of each φ-feature in the L1 German/Japanese reflexives and their syntactic properties in the transitional grammar of JLsG/GLsJ. We will next provide our experimental data to ensure that they are consistent with the prediction by FTFL.

Beginner/intermediate JLsG who participated in our experimental surveys were divided into three groups consisting of 31, 33, and 13 students, all of whom were native Japanese and at the time of our experiment they had studied German at university for more than two years. An advanced JLG who participated in our experimental surveys was a graduate student, majoring in German at the Department of German literatures and language. He was a native Japanese and at the time of our experiment he had studied German as a second language for more than nine years.

First we contrived the following experiments in order to disclose the precise locality on the binding dependency of *sich* and *sich selbst* in the transitional grammar of JLsG. The subjects were beforehand explained how to answer to each test sentence: They were instructed to answer to a question as to whether they are grammatical or not. We have utilized the following test sentences in which the German reflexives are contained either within an embedded tensed clause (as in (5.38)), or within an embedded non-tensed clause, such as a perceptive verb construction (as in (5.39)):[9]

(5.38) a. *Die Studenten$_k$ glauben, [$_{CP}$ daß Ich *sich$_k$* liebe].
The students believe that I SELF love
Lit. 'The students believe that I love SELF.'

b. *Die Studenten$_k$ glauben, [$_{CP}$ daß Ich *sich selbst$_k$* liebe].
The students believe that I SELF-self love
Lit. 'The students believe that I love SELF-self.'

(5.39) a. ^{OK}Die Studenten$_k$ hörten [$_{VP}$ die Lehrer über *sich$_k$* sprechen].
The students hear the teacher about SELF speak
Lit. 'The students hear the teacher speak about SELF.'

CHAPTER 5   CROSSLINGUISTIC INVESTIGATIONS ON TG REFLEXIVES

    b. *<u>Die Studenten</u>$_k$ hörten [$_{VP}$ die Lehrer über   <u>sich selbst</u>$_k$
        The students   hear   the teacher about SELF-self
        sprechen].
        speak
        Lit. 'The students hear the teacher speak about SELF-self.'

If our JLG subject judges (5.38a) as acceptable under the interpretation that *sich* is coreferential with *Die Studenten*, he/she is alleged to interpret *sich* as being bound astride a tensed clause boundary; namely, he/she regards *sich* within a tensed clause as showing LD. If our JLG subject judges (5.38a) as unacceptable, he/she is alleged to interpret *sich* as not being bound astride a tensed clause boundary; namely, he/she regards *sich* within a tensed clause as showing LC. If a subject judges (5.38b) as acceptable, he/she regards *sich selbst* within a tensed clause as showing LD. If a subject judges (5.38b) as unacceptable, he/she regards *sich selbst* within a tensed clause as showing LC.

    Moreover, we examined the locality on the binding dependency of their German reflexives within a non-tensed clause. With respect to a non-tensed clause, we have utilized the test sentences in (5.39): The examples in (5.39) are acceptable when *sich/sich selbst* are locally bound. Our JLG subjects were asked whether (5.39) are acceptable when *sich/sich selbst* are coreferential with *Die Studenten*. Those who judge (5.39a) as acceptable regard *sich within* a non-tensed clause as showing LD, and those who judge (5.39a) as unacceptable regard *sich* within a non-tensed clause as showing LC. Those who judge (5.39b) as acceptable regard *sich selbst* within a non-tensed clause as showing LD, and those who judge (5.39b) as unacceptable regard *sich selbst* within a non-tensed clause as showing LC. The results of our experimental tests are shown in Table 3.1 and Table 3.2:

TABLE 3.1. Locality for the Binding Dependency (*Sich*)

(%)		JLsG[a]	
		Tensed	Non-tensed
(a)	LC	19.4	0.0
(b)	LD	**80.6**	*100.0*

[a]$n=31$.

TABLE 3.2. Locality for the Binding Dependency (*Sich selbst*)

(%)		JLsG[a]	
		Tensed	Non-tensed
(c)	LC	**83.9**	48.4
(d)	LD	16.1	**51.6**

[a]$n=31$. *Notes.* Statistically, there are significant differences: $t=-7.385$, $p<.001$ (between (a) and (c)), $t=4.062$, $p<.001$ (between (c) and (d)).

Notice here that 80.6% of the JLG subjects mistakenly regard *sich* within an embedded tensed clause (as in (5.38a)) as showing LD, though *sich* in the grammar of L1 German shows LC in a tensed clause. Of another empirical interest is the fact that 51.6% of our JLG subjects regard *sich selbst* within a non-tensed clause (as in (5.39b)) as showing LD, although 83.9% of them correctly regard *sich selbst* within a tensed clause (as in (5.38b)) as showing LC.

Next, in order to confirm whether the *person*-feaure of *sich(-selbst)* in the transitional grammar of JLsG is underspecified or not, we presented both of the beginner/intermediate JLG group and the advanced JLG with the sentence in (5.40), which is acceptable in the grammar of L1 German, and (5.41) and (5.42), which are unacceptable in the grammar of L1 German.

(5.40) ^{OK}Die Damen washen *sich*.
       The ladies wash SELF
       Lit. 'The ladies wash themselves.'

(5.41) *Du und deiner Familie washen *sich.*
You and your family wash SELF
Lit. 'You and your family wash yourselves.'

(5.42) *Wir washen *sich.*
We wash SELF
Lit. 'We wash ourselves.'

The results of the test are shown in Table 3.3 below:

TABLE 3.3. Acceptability of the *Person*-Neutral Interpretation

(%)	Beginner/Intermediate JLsG[a]	Advanced JLG[b]
acceptable	**73.1**	*0.0*
unacceptable	*26.9*	**100.0**

[a]n=13. [b]n=1.

As shown in Table 3.3, 73.1% of our beginner/intermediate JLG subjects mistakenly regard the given sentences of (5.41) and (5.42) as acceptable; that is, they mistakenly regard *sich* as being bound by 1st and/or 2nd person antecedents. Note that 100% of our beginner/intermediate JLG correctly regard (5.40) as acceptable. It can be concluded that the *person*-feature of *sich* in the transitional grammar of beginner/intermediate JLsG is underspecified. On the other hand, 100% of our advanced JLG subject correctly regarded the sentences in (5.41) and (5.42) as unacceptable. It can be safely said that the *person*-feature of the German reflexives in the transitional grammar of advanced JLsG is strictly specified.

In addition, we presented our beginner/intermediate JLsG subjects with the sentence in (5.43) and (5.44), which are acceptable in the grammar of L1 German in order to confirm whether the *gender*-feature of their German reflexives is underspecified, and its result is shown in Table 3.4.

(5.43) ᴼᴷEine Dame wascht *sich.*
A lady washes SELF
Lit. 'A lady washes herself.'

(5.44) ᴼᴷEin Herr waschst *sich.*
A gentleman washes SELF
Lit. 'A gentleman washes himself.'

TABLE 3.4. **Acceptability of the *Gender*-Neutral Interpretation**

(%)	Beginner/Intermediate JLsG[a]	Advanced JLG[b]
acceptable	**84.6**	***100.0***
unacceptable	*15.4*	*0.0*

[a]$n=13$. [b]$n=1$.

As shown in Table 3.4, 84.6% of our beginner/intermediate JLG subjects correctly regard both of (5.43) and (5.44) as acceptable; that is, they correctly regard *sich* as being bound by a masculine or a feminine antecedent. It can be safely concluded that the *gender*-feature of *sich* in the transitional grammar of JLsG is underspecified.

Next, in order to discern whether JLsG consider the *number*-feature of *sich* in their transitional grammar to be specified or underspecified, we presented both of beginner/intermediate JLsG and advanced JLsG in our experimental surveys with the test sentence in (5.45), which is acceptable in the grammar of L1 German:

(5.45) [Karl und Maria]$_i$ sehen sich$_i$.
Charles and Mary see SELF
Lit. '[Charles and Mary] see [Charles and Mary].' (*group reading*)

Sich in the grammar of L1 German can be bound by the plural antecedents, here *Karl* and *Maria* because the *number*-feature of *sich* is underspecified. It is therefore acceptable that the sentence in (5.45) means '(the group of)

Charles and Mary see (the group of) Charles and Mary,' which we call *group reading*. Our JLG subjects were asked whether (5.45) has the interpretation '(the group of) Charles and Mary see (the group of) Charles and Mary.' If our JLG subjects regard the sentence in (5.45) as acceptable, we conclude that *sich* in their transitional grammar is underspecified in terms of the *number*-feature because underspecification in terms of the *number*-feature leads to arbitrarily any interpretation in *number*. The result of this survey is delineated in Table 3.5:

TABLE 3.5. **Acceptability of the *Number*-Neutral Interpretation**

(%)	Beginner/Intermediate JLsG[a]	Advanced JLG[b]
acceptable	33.3	**100.0**
unacceptable	**66.7**	0.0

[a]$n=33$. [b]$n=1$.

As Table 3.5 shows, 66.7% of our 33 beginner/intermediate JLG subjects rejected the sentence in (5.45); therefrom, we infer that the *number*-feature within *sich* in the transitional grammar of beginner/intermediate JLsG is ***not underspecified***. Empirically, highly interesting is the fact that our advanced JLG subject regarded the sentence in (5.45) as acceptable. The result shown in Table 3.5 leads us to conclude that the *number*-feature of *sich* in the transitional grammar of advanced JLsG is underspecified. FTFL predicts that the *number*-feature in *sich* in the transitional grammar of beginner/intermediate JLsG is (partially) specified due to Feature Transfer but that of *sich* for advanced JLsG is replaced by the target feature, which is underspecified, due to Feature Learning, as shown in (α) and (β) in (5.30). As a consequence of FTFL, it is predicted that beginner/intermediate JLsG mistakenly regard *sich* as disallowing the *number*-neutral interpretation, but at the later stage in their transitional grammar, advanced JLsG correctly regard it as allowing the *number*-neutral interpretation, as shown in (*f*) and (*g*) in (5.30), and our experimental results are consistent with the prediction by FTFL.

Now we will offer a piece of evidence in support of FTFL: We have to investigate precisely whether *sich* in the transitional grammar of beginner/

intermediate JLsG is strictly specified or partially specified in terms of the *number*-feature. In Table 3.5, its result only indicates that the *number*-feature of *sich* in the transitional grammar of beginner/intermediate JLsG is somehow specified. It has not yet been revealed whether it is specified strictly or partially. Then, we adopted the test sentence in (5.46) below:

(5.46) Hans$_k$ und Maria$_j$ lichen über sich$_{k \otimes j}$.
John and Mary laugh at/about SELF
Lit. 'John laughs at John, and Mary laughs at Mary.'

Sich in the grammar of L1 German allows the distributive reading because its *number*-feature is not strictly specified. Our JLG subjects were asked whether (5.46) has the interpretation 'John laughs at John, and Mary laughs at Mary.' We intended this test to make it clear whether *sich* in JLsG's transitional grammar is tolerable with the distributive reading. If a subject cannot accept this reading, it can be safely concluded that the *number*-feature of *sich* in their transitional grammar is strictly specified. On the other hand, if a subject can accept this reading, we can conclude that *sich* in their transitional grammar is not strictly specified in terms of its *number*-feature. Their results are shown in Table 3.6:

TABLE 3.6. **Acceptability of the Distributive Reading**

(%)	Beginner/Intermediate JLsG[a]	Advanced JLG[b]
acceptable	**57.6**	***100.0***
unacceptable	42.4	*0.0*

[a]n=33. [b]n=1.

As shown in Table 3.6, 57.6% of our 33 JLG subjects, all of whom are beginners/intermediate learners, regarded the sentence in (5.46) as acceptable. That is to say, *sich* in their transitional grammar is ***not strictly specified*** in terms of the *number*-feature. As we have inferred from the results in Table 3.5, the *number*-feature in *sich* in their transitional grammar is ***not underspecified*** either. We can conclude from the results in Table 3.5

together with the result in Table 3.6 that the *number*-feature of *sich* in the transitional grammar of beginner/intermediate JLsG is ***partially specified***.

Given that *sich* in the transitional grammar of JLsG has more than one feature that is not strictly specified(i.e., the *gender*- and *number*-features), *sich* in their transitional grammar counts as φ-defective. Then we predict that *sich* in their transitional grammar shows the subject orientation, as shown in (*b) in (5.30). In order to examine whether *sich* in the transitional grammar of JLsG show the subject orientation or not, we utilized the test sentence in (5.47):

(5.47) Willi dachte, [$_{CP}$ daß Hans   mit Fritz   über   *sich*
      Willy thought   that Hans   with Fritz   about   SELF
      gesprochen   hat].
      spoken   has
      Lit. 'Willy thought that Hans spoke with Fritz about SELF.'

The sentence in (5.47) is well-formed in the grammar of L1 German when *sich* is bound by the subject of the embedded CP, here *Hans*. *Sich* cannot be bound by the object of the embedded CP *Fritz*; for, *sich* is always subject oriented. Our JLG subjects were given the test sentence in (5.47) and were asked whether *sich* in (5.47) can be coreferential with the object *Fritz* or not. If a subject cannot accept the interpretation, he/she is alleged to regard *sich* in their transitional grammar as showing the subject orientation. The results of the above test are shown in Table 3.7:

TABLE 3.7. Acceptability of Object Antecedents

(%)	Beginner/Intermediate JLsG[a]
acceptable	*37.5*
unacceptable	**62.5**

[a]n=31.

As shown in Table 3.7, 62.5% of our JLG subjects correctly regard *sich* in their transitional grammar as showing the subject orientation. This is exactly what FTFL predicts, and hence it also proves the validity of FTFL.

5.2.4. Residual Issue

In addition to our discussion on the Chinese reflexives in the transitional grammar for JLsC in § 5.1, we have thus far investigated the syntactic properties of the German reflexives in the transitional grammar of JLsG. Strictly speaking, however, the JLG subjects in our experiments started to study German after they had started to study English as their L2. A relevant issue to be settled is: Is there any effect of JLsG's learning of the English reflexives on their learning of the German reflexives? In this regard, it might be possible to conjecture that it is only JLsG's transitional grammar of English, but not the grammar of L1 Japanese, that affects their learning of the German reflexives. To put it differently, one might conjecture that there is no direct connection between JLsG's knowledge of the reflexives in their L1 Japanese and their learning of the German reflexives, which is contrary to what we have so far argued in this dissertation.

It has been widely admitted (*inter alia*, Hirakawa 1990) that JLsE are specifically apt to misunderstand the binding dependency of the English reflexives in their transitional grammar. JLsE tend to regard an English reflexive as showing LC when it is embedded within a tensed clause, though regarding one as showing LD when it is embedded within a non-tensed clause. Note again that this behavior of the English reflexives in the transitional grammar of JLsE is unacceptable in the grammar of L1 English.

As we have confirmed in Chapter 4, the English reflexives in the transitional grammar of JLsE show LD in a non-tensed clause, while they show LC in a tensed clause. The locality on the binding dependency of the English reflexives in JLsE's transitional grammar therefore corresponds exactly to that of *sich selbst* in JLsG's transitional grammar, as have been observed in this section.

It seems that this result supports the aforementioned conjecture that JLsG's transitional grammar of English affects their transitional grammar of German with respect to their use of the German reflexives. It is quite the contrary: the learning of the German simplex reflexive *sich* is utterly unexplainable with this conjecture, simply because there is no simplex reflexive in the transitional grammar of English. Thus, there is no way to explain the remarkable correspondence between *sich* in JLsG's transitional grammar and *zibun* in their native grammar, the correspondence of which we have detected in our experimental research. Moreover, we should notice here that the φ-feature specification of the German reflexives in the transitional grammar of JLsG can be decomposed to the feature compoisition of {+,Ø,Ø} through FTFL. Empirically, it has been indeed revealed that the German complex reflexive *sich selbst* in the transitional grammar of JLsG behaves the same as the English reflexives in the transitional grammar of JLsE with respect to their locality; for both of them are φ-defective and morphologically complex. In terms of the φ-feature specification, the German reflexive *sich selbst* in the transitional grammar of JLsG includes the feature composition of {+,Ø,Ø}, but the English reflexives in the transitional grammar of JLsE includes the feature composition of {+,+,−}, so that they are totally distinct from each other. The conclusion we would like to draw here is that there is no direct effect of JLsG's knowledge of the English reflexives on their learning of the German reflexives.

5.3. Crosslinguistic Variations

As we have thus far argued throughout this chapter, FTFL, which gives a feature-based account to transitional grammar of crosslinguistic variations concerning the syntactic properties of reflexive binding, is theoretically superior to other previous proposals in the field of the L2 learning of reflexive binding. Other piece of evidence in support for FTFL will be provided in what follows.

5.3.1. The English Reflexives in the Transitional Grammar of Chinese Learners of English

First, let us consider the English reflexives in the transitional grammar of Chinese learners of English (CLsE), as shown in (5.48) below:

(5.48) Prediction of the properties of *himself* in the transitional grammar of beginner/intermediate and advanced CLsE:

(i) level	L1 Chinese	TG *himself* Beginner/ Intermediate	TG *himself* Advanced	Target English *himself*
(ii) φ-features				
person	{Ø, +} →	+	+	+
gender	{Ø} → Ø ⇒		+ ←------	+
number	{Ø, +} →	+	+	+
(iii) φ-completeness		φ-defective (*a)	φ-complete (*b)	φ-complete
(iv) syntactic properties		syntactic binding	reflexivizer	reflexivizer
Subject Orientation		yes (*c)	no (*d)	no
Binding Dependency Tensed/Non-tensed		LC / LD (*α)	LC / LC	LC / LC
Distributive Reading		no (*f)	no	no

From the perspective of the specification of each φ-feature in a reflexive, it is assumed that the L1 English reflexives, which are φ-complete, have the same feature specification as PRONOUN+*zisin* in L1 Japanese does because it also counts as φ-complete. The prediction by FTFL therefore indicates that the feature set of *himself* in the transitional grammar of CLsE is the same as the feature set of *kare-zisin* in the transitional grammar of CLsJ, as we have argued in § 5.1.2.

With respect to the *person-/number*-features, the strictly specified features in the L1 feature inventory of CLsE should be transferred to their transitional grammar. It is therefore expected that CLsE correctly regard *himself* as disallowing the *person*-neutral interpretation nor the *number*-neutral interpretation. With respect to the *gender*-feature, their L1 feature is different from the target one in terms of the markedness of the feature specification.

It should be noticed that the feature specification of *himself* in the transitional grammar of CLsE is expected to be φ-defective in their early stage of the transitional grammar, as shown in (*a*) in (5.48) because it includes the *gender*-feature, which is underspecified, but at the later stage of their transitional grammar, it is expected to become φ-complete, as shown in (*b*) in (5.48) because its *gender*-feature turns out to be strictly specified due to Feature Learning. That is to say, *himself* in the transitional grammar of advanced CLsE is regarded as a reflexivizer: Consequently, beginner/intermediate CLsE regard *himself* as showing the subject orientation, but advanced CLsE correctly reject its subject orientation (as shown in (*c*) and (*d*) in (5.48)). It is also predicted that CLsE correctly regard *himself* as disallowing the distributive reading because its *number*-feature is strictly specified, as shown in (*f*) in (5.48).

Next, we will provide results of our small experimental surveys to support FTFL: We set out the following test to 13 beginner/intermediate CLsE, all of whom are native Chinese speakers and had studied English for more than seven years at the time of our experiment. In order to examine whether *himself* in the transitional grammar of CLsE is strictly specified or not in terms of the *number*-feature, we adopted the test sentence in (5.49), which is unacceptable in the grammar of L1 English:

(5.49) *John and Bill talked about *himself.*
Lit. 'John talked about John, and Bill talked about Bill.'

Himself in the grammar of L1 English disallows the distributive reading because its *number*-feature is strictly specified. Our CLE subjects were asked whether (5.49) is acceptable or not. We intended this test to make it clear whether *himself* in the transitional grammar of CLsE is tolerable with the distributive reading. If our CLE subject cannot accept this reading, it can be safely concluded that the *number*-feature of *himself* in their transitional grammar is strictly specified. On the other hand, if a subject can accept this reading, we can conclude that *himself* in their transitional grammar is not strictly specified in terms of its *number*-feature. Their results are shown in Table 4.1:

TABLE 4.1. Acceptability of the Distributive Reading

(%)	JLsE[a]	CLsE[b]	Control[c]
acceptable	**62.2**	**30.8**	**0.0**
unacceptable	37.8	69.2	100.0

[a]$n=154$. [b]$n=13$. [c]$n=20$.

For comparison, the results of our test for the acceptability of the distributive reading of *himself* in the transitional grammar of JLsE and that of *himself* in the grammar of L1 English are also shown in Table 4.1. Our 154 JLE subjects in this test and the control group are those who participated in our Test 1.4, as observed in § 4.3.5.

As shown in Table 4.1, 69.2% of our 13 CLsE subjects, all of whom are beginners to intermediate learners, regarded the sentence in (5.49) as unacceptable. That is to say, *himself* in their transitional grammar is **strictly specified** in terms of the *number*-feature. Empirically interesting is the experimental result that JLsE are mistakenly apt to regard *himself* as having the distributive reading, while CLsE correctly regard *himself* as disallowing it.

FTFL predicts that *himself* in the transitional grammar of beginner/intermediate CLsE is φ-defective, but it becomes φ-complete in the transitional grammar of advanced CLsE. We therefore expect that the subject orientation disappears from *himself* in the transitional grammar of advanced CLsE. In order to examine whether *himself* in the transitional grammar of CLsE show the subject orientation or not, we utilized the test sentence in (5.50), which is acceptable because *himself* is not subject oriented in the grammar of L1 English:

(5.50) ^{OK}These girls told Bill about *himself*.

Our CLE subjects were given the test sentence and were asked whether it is acceptable or not. If our CLE subject cannot accept the sentence, he/she is alleged to regard *himself* in their transitional grammar as showing the subject orientation. The results of the above test are shown in Table 4.2:[10]

TABLE 4.2. Acceptability of Object Antecedents

(%)	Beginner/Intermediate JLsE[a]	Advanced JLsE[b]	Beginner/Intermediate CLsE[c]	Advanced CLsE[d]
acceptable	20.6	9.1	30.8	**66.7**
unacceptable	**79.4**	**90.9**	**69.2**	33.3

[a]$n=253$. [b]$n=11$. [c]$n=13$. [d]$n=3$.

As shown in Table 4.2, with respect to beginner/intermediate JLsE/CLsE, 79.4% of our JLE subjects and 69.2% of our CLE subjects regard *himself* in their transitional grammar as showing the subject orientation. Of empirically interesting point in the results of advanced JLsE/CLsE is that 90.9% of our advanced JLE subjects still mistakenly consider *himself* as showing the subject orientation, but 66.7% of our advanced CLsE subjects correctly reject the subject orientation of the English reflexives.

With respect to the locality on the binding dependency of the English reflexives in the transitional grammar of CLsE, FTFL predicts that beginner/intermediate CLsE are mistakenly apt to regard them as φ-defective, resulting in the LD/LC-property, as shown in (*α) in (5.48), but advanced CLsE correctly regard them as φ-complete thanks to Feature Learning. As a result the English reflexives in the transitional grammar of advanced CLsE always show LC in any context. It has been borne out empirically. Jiang (2009) provided an experimental result indicating the finite/non-finite asymmetry in the LD-properties was strongest for intermediate CLsE, but much weaker for advanced CLsE.

Since Japanese and Chinese have two types of SELF-type reflexives (*zibun/zibun-zisin* and *ziji/ta-ziji*), each of which shares the syntactic properties with respect to the subject orientation and the locality on the binding dependency, these two asymmetries (i.e., the existence/absence of the distributive reading for the English reflexives in transitional grammar and the persistence/disappearance of the subject orientation for the English reflexives at the advanced stage in transitional grammar) between JLsE and CLsE are highly resistant to a coherent explanation under two widely advocated approaches to the L2 learning of reflexive binding.

5.3.2. The English Reflexives in the Transitional Grammar of German Learners of English

Let us next consider the syntactic properties of the English reflexives in the transitional grammar of German learners of English (GLsE), as shown in (5.51) below:

(5.51) Prediction of the properties of *himself* in the transitional grammar of beginner/intermediate and advanced GLsE

		L1 German	TG *himself*		Target *English himself*
(i)	level		Beginner/ Intermediate	Advanced	
(ii)	φ-features				
	person	{+} ⟶ +	+	+	
	gender	{∅} ⟶ ∅ ⟹	+ ⟵------ +		
	number	{∅} ⟶ ∅ ⟹	+ ⟵------ +		
(iii)	φ-completeness		φ-defective (*a)	φ-complete (*b)	φ-complete
(iv)	syntactic properties		syntactic binding	reflexivizer	reflexivizer
	Subject Orientation		yes	no	no
	Binding Dependency Tensed/Non-tensed		LC/LD	LC/LC	LC/LC
	Distributive Reading		yes	no	no

FTFL predicts that the *gender-/number*-features of *himself* in the transitional grammar of advanced GLsE become strictly specified thanks to Feature Learning. It is therefore predicted that *himself* in the transitional grammar of advanced GLsE becomes φ-complete, as shown in (*b*) in (5.51). Theoretically significant point here is that *himself* in the transitional grammar of beginner/intermediate GLsE shows the subject orientation, but it disappears in *himself* in the transitional grammar of advanced GLsE. The distributive reading of *himself* in the transitional grammar of advanced GLsE is also

CHAPTER 5   CROSSLINGUISTIC INVESTIGATIONS ON TG REFLEXIVES

expected to disappear, according to Feature Learning in the *number*-feature.

We see it as essential that the theoretical prediction by FTFL with respect to the L2 learning of the English reflexives by GLsE is comfirmed empirically, but unfortunately we have not yet found beginner/intermediate GLE subjects. We leave it open for our future research.

5.3.3. The Japanese Reflexives in the Transitional Grammar of English Learners of Japanese

Finally, we will investigate the syntactic properties of the Japanese reflexives in the transitional grammar of English learners of Japanese (ELsJ). The prediction by FTFL comes about as follows: Take a look at the properties of *zibun(-zisin)*, as shown in (5.52):

(5.52) Prediction of the properties of *zibun(-zisin)* in the transitional grammar of beginner/intermediate and advanced ELsJ

		L1 *English*	TG *zibun(-zisin)*		Target *Japanese zibun(-zisin)*
			Beginner/ Intermediate	Advanced	
(i)	level				
(ii)	φ-features				
	person	{+} ⟶	+ ▭▭ ⟹	∅ ◂------	∅
	gender	{+} ⟶	+ ▭▭ ⟹	∅ ◂------	∅
	number	{+} ⟶	+ (α)	(+)(β)	−
(iii)	φ-completeness		φ-complete (*a*)	φ-defective (*b*)	φ-defective
(iv)	syntactic properties		reflexivizer	syntactic binding	syntactic binding
	Subject Orientation		no (*c*)	yes (*d*)	yes
	Binding Dependency Tensed/Non-tensed		LC / LC (*zibun*) LC / LC (*zibun-zisin*)	LD / LD (*zibun*) LC / LD (*zibun-zisin*)	LD / LD (*zibun*) LC / LD (*zibun-zisin*)
	Distributive Reading		no (*e*)	no (*f*)	yes

With respect to the *person-/gender*-features, the strictly specified ones in the L1 feature inventory of ELsJ should be transferred to their transitional grammar. The transferred L1 features are distinct from the target ones in terms of the markedness of their specification. Then, it is predicted that the *person-/gender*-features of *zibun(-zisin)* in the transitional grammar of advanced ELsJ should be replaced by the target features, which are underspecified, thanks to Feature Learning. We predict that advanced ELsJ correctly regard *zibun(-zisin)* as having the *person-/gender*-neutral interpretation; however, Feature Learning does not take place with respect to the *number*-feature in the transitional grammar of ELsJ because the transferred L1 feature is the same as the target one in terms of the markedness of its specification, although it is distinct from the target one in terms of the specification. Therefore, FTFL predicts that the *number*-feature of *zibun(-zisin)* in the transitional grammar of advanced ELsJ is strictly specified, as shown in (α) and (β) in (5.52).

Notice here that the feature specification of *zibun(-zisin)* in the transitional grammar of beginner/intermediate ELsJ is expected to be φ-complete (as shown in (*a*) in (5.52)), but at the later stage of their transitional grammar, it is expected to become φ-defective (as shown in (*b*) in (5.52)) because it includes the *person-/gender*-features which are deemed to be underspecified. As a consequence, *zibun(-zisin)* in the transitional grammar of beginner/intermediate ELsJ behaves like a reflexivizer; however, it requires the syntactic binding at the later stage in their transitional grammar. Accordingly, beginner/intermediate ELsJ reject the subject orientation of *zibun(-zisin)*, but advanced ELsJ correctly consider that it is subject oriented (as shown in (*c*) and (*d*) in (5.52)). It is also predicted that ELsJ mistakenly regard *zibun(-zisin)* as disallowing the distributive reading because its *number*-feature is strictly specified, as shown in (*e*) and (*f*) in (5.52).

Next, we will provide results of our small experimental surveys in support of FTFL: We set out the following test to 30 beginner/intermediate ELsJ, all of whom were native English speakers and had studied Japanese for more than three years. An advanced ELJ in our experiment was a native English speaker and had lived in Japan for more than 10 years. In order to confirm whether the *person*-feaure of *zibun(-zisin)* in the transitional gram-

CHAPTER 5 CROSSLINGUISTIC INVESTIGATIONS ON TG REFLEXIVES

mar of ELsJ is underspecified or not, we presented beginner/intermediate ELJ group with the sentence in (5.53), which is acceptable in the grammar of L1 Japanese.

(5.53) [OK]Watasi/anata/kare-wa zibun(-zisin)-o   hihan-sita.
        I/you/he-TOP   SELF-self-ACC   criticize-PAST
        Lit. 'I/you/he criticized myself/yourself/himself.'

The result of the test is shown in Table 5.1 below:

TABLE 5.1. Acceptability of the *Person*-Neutral Interpretation

(%)	ELsJ[a]	Control[b]
acceptable	*13.3*	*100.0*
unacceptable	*86.7*	*0.0*

[a]$n=30$. [b]$n=20$.

Only 13.3% of our experimental subjects considered *zibun-zisin* as allowing all of the 1st/2nd and 3rd person interpretation. In addition, we presented our ELJ subjects with the sentence in (5.54), which is acceptable in the grammar of L1 Japanese in order to confirm whether the *gender*-feature of their Japanese reflexives is underspecified. Its result is shown in Table 5.2.

(5.54) [OK]Kare/kanojo-wa zibun(-zisin)-o   hihan-sita.
        he/she-TOP   SELF-self-ACC   criticize-PAST
        Lit. 'He/she criticized himself/herself.'

TABLE 5.2. Acceptability of the *Gender*-Neutral Interpretation

(%)	ELsJ[a]	Control[b]
acceptable	*26.6*	*100.0*
unacceptable	*73.4*	*0.0*

[a]$n=30$. [b]$n=20$.

Only 26.6% of our experimental subjects allowed *zibun-zisin* to be coreferent both with a masculine and a feminine antecedent. Finally, in order to confirm whether the *number*-feaure of *zibun(-zisin)* in the transitional grammar of ELsJ is underspecified or not, we presented them with the sentence in (5.55), which is not acceptable in the grammar of L1 Japanese.

(5.55) *Karera-wa   *zibun(-zisin)*-o   hihan-sita.
They-TOP   SELF-self-ACC   criticize-PAST
Lit. 'They criticized themselves.'

The result of the test is shown in Table 5.3 below:

TABLE 5.3. **Acceptability of the *Number*-Neutral Interpretation**

(%)	ELsJ[a]	Control[b]
acceptable	*13.3*	*0.0*
unacceptable	**86.7**	*100.0*

[a]$n=30$. [b]$n=20$.

86.7% of our experimental subjects rejected the number-neutral interpretation of *zibun-zisin*. From our results above, we can conclude that the *person-/gender-/number*-features of *zibun(-zisin)* in the transitional grammar of ELsJ are specified.

Next, in order to precisely examine whether *zibun(-zisin)* in the transitional grammar of ELsJ is strictly specified or not in terms of the *number*-feature, we adopted the test sentence in (5.56), which is acceptable in the grammar of L1 Japanese:

(5.56) [OK]John to Bill-wa   *zibun(-zisin)*-o   home-ta.
John and Bill-TOP   SELF(-self)-ACC   praise-PAST
Lit. 'John praised John, and Bill praised Bill.'

Zibun(-zisin) in the grammar of L1 Japanese allows the distributive reading because its *number*-feature is not strictly specified. Our ELJ subjects (both

CHAPTER 5 CROSSLINGUISTIC INVESTIGATIONS ON TG REFLEXIVES

the beginner/intermediate learners and the advanced learners) were asked whether (5.56) has the interpretation 'John praised John, and Bill praised Bill.' If our ELJ subject cannot accept this interpretation, we conclude that the *number*-feature of *zibun(-zisin)* in their transitional grammar is strictly specified. Their results are shown in Table 5.4.

TABLE 5.4. Acceptability of the Distributive Reading

(%)	Beginner/ Intermediate ELsJ[a]	Advanced ELsJ[b]	Control[c]
acceptable	27.6	0.0	*100.0*
unacceptable	*72.4*	*100.0*	0.0

[a]$n=30$. [b]$n=1$. [c]$n=12$.

72.4% of our 30 ELJ subjects and the advanced ELJ subject mistakenly regarded the sentence in (5.56) as unacceptable. That is to say, *zibun(-zisin)* in their transitional grammar is **strictly specified** in terms of its *number*-feature. FTFL predicts that ELsJ mistakenly regard *zibun(-zisin)* as disallowing the distributive reading, as shown in (*e) and (*f) in (5.52). Thus, our experimental result is consistent with the prediction by FTFL.

We next confirm whether *zibun(-zisin)* in the transitional grammar of ELsJ show the subject orientation or not. We utilized the Japanese test sentences in (5.57) and (5.58) below:

(5.57) *Iinkai-wa   John-ni   *zibun(-zisin)* nituite hanashi-ta.
        The committee-TOP John-DAT SELF(-self) about tell-PAST
        Lit. 'The committee told John about himself.'

(5.58) ^{OK}John-wa keisatu-ni   *zibun(-zisin)* nituite hanashi-ta.
        John-TOP the police-DAT him-self about tell-PAST
        Lit. 'John told the police about himself.'

The sentence in (5.57) is unacceptable in the grammar of L1 Japanese because the subject-oriented anaphor *zibun(-zisin)* is bound by the object, here *John*. On the other hand, the sentence in (5.58) is acceptable in L1 Japanese because *zibun(-zisin)* is bound by the subject *John*. If our ELJ subjects cannot accept the test sentence in (5.57), he/she is alleged to regard their transitional reflexives as showing the subject orientation. The results of the above tests are shown in Table 5.5 and 5.6.

TABLE 5.5. **Acceptability of Object Antecedents**

(%)	Beginner/Intermediate ELsJ[a]	Advanced ELsJ[b]
acceptable	*51.7*	*0.0*
unacceptable	*48.3*	*100.0*

[a]$n=30$. [b]$n=1$.

TABLE 5.6. **Acceptability of Subject Antecedents**

(%)	Beginner/Intermediate ELsJ[a]	Advanced ELsJ[b]
acceptable	*58.6*	*100.0*
unacceptable	*41.4*	*0.0*

[a]$n=30$. [b]$n=1$. *Notes.* There is no statistically significant deference between the acceptability of object antecedents by beginner/intermediate ELsJ and the acceptability of subject antecedents by beginner/intermediate ELsJ: $p>.05$.

Statistically, there is no significant difference between the result in Table 5.5 and that in Table 5.6 with respect to our beginner/intermediate ELJ subjects, the result which implies that *zibun(-zisin)* in the transitional grammar of beginner/intermediate ELsJ does not show the subject orientation. On the other hand, with respect to the advanced ELJ subject, he correctly regards the sentence in (5.57) as unacceptable and *zibun(-zisin)* is always subject oriented. (Additionally, we have also confirmed that the advanced ELJ subject correctly regard that *kare-zisin* lacks the subject orientation.) That is to say, *zibun(-zisin)* in the transitional grammar of beginner/intermediate

CHAPTER 5 CROSSLINGUISTIC INVESTIGATIONS ON TG REFLEXIVES

ELsJ is φ-complete and lacks the subject orientation, but *zibun(-zisin)* for advanced ELsJ is φ-defective and shows the subject orientation, as shown in (*c*) and (*d*) in (5.52).[11]

Given the prediction by FTFL that the compositional property of the φ-feature in *zibun(-zisin)* in the transitional grammar of beginner/intermediate ELsJ is φ-complete, whereas that in the transitional grammar of advanced ELsJ is φ-defective, it is predicted that the locality on the binding dependency of *zibun(-zisin)* in their transitional grammar is expected to change depending on the stage in their transitional grammar. We contrived the following experiment: We have utilized the following test sentences in which *zibun(-zisin)* is contained either within an embedded tensed clause (as in (5.59)), or within an embedded non-tensed clause, such as a causative construction (as in (5.60)):

(5.59) *John$_j$-wa   iinkai-ga   zibun-zisin$_{*j}$-o   hihansi-ta
       John-TOP   the committee-NOM   SELF-self-ACC   criticize-PAST
       to   omot-ta.
       C   think-PAST
       Lit. 'John thought that the committee criticized SELF.'

(5.60) ^{OK}John$_j$-wa   iinkai-ni   zibun-zisin$_j$-o
       John-TOP   the committee-DAT   SELF-self-ACC
       hihans-ase-ta.
       criticize-CAUSE-PAST
       Lit. 'John made the committee criticize SELF.'

If a subject judges (5.59) as acceptable, he/she is alleged to interpret *zibun-zisin* as being bound astride a tensed clause boundary; namely, he/she regards *zibun-zisin* within a tensed clause as showing LD. If a subject judges (5.59) as unacceptable, he/she regards *zibun-zisin* within a tensed clause as showing LC. If a subject judges (5.60) as acceptable, he/she regards *zibun-zisin* within a non-tensed clause as showing LD. If a subject judges (5.60) as unacceptable, he/she regards *zibun-zisin* within a non-tensed clause as showing LC. The results of our experimental tests are shown in Table 5.7:

TABLE 5.7. Locality for the Binding Dependency

(%)		Beginner/Intermediate ELsJ[a]		Advanced ELsJ[b]	
		Tensed	Non-tensed	Tensed	Non-tensed
(a)	LC	65.5	62.1	100.0	0.0
(b)	LD	34.5	37.9	*0.0*	*100.0*

[a]$n=20$. [b]$n=1$. *Notes.* Statistically, there is not a significant difference ($p>.05$) between (a) and (b) for beginner/intermediate ELsJ.

Notice here that 65.5% of our beginner/intermediate ELJ subjects regarded *zibun-zisin* within an embedded tensed clause (as in (5.59)) as showing LC, and 62.1% of them regarded *zibun-zisin* within an embedded non-tensed clause (as in (5.60)) as showing LC. There is no significant difference between the result of the tensed clause and that of the non-tensed clause. On the other hand, with respect to the advanced ELJ subject, he correctly regarded the sentence in (5.60) as acceptable and *zibun(-zisin)* syntactically behaves as a long-distant anaphor only when it is embedded in a non-tensed clause. We infer from our results that *zibun-zisin* is always locally-bound in the transitional grammar of beginner/intermediate ELsJ, whereas it allows the long-distance binding when it is embedded in a non-tensed clause in the transitional grammar of advanced ELsJ. FTFL predicts that the feature specification of *zibun(-zisin)* in the transitional grammar of beginner/intermediate ELsJ is φ-complete, but it should become φ-defective along with Feature Learning applying to the *person-/gender*-features, as shown in (*a) and (*b) in (5.52). It has been revealed through our experimental surveys that the prediction by FTFL is indeed borne out.[12]

In this chapter, aiming to give a theoretically universal account to the syntactic mechanism for reflexive binding in transitional grammar, we have so far demonstrated that FTFL is crosslinguistically applicable to all syntactic properties of various reflexives in transitional grammar. For example, the English reflexives of JLsE, the Chinese reflexives of JLsC, the Japanese reflexives of CLsJ, the German reflexives of JLsG, the Japanese reflexives of GLsJ, the English reflexives of CLsE, and the Japanese reflex-

CHAPTER 5   CROSSLINGUISTIC INVESTIGATIONS ON TG REFLEXIVES

ives of ELsJ, at every stage in their transitional grammar. Thus far, we have reached the conclusion that all of our experimental surveys are consistent to the prediction by FTFL and they have hence proved the validity of FTFL. In the following chapters in Part II, we will demonstrate that FTFL, which is based on the idea utilizing the φ-feature (de)composition, is not only applicable to reflexive binding in transitional grammar but also coherently applicable to the existence/absence of multiple Specifiers in transitional grammar.

NOTES

1 Portions of this chapter were reported in Ishino and Ura (2010, 2011d).
2 We exclude the feature specification of *kare-zisin* from the L1 feature inventory of JLsC because *kare-zisin*, which is defined as φ-complete and marked, is regarded as a reflexivizer; as a consequence, Japanese learners do not recognize it as an anaphor in syntax. Only the φ-specification of *zibun(-zisin)*, which is unmarked, is in the L1 feature inventory of Japanese learners.
3 The locality on the binding dependency of *ziji*, which shows LD in a tensed clause, is not explained straightforwardly from FTFL because we attribute its locality in a tensed clause to its movement property.
4 In the case where the L1 feature inventory includes more than one feature specification, it is logically possible that a certain feature in the L1 inventory has a strictly specified feature and a partially specified one, both of which are classified as unmarked. Theoretically speaking, FTFL states that either of them can be transferred to transitional grammar; however, from an empirical perspective, we have not yet found such situation where a certain feature in the L1 inventory has both of a strictly specified feature and a partially specified one. We would like to leave this issue open for our future research.
5 Note that *ta-ziji* in L1 Chinese is underspecified in terms of the *gender*-feature although there are two morphological variants for *ta-ziji* 他自己 and 她自己 in Chinese characters, but 他自己 and 她自己 are the same in their phonological property *tā-zìjǐ*; for, as discussed in § 2.1.1, it is stipulated that (α) a feature *F* within a lexical item *LI* is *underspecified* iff every morphophonologically possible variation of *F* in a language *L* allows arbitrarily free (or neutral) interpretation. Accordingly, we regard the *gender*-feature of *ta-ziji* in L1 Chinese as underspecified.
6 *Sich* can be bound by a long-distant antecedent over a non-tensed clause boundary, when it is embedded in causative or perception verb complements; however, it is

strictly locally bound when it is embedded in a non-tensed clause of *to*-infinitive. See Safir (2004) and Reuland (2011), for more discussion on German anaphors.

7 The existence/absence of the multiple Specifiers is attributed to the feature checking ability of φ (not to the checking ability of √φ) because the feature checking which is concerned with the multiple Specifiers takes place before Spell-Out. The relevancy of the φ-feature checking ability to the multiple Specifiers will be analyzed in Chapter 9. Moreover, it is very important to investigate the relevancy of the feature checking ability of φ and that of √φ, the study of which we wish to pursue in a future research.

8 In analogy with the properties of *sich(-selbst)* in JLsG's transitional grammar, other factors (e.g., T's checking ability) affect the locality on the binding dependency of *zibun(-zisin)* in GLsJ's transitional grammar. As long as this dissertation aims to investigate the L2 learning of the φ-feature specification and to elucidate the syntactic properties of a target item through decomposing its φ-feature specification, in what follows we will concentrate our attention only on the φ-features in transitional grammar.

9 We insert the brackets, which were not shown to the subjects in our experiment, in order to display the binding dependencies of *sich* and *sich selbst* in the grammar of L1 German for the sake of argumentation herein.

10 Advanced JLsE in Table 4.2 were graduate students, all of whom were native Japanese and had studied English as a second language for more than 15 years. Advanced CLsE in Table 4.2 were Chinese teachers who were advanced L2 learners of Japanese. They teach Chinese to Japanese undergraduate students in Japan. They are also regarded as highly-advanced L2 learners of English because they have been professionally trained with respect to the L2 learning of English before (or at the same time) they have studied Japanese in order to qualify as a teacher at Japanese university.

11 More interestingly, Yuan (1998) provided an experimental result indicating that it is also difficult for ELsC to regard *ziji* as having the subject orientation.

12 In Thomas (1995), it has been empirically confirmed that advanced ELsJ correctly regard *zibun* as having the LD-property in a tensed clause.

CHAPTER 6

Multiple Specifiers and Φ-Feature Specification

Since Kuroda (1965), it has widely been observed in the literature on Japanese syntax that Japanese allows so-called *Multiple Nominative Construction* (or *Multiple Subject Construction*) (which is hereafter abbreviated as MNC) (as exemplified in (6.1a)) and so-called *Multiple Genitive Construction* (hereafter MGC) (as exemplified in (6.1b)), both of which are disallowed in L1 English (as shown in (6.2) below).[1]

(6.1) a. ᴼᴷ[TP Kare-**ga** imooto-**ga** [T' utsukusi-i T]](koto).
      He-NOM   sister-NOM   beautiful   (fact)
      Lit. '(the fact that) His sister is beautiful.'

  b. ᴼᴷMary-wa [DP a-**no** John-**no** [D' uta D]]-o kii-ta.
     Mary-TOP that-GEN John-GEN song-ACC hear-PAST
     Lit. 'Mary heard that song sung by John.'

(6.2) a. *He sister is beautiful.
  b. *Mary heard John's that song.

In the minimalist Case theory (Chomsky 1995 and its subsequent work), it has been extensively argued that the (structural) Case of a DP is morphosyntactically realized when it is valued/checked by a functional head (such as, T(Infl) and D) with the ability to check the φ-feature of a DP which is located at its Spec. Following the general assumption that T values/

checks the nominative Case of a DP at T's Spec and D values/checks the genitive Case of a DP at D's Spec, Ura (1994, 1996) has hypothesized that T and D in Japanese should have the ability to value/check Cases for more than one DP, owing to the fact that T and D in Japanese can project multiple Specs; as a consequence, it follows with the assumption that T values/checks the nominative Case and D values/checks the genitive Case, that Japanese allows MNC and MGC. It has been argued (cf. Kuroda 1988, Ura 1994, and Ogawa 1996) that this type of multiple licensing ability of a given functional head stems from the defectiveness of the head; in other words, a functional head can project multiple Specs when its φ-features are defective in the sense of Burzio (1991).[2] More specifically, Ura (1994, 1996) has hinted, under the minimalist framework, that the multiple Case-feature checking ability of T and D in a language allowing MNC and/or MGC should be attributed to the featural defectiveness of the φ-features within a head relevant to Case-checking. To put it differently, when the φ-feature of the relevant head is defective, the head is expected to retain the multiple Case-checking ability, resulting in the emergence of its multiple Specs, and, hence, multiple Specs cannot be projected by a φ-complete head.

Developing Ura's (1994, 1996) hypothesis concerning the correlation between multiple Specs and the featural completeness/defectiveness, we will assume, basically following an inductive generalization provided in Ishino and Ura (2011b), that the completeness/defectiveness of the φ-features in T and D determines whether these relevant functional heads can project multiple Specs or not.

This chapter aims at providing a detailed analysis to the syntactic mechanism for the English nominative/genitive Case licensing in the transitional grammar of JLsE. More specifically, the following question will be addressed attentively in this chapter: Do T and/or D retain the ability to project multiple Specs in the transitional grammar of JLsE? This question is especially interesting and highly consequential also in the field of the generative studies on L2 learning because a solution to this question may reveal how L2 learning progresses when a parameter in an L1 is different radically from the relevant parameter in a target language; for, L1 Japanese has the parameter that allows multiple Specs both in T and in D while L1 English has the parameter that does not allow multiple Specs at all.

6.1. Multiple Specifiers in L1 Japanese

Before entering into the discussion about the acceptability of MNC and MGC in the transitional grammar of JLsE, we will briefly illustrate whether MNC/MGC are allowed or disallowed in L1 Japanese and in L1 English, respectively, and explicate the syntactic mechanism for MNC/MGC.

It has widely been recognized that L1 Japanese allows MNC (as shown by the well-formedness of the example in (6.3)) and also allows MGC (as shown by the well-formedness of the example in (6.4)), both of which are disallowed in L1 English, as the ill-formedness of the examples in (6.5) and (6.6) shows (see Fukui 1986, and Kuroda 1988):

(6.3) a. ^{OK}[$_{TP}$ Zoo-**ga**   hana-**ga** [$_{T'}$ nagai T]](koto).
             elephant-NOM   nose-NOM   long   (fact)
             Lit. '(the fact that) elephants' noses are long.'

     b. ^{OK}[$_{TP}$ John-**ga**   imooto-**ga**   [$_{T'}$ kawai-i T]](koto).
             John-NOM   sister-NOM   pretty   (fact)
             Lit. '(the fact that) John's sister is pretty.'

     c. ^{OK}[$_{TP}$ John-**ga**   imooto-ga ke-ga   [$_{T'}$ naga-i T]](koto).
             John-NOM   sister-NOM hair-NOM   long   (fact)
             Lit. '(the fact that) John's sister's hair is long.'

(6.4) a. ^{OK}Watasi-wa [$_{DP}$ Mary-**no**   sorera-**no**   [$_{D'}$ inu D]]-o
             I-TOP   Mary-GEN   these-GEN   dogs-ACC
             mi-ta.
             see-PAST
             Lit. 'I saw these dogs that Mary had.'

b. ᴼᴷJohn-wa [_DP ko-**no**   watasi-**no** [_D' kuruma D]]-ni
   John-TOP   this-GEN   I-GEN   car-DAT
   not-ta.
   ride-PAST
   Lit. 'John has ridden in this car of mine.'

c. ᴼᴷJohn-wa [_DP sorera-**no** anata-**no** [_D' hon D]]-o yon-da.
   John-TOP   these-GEN   you-GEN   books-ACC   read-PAST
   Lit. 'John has read these books of yours.'

(6.5) a. *He sister is beautiful.
      b. *John sister is pretty.
      c. *John sister hair is long.

(6.6) a. *I saw Mary's these dogs.
      b. *John has riddern in this my car.
      c. *John has read these your books.

In a Japanese MNC (such as (6.3a)), the preceding DP has the inalienable possession relation to the following DP, both of which are alleged, under the minimalist syntax (Ura 1994, 1996), to have its nominative Case valued/checked by T when they are located at T's multiple Specs. In a Japanese MGC (such as (6.4a)), both DPs have their genitive Cases valued/checked at D's multiple Specs (Ura 1994). On the other hand, as the examples in (6.5) and (6.6) show, multiple Specs are not at all allowed in the grammar of L1 English.

What we extensively discuss throughout this dissertation is that the idea about the φ-feature decomposition of a lexical item plays the most significant role in determining syntactic properties of its relevant item in transitional grammar. As argued throughout Part I, the specification of the φ-features in a lexical item (for example, a reflexive) in L2 learners' native language should be transferred to their transitional grammar and the specification of the transferred L1 feature should/should not be overwritten by a target feature depending on the markedness of the feature specification.

CHAPTER 6   MULTIPLE SPECIFIERS AND Φ-FEATURE SPECIFICATION

Then the specification of transferred L1 features and learned features from a target item compositionally determine the feature specification of the relevant item in transitional grammar and its various syntactic properties in transitional grammar. In Part II, we assume, supporting Ura (1994, 1996), that the multiple Case-feature checking ability of T and D in a language allowing MNC and/or MGC should be attributed to the featural defectiveness of the φ-features within a head (i.e., T or D) which is relevant to Case-checking. To be more specific, Ishino and Ura (2011b), which have conducted a parametric study of the existence/absence of multiple Specs, have inductively generalized about the φ-feature composition of a functional head which determines how many Specs can be projected: A head whose φ-features are all underspecified (i.e., the feature compoisition of {Ø,Ø,Ø}) and a head which has the three distinct specifications for its φ-feature (i.e., the feature composition of {+,Ø,−}) can project multiple Specs. Look at Chart 5 below:

CHART 5. Φ-Feature Specification and the Number of Specifiers
(Ishino and Ura (2011b))

Feature Specification[3]			Multiple Specs	Null Subject	The Number of Specs	Languages
Ø	Ø	Ø	OK	OK	(i) 0, 1, 2≦	*Japanese* T, *Chinese* D, *Korean* T *Quechua* T
+	Ø	−	OK	OK	0, 1, 2≦	*Japanese* D, *Arabic* T *Perusian* T
+	Ø	Ø	*	OK	(ii) 0, 1	*Chinese* T
+	+	Ø	*	OK	0, 1	*English* D, *Italian* T
+	+	−	*	OK	0, 1	Not Found
+	+	+	*	OK	0, 1	*Modern Greek* T, *Russian* T
−	Ø	Ø	*	*	(iii) 1	Not Found
−	−	Ø	*	*	1	*English* T, *French* T
−	−	+	*	*	1	Not Found
−	−	−	*	*	1	Not Found

Ishino and Ura (2011b) propose that the number of Specs that T or D can project varies in the following three ways: (I) If the number of Specs that a head can project is not fixed, the relevant head allows either multiple subjects or a null subject (as indicated by "(i) 0, 1, 2≦" in Chart 5); (II) if a head can project one Spec or if a head is allowed to project no Spec, the relevant head allows only a null subject (as indicated by "(ii) 0, 1" in Chart 5); and (III) if a head can project only one Spec, the relevant head disallows multiple subjects nor a null subject (as indicated by "(iii) 1" in Chart 5). It has been widely admitted that if a language L_1 allows multiple Specs, a null subject is unexceptionally allowed in L_1, but it is not necessarily the case that if a language L_2 allows a null subject, multiple Specs are allowed in L_2. To put it differently, there is not a language L_x whose T and/or D can project multiple Specs but cannot allow a null subject. See Ishino and Ura (2011b) for more detailed discussion, with the aid of the idea utilizing the φ-feature decomposition, on the crosslinguistically parametric difference concerning the number of Specs.

In what follows we will demonstrate that FTFL is applicable coherently to the number of Specs that is allowed by T and D in the transitional grammar of JLsE. We will first stipulate that it is essential for us to explicate the φ-feature specification of T/D in L1 Japanese and L1 English. In the next section, we will show the specification of each φ-feature within T/D in L1 Japanese and L1 English and their compositional properties of the φ-features.

6.2. Φ-Feature Specification of T

6.2.1. *Person*-Feature Specification of T

Let us first examine the specification of the *person*-feature of T in L1 Japanese and that of the *person*-feature of T in L1 English. Consider the examples in (6.7) and (6.8) below:

(6.7) [Watasi /Anata /Kare]-ga piano-o *hiku*$_{[peson:\ 1st/2nd/3rd]}$ (koto).
I /you /he-NOM piano-ACC play-PRES (the fact)
Lit. '(The fact) that [I play / you play / he plays] the piano.'

(6.8) a. I
 b. You play$_{[peson:\ 1st/2nd]}$ the piano.
 c. He play**s** $_{[peson:\ 3rd]}$

It is quite natural to assume that a DP in the Spec of T has a φ-feature checking relation with T when it induces a morphophonologically visible inflection upon V. As the examples in (6.7) show, it has widely been recognized that a subject DP in L1 Japanese does not induce a morphologically overt φ-feature agreement upon V, irrespective of the *person*-feature of the DP located at the Spec of T. Because L1 Japanese has only one morphological form for V, T's *person*-feature in L1 Japanese has only one morphological variation, which allows arbitrarily free interpretation (i.e., it allows either 1st person, 2nd person, or 3rd person interpretation), as shown in (6.7). This leads us to conclude that T in L1 Japanese has the ***underspecified*** *person*-feature.

On the other hand, as the examples in (6.8) show, a subject DP in L1 English manifestly induces a morphologically overt *person*-feature agreement upon V. We can, therefore, conclude that the *person*-feature of T in L1 English is ***not underspecified***; that is, it is either strictly or partially specified. With respect to the V's third-person, singular, present suffix (i.e., -*(e)s*) in L1 English, its morphological reflex allows only one interpretation, as shown in (6.8c); however, the V-Ø form (i.e., a verb without the suffix) allows either 1st or 2nd person interpretation, as shown in (6.8a,b). As a consequence, we conclude that T in L1 English has the ***partially specified*** *person*-feature.

6.2.2. *Gender*-Feature Specification of T

Next, with respect to the *gender*-feature, look at (6.9) and (6.10) below:

(6.9) [Kare / kanojo]-ga piano-o *hiku*_[gender: masculine/feminine] (koto).
      He / she-NOM piano-ACC play-PRES (the fact)
      Lit. '(The fact) that [he / she] plays the piano.'

(6.10) a. He
       b. She } plays$_{[gender:\ masculine/feminine]}$ the piano.

As the examples in (6.9) show, T's *gender*-feature in L1 Japanese has only one morphological variation, which allows arbitrarily free interpretation (i.e., it allows either masculine or feminine interpretation). We conclude that T in L1 Japanese has an **underspecified** *gender*-feature. As shown in (6.10), a subject DP in L1 English does not induce a morphologically overt *gender*-feature agreement upon V. We can therefore conclude that the *gender*-feature of T in L1 English is **underspecified**, too.

6.2.3. *Number*-Feature Specification of T

Finally, let us examine the specification of the *number*-feature of T in L1 Japanese and that of T in L1 English. Look at the examples in (6.11) and (6.12):

(6.11) [Watasi(-tati)/Anata(-tati) /Kare(-ra)]-ga piano-o
       I(-PL) / you(-PL) / he(-PL)-NOM piano-ACC
       hiku$_{[number:\ sing/pl]}$ (koto).
       play-PRES (the fact)
       Lit. '(The fact) that [I play/we play/you play/he plays/they play] the piano.'

(6.12) a. I / We
       b. You } play$_{[number:\ 1st/2nd\ (no\ singular/plural\ contrast)\ 3rd\ (pl)]}$ } the piano.
       c. They
       c'. He   play<u>s</u> $_{[number:\ 3rd,\ sing]}$

We regard T's *number*-feature (as well as the other φ-features) in L1 Japanese as having only one morphological variation, which allows arbitrarily

CHAPTER 6 MULTIPLE SPECIFIERS AND Φ-FEATURE SPECIFICATION

free interpretation (i.e., it allows either singular or plural interpretation), as shown in (6.11). This leads us to conclude that T in L1 Japanese has the **underspecified** *number*-feature.

On the other hand, as the examples in (6.12) show, a subject DP in L1 English manifestly induces a morphologically overt *number*-feature agreement upon V with respect to the 3rd person, as shown in (6.12c,c'). We can therefore conclude that the *number*-feature of T in L1 English is **not underspecified**; that is, it is either strictly or partially specified. V's third-person, singular, and present suffix (i.e., *-(e)s*) in L1 English allows only one interpretation; that is to say, it disallows the plural interpretation; however, with respect to the first/second-person agreement, it is not necessarily the case that a subject DP in L1 English induces a morphologically overt *number*-feature agreement upon V. As a consequence, we conclude that T in L1 English has the **partially specified** *number*-feature.

Now we summarize the feature composition of T in L1 Japanese and that of T in L1 English, as shown in (6.13) below:

(6.13)

T	L1 Japanese	L1 English
Person	Ø	–
Gender	Ø	Ø
Number	Ø	–
Multiple Specs	*yes*	*no*

Here it is important to notice, given Ishino and Ura's (2011b) hypothesis, that T in L1 Japanese (as indicated by the feature composition of {Ø,Ø,Ø} in (6.13)) allows multiple Specs (as well as a null subject) because the φ-feature compoisition of T in L1 Japanese is *defective*, and T in L1 English (as indicated by the feature composition of {–,Ø,–} in (6.13)) disallows multiple Specs.

6.3. Φ-Feature Specification of D

6.3.1. *Person*-Feature Specification of D

In this subsection, we investigate the specification of D's *person*-feature in L1 Japanese and D's *person*-feature in L1 English. With respect to L1 Japanese, we assume the following internal structure of DP in (6.14):

(6.14)

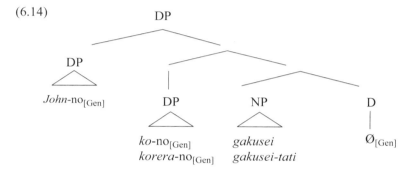

Then we examine the agreement between the head D and its complement NP) in terms of the φ-features. More specifically, we examine the existence of the agreement between the Spec of D (such as *kono* 'this', *korera(no)* 'these', *sono/ano* 'that' and *sorera(no)/arera(no)* 'those') and the complement of D because Japanese D is morphophonologically invisible. Consider the examples in (6.15) below:

(6.15) a. *kono/sono/ano* *watasi$_{[1st]}$ /*anata$_{[2nd]}$ /^{OK}otoko$_{[3rd]}$
this/that   I   / you   /   man
Lit. 'this/that man'

b. *korerano/sorerano/arerano*   *watasi$_{[1st]}$-tati
these/those   I-PL
/ *anata$_{[2nd]}$-tati   / ^{OK}otoko$_{[3rd]}$-tati
/ you-PL   /   man-PL
Lit. 'these/those men'

CHAPTER 6 MULTIPLE SPECIFIERS AND Φ-FEATURE SPECIFICATION

Next, with respect to D in L1 English, we assume the following structures in (6.16):[4]

(6.16)

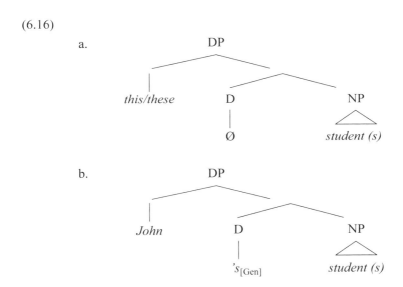

Then, we examine the agreement between D and its complement NP. Consider the examples in (6.17) below:

(6.17) a. this/that [*I$_{[1st]}$/*you$_{[2nd]}$/^{OK}student$_{[3rd]}$]
       b. these/those [*we$_{[1st]}$/*you$_{[2nd]}$/^{OK}students$_{[3rd]}$]

As shown in (6.15) and (6.17), D in L1 Japanese and D in L1 English only select NP[*person*: 3rd]. The ill-formed examples in (6.15) and (6.17) indicate that D both in L1 Japanese and in L1 English are **strictly specified** in terms of their *person*-features; for, they disallow the 1st person or the 2nd person interpretations.

6.3.2. *Gender*-Feature Specification of D

Next, let us consider the examples in (6.18) and (6.19) below:

(6.18) a. *kono/sono/ano* ^{OK}otoko_{[masculine]} /^{OK}onna_{[feminine]}
this/that   man   / woman
Lit. 'this/that [man/woman]'

b. *korerano/sorerano/arerano* ^{OK}otoko_{[masculine]}-tati
these/those   man-PL
/ ^{OK}onna_{[feminine]}-tati
/ woman-PL
Lit. 'these/those [men/women]'

(6.19) a. this/that [^{OK}boy_{[masculine]}/^{OK}girl_{[feminine]}]
b. these/those [^{OK}boys_{[masculine]}/^{OK}girls_{[feminine]}]

As the well-formed examples in (6.18) and (6.19) indicate, D both in L1 Japanese and in L1 English both allows arbitrarily free interpretation (i.e., it allows either the masculine or the feminine interpretation). This leads us to conclude that D both in L1 Japanese and in L1 English are **underspecified** in terms of its *gender*-features.

6.3.3. *Number*-Feature Specification of D

Now, let us examine the specification of the *number*-feature of D in L1 Japanese and that of D in L1 English. Look at (6.20) and (6.21) below:

(6.20) a. [_{DP} ^{OK}[_{DP} *kono/sono/ano*] [_{D'} [_{NP[-plural]} hitori-no
              this/that   one-COPULAR
gakusei] D]]
student
Lit. 'this/that student'

b. [_{DP} *[_{DP} *korerano/sorerano/arerano*] [_{D'} [_{NP[-plural]} hitori-no
              these/those   one-COPULAR
gakusei] D]]
student
Lit. '*these/those student'

CHAPTER 6   MULTIPLE SPECIFIERS AND Φ-FEATURE SPECIFICATION

    c. [$_{DP}$ ^{OK}[$_{DP}$ *kono/sono/ano*] [$_{D'}$ [$_{NP[+plural]}$ sannin-no
        this/that   three-COPULAR
    gakusei-tati] D]]
    student-PL
    Lit. '*this/that three students'

    d. [$_{DP}$^{OK}[$_{DP}$ *korerano/sorerano/arerano*] [$_{D'}$ [$_{NP[+plural]}$ san-nin-no
        these/those   three-COPULAR
    gakusei-tati] D]]
    student-PL
    Lit. 'these/those three students'

(6.21) a. [$_{DP}$ ^{OK}[$_{DP}$ this/that] [$_{D'}$ D [$_{NP[-plural]}$ student]]]
     b. [$_{DP}$ *[$_{DP}$ these/those] [$_{D'}$ D [$_{NP[-plural]}$ student]]]
     c. [$_{DP}$ *[$_{DP}$ this/that] [$_{D'}$ D [$_{NP[+plural]}$ three students]]]
     d. [$_{DP}$ ^{OK}[$_{DP}$ these/those] [$_{D'}$ D [$_{NP[+plural]}$ three students]]]

Notice that (6.20a), as well as (6.20d), is acceptable in the grammar of L1 Japanese and that (6.20b) is ill-formed, but (6.20c) is acceptable. It follows that the *number*-feature of D in the grammar of L1 Japanese is ***not underspecified*** because the ill-formedness of (6.20b) indicates that *korerano* ('these') and *sorerano/arerano* ('those'), which are the two variants of D's plural *number*-feature in L1 Japanese, never allow the singular interpretation; that is, the plural form of the Spec of D (such as *korerano* and *sorerano/arerano*) never selects NP[-plural]. If it were the case that the *number*-feature of D in L1 Japanese is strictly specified, then *kono* and *sono/ano* would never allow the plural interpretation; that is, the singular form of the Spec of D (such as *kono* and *sono/ano*) does not select NP[+plural], but it indeed selects NP[+plural], as shown in (6.20c). It can be inferred from the facts shown in (6.20) that the *number*-feature of D in the grammar of L1 Japanese is not strictly specified. Now we have reached the conclusion that the *number*-feature of D in L1 Japanese is ***partially specified***.

As for L1 English, all of the examples in (6.21) apparently show that the *number*-feature of D is ***strictly specified*** because *this* and *that*, which are the two variants of D's singular *number*-feature in L1 English, disallow the plural interpretation, as shown in (6.21c), and *these* and *those*, which are the two variants of D's plural *number*-feature in L1 English, disallow the singular interpretation, as shown in (6.21b). We thereby conclude that the *number*-feature of D in L1 English is **strictly specified**.

Now we summarize the feature composition of D in L1 Japanese and L1 English, as in (6.22) below:

(6.22)

D	L1 Japanese	L1 English
Person	+	+
Gender	Ø	Ø
Number	−	+
Multiple Specs	*yes*	*no*

We should notice that, according to Ishino and Ura (2011b), the feature composition of D in L1 Japanese (as indicated by the feature composition of {+,Ø,−} in (6.22)) indicates that D in L1 Japanese allows multiple Specs, and that of D in L1 English (as indicated by the feature composition of {+,Ø,+} in (6.22)) indicates that D in L1 English disallows multiple Specs, according to the generalization presented in Ishino and Ura (2011b).

Now an empirically interesting question in the field of SLA arises: Do JLsE allow multiple Specs of T and/or D in their transitional grammar? We will next reveal the specification of each φ-feature in T and D in their transitional grammar deductively through FTFL and then demonstrate that the prediction by FTFL consists empirically with the results of our experimental surveys on the existence/absence of multiple Specs of T and D in the transitional grammar of JLsE.

Notes

1 Portions of this chapter were reported in Ishino (2011b).
2 For Kuroda (1988), MNC (and MGC) is ascribed to T/D's lack of agreement; for Ura

CHAPTER 6 MULTIPLE SPECIFIERS AND Φ-FEATURE SPECIFICATION

(1994), it is ascribed to the imperfect specification of T's (and D's) φ-features; for Ogawa (1996), it is ascribed to the semantically vacuous nature of T/D.
3   The order of the φ-features (*person, gender* and *number*) is irrelevant.
4   We assume that *this/that* and *these/those* are localted at the Spec of DP. They may induce a rather strong blocking effect on the movement out of DP (what is called "Specificity Effect"). We assume that *a* and *the* are located at the head D; for, they may not induce such a strong blocking effect on the extraction from DP.

CHAPTER 7

Φ-Feature Specification of T/D in Transitional Grammar: Prediction by FTFL and Experimental Results

In this chapter, we will first discuss what is predicted with some previously proposed L2 hypotheses concerning the acceptability of multiple Specs in the transitional grammar of JLsE.

7.1. Prediction by Previous Studies (PRA and LTA)

First, it is important to notice that there has been very scarce discussion in the literature on L2 learning concerning the issue as to whether JLsE allow multiple Specs in their transitional grammar or not, the issue to which this dissertation will directly address itself.

7.1.1. PRA with Subset Principle

Under Subset Principle (Berwick 1985), it has been argued that a parameter *P1* is less marked than another parameter *P2* if *P2* is less restrictive than *P1* (more precisely, the set of what is generated under *P2* subsumes the set of what is generated under *P1* as its proper subset), and PRA stipulates that resetting a restrictive parameter value with a less restrictive one is much easier for learners than resetting in the opposite direction because only positive evidence suffices for the former, but not for the latter.

Given that there is a syntactic parameter concerning the availability of multiple Specs, it is natural to presume that the parametric value for L1 English is more restrictive than the one for L1 Japanese because T and D in

L1 English are specified in terms of the number of their Specs whereas the number of the Specs of T and that of D in L1 Japanese is, hypothetically, not restricted. Under Subset Principle, therefore, it is predicted that it is more difficult for JLsE to recognize that T and D in English in their transitional grammar cannot project more than one Spec because their L1 Japanese parameter value concerning the availability of multiple Specs subsumes the L2 English value as a proper subset.

7.1.2. LTA

As we have argued in § 1.6.2, LTA demands that the lexical/syntactic properties of an L1 lexical item should be transferred to transitional grammar. If we apply LTA to the L2 learning of functional categories, it is predicted that T and D of English in the transitional grammar of JLsE are able to project more than one Spec; for, T and D in L1 Japanese have the characteristics of allowing multiple Specs. Consequently, the prediction follows that it is difficult for JLsE to recognize that neither MNC nor MGC is allowed in English.

Of theoretical significance is the fact that, no matter which of the above approaches (PRA and LTA) might be taken as a theory of JLsE's learning of English Specifiers, both approaches predict that T of English in the transitional grammar of JLsE and D of English in their transitional grammar syntactically behave exactly the same: To be precise, if T of English in the transitional grammar of JLsE can project multiple Specs, it is predicted that English D in their transitional grammar can also project multiple Specs. On the other hand, if T of English in the transitional grammar of JLsE cannot project multiple Specs, English D in their transitional grammar cannot, either. The difference between the L2 learning of T and that of D is not therefore expected under these L2 hypotheses.

7.2. Prediction by FTFL

Now we show that FTFL can be applied to the properties of T and D in the transitional grammar of beginner/intermediate and advanced JLsE with the idea of the φ-feature (de)composition, as shown in (7.1):

CHAPTER 7 Φ-FEATURE SPECIFICATION OF T/D IN TRANSITIONAL GRAMMAR

(7.1) Prediction of the properties of T in the transitional grammar of beginner/intermediate and advanced JLsE:

T	(L1) Japanese	(TG) Beginner/ Intermediate	(TG) (High-Intermediate) Advanced	(Target) English
Person	{Ø} ⟶	Ø ⟹	— ◁------	—
Gender	{Ø} ⟶	Ø	Ø	Ø
Number	{Ø} ⟶	Ø ⟹	— ◁------	—
Multiple Specs	*yes*	*yes*	*no*	*no*

First, with respect to the *person-/number*-features, L1 features are different from target ones in terms of the markedness of their feature specification; that is, the L1 features which are underspecified count as marked, but the target features which are partially specified are unmarked, as previously indicated in (2.4) (repeated as (7.2) below):

(7.2) L1 *Marked* and Target *Unmarked* (partially specified): Transferred and overwritten

Stage in L2 Learning	L1 Feature Inventory	TG (Beginner/ Intermediate)	TG (Advanced)	Target Item
earlier	{Ø} ⟶	Ø		
later		Ø ⟹	(—) ◁------	—

The L1 value changes to the target value later in transitional grammar.

FTFL demands that the *person-/number*-features in English T in the transitional grammar of beginner/intermediate JLsE be underspecified due to Feature Transfer, but those in English T in the transitional grammar of advanced JLsE become partially specified thanks to Feature Learning, which stipulates that an L1 feature should be overwritten by a target feature when the L1 feature is distinct from the target one in terms of its markedness.

With respect to the *gender*-feature, the L1 feature is the same as the target one in terms of its feature specification; that is, both of the L1 feature and the target one are underspecified. FTFL therefore demands that the *gender*-feature in English T in the transitional grammar of beginner/intermediate JLsE be underspecified due to Feature Transfer, and the *gender*-feature in English T in the transitional grammar of advanced JLsE should be the same. As a consequence, FTFL demands that the φ-feature composition of English T in a later stage of the transitional grammar of JLsE be in the combination of {−,Ø,−}, as shown in (7.1) above. It should be noticed here that if we apply the φ-feature composition to the generalization in Ishino and Ura (2011b) (as indicated in Chart 5), it can be safely said that English T in the transitional grammar of advanced JLsE cannot project multiple Specs.

Next we apply FTFL to the properties of English D in the transitional grammar of beginner/intermediate JLsE and advanced JLsE, as shown in (7.3) below:

(7.3)   Prediction of the properties of D in the transitional grammar of beginner/intermediate and advanced JLsE:

D	(L1) Japanese	(TG) Beginner/ Intermediate	(TG) (High-Intermediate) Advanced	(Target) English
Person	{+} ⟶	+	+	+
Gender	{Ø} ⟶	Ø	Ø	Ø
Number	{−} ⟶	− ⟶	(−)	+
Multiple Specs	*yes*	*yes*	*yes*	*no*

With respect to the *person*-feature, the strictly specified feature in the L1 feature inventory of JLsE should be transferred to their transitional grammar, and the same holds true in the transitional grammar of advanced JLsE, because the L1 feature is the same as the target one in terms of its feature specification. With respect to the *gender*-feature, the L1 feature is the same as the relevant feature in the target language in terms of its feature specifi-

CHAPTER 7   Φ-FEATURE SPECIFICATION OF T/D IN TRANSITIONAL GRAMMAR

cation; that is, both of the L1 feature and the target one are underspecified. FTFL therefore demands that the *gender*-feature in English D in the transitional grammar of beginner/intermediate JLsE be underspecified due to Feature Transfer, and the *gender*-feature in English D in the transitional grammar of advanced JLsE should be the same.

Here, a special attention should be paid to the *number*-feature of English D in transitional grammar, because the L1 feature is the same as the target feature in terms of the markedness of its specification, whereas the L1 feature is distinct from the target one in terms of its specification. It is therefore predicted under FTFL that Feature Learning does not take place when both of the L1 feature and the target one are unmarked, as was previously argued in (2.11) (repeated as (7.4) below):

(7.4)   L1 *Unmarked* (partially specified) and Target *Unmarked* (strictly specified): Transferred and retained

Stage in L2 Learning	L1 Feature Inventory	TG (Beginner/ Intermediate)	TG (Advanced)	Target Item
earlier	{−} ⟶	−		
later		−	(−)	+

No FEATURE LEARNING and the L1 value persists.

Consequently, the L1 feature which is transferred to the transitional grammar of beginner/intermediate JLsE should be retained in the transitional grammar of advanced JLsE. As a consequence, the φ-feature composition of English D in the transitional grammar of advanced JLsE has the feature composition of {+,∅,−}, as shown in (7.3). Of theoretically significant point here is that if we apply the feature composition of {+,∅,−}, which we have deductively concluded from FTFL, to the generalization in Ishino and Ura (2011b) provided in Chart 5, it leads us to predict that English D in the transitional grammar of advanced JLsE can project multiple Specs.

In the following sections, we will investigate, through conducting several experimental surveys, whether multiple Specs of English T and/or D are allowed or not in the transitional grammar of JLsE.

7.3. Experimental Results on JLsE's Specifiers

7.3.1. Subjects and Aims of Experiments

59 college students, all of whom were native Japanese and had studied English as a second language for more than seven years at the time of our experiment, participated in our experiments. Their average score of TOEFL(P) (TOEFL Papre-based Test) is approximately 505, so that they were regarded as high-intermediate learners of English. In order to disclose the existence/absence of the multiple Specifiers of T and of D in their transitional grammar, we set out the following two surveying tests and examined (i) whether JLsE regard MNC as acceptable or not in their transitional grammar, and (ii) whether JLsE regard MGC as acceptable or not in their transitional grammar. In addition, there was one control group consisting of 20 native speakers of English, who were exchange students studying at an university in Japan.

7.3.2. Test 1: Multiple Nominative Construction

First, in order to detect whether more than one DP within a single clause can be assigned nominative Case or not, our experimental subjects were asked whether multiple subjects within a single clause are acceptable or not in English. We adopted the test sentences in (7.5), (7.6), and (7.7) below:

(7.5) *Those men CD is nice.
(7.6) *John sister is pretty.
(7.7) *John sister hair is long.

Notice that the sentences in (7.5), (7.6) and (7.7) are all ill-formed in the grammar of L1 English because more than one DP is supposed to be a subject within a single clause. The results of the above tests are provided in Table 6.1:

CHAPTER 7 Φ-FEATURE SPECIFICATION OF T/D IN TRANSITIONAL GRAMMAR

TABLE 6.1. Acceptalibity of MNC

(%)	JLsE[a]	Control[b]
acceptable	9.3	0.0
unacceptable	**90.7**	100.0

[a]n=59. [b]n=20. *Notes.* There is no statistically significant difference between the JLE group and the control group (p>.05).

As shown in Table 6.1, 90.7% of the JLE subjects in our experiment correctly recognized that multiple subjects in a single clause are disallowed in English. Notice also that, statistically speaking, there is no significant difference in the acceptability of multiple subjects between the JLE group and our control group. Our conclusion therefore is that JLsE are very apt to allow multiple subjects within a single clause in English. Because DPs in L1 English (except pronouns) are usually not declined mophophonologically for nominative Case, we would like to interpret this experimental result as indicating that JLsE in their transitional grammar correctly regard MNC as unacceptable in English.

7.3.3. Test 2: Multiple Genitive Construction

Next, in order to detect whether more than one DP within a single DP can be assigned genitive Case or not, our experimental subjects were asked whether MGC in English are acceptable or not. We adopted the test sentences in (7.8), (7.9), and (7.10) below:

(7.8) *Mary heard John's that song.
(7.9) *I saw Mary's these dogs.
(7.10) *John read these your books.

Note that the given test sentences in (7.8), (7.9) and (7.10) are all ill-formed in the grammar of L1 English because more than one DP in a single DP are assigned genitive Case by D. The results of the above tests are delineated in Table 6.2:

TABLE 6.2. Acceptalibity of MGC

(%)	JLsE[a]	Control[b]
acceptable	**81.1**	*20.0*
unacceptable	*18.9*	*80.0*

[a]$n=59$. [b]$n=20$. *Notes.* There is a statistically significant difference between the JLE group and the control group: ($t=8.71$, $p<.01$.)

As shown in Table 6.2, 81.1% of the JLE subjects in our experiment erroneously recognized that MGC is acceptable in English. This is endorsed by the fact that there is a statistically significant difference in the acceptability of MGC between the JLE group and our control group.

7.3.4. Summary

In the preceding subsections, we have observed, through our experimental surveys, that JLsE mistakenly regard MGC in English as acceptable in their transitional grammar, but they correctly reject MNC in English in their transitional grammar. We can summarize our experimental discovery concerning the Case-licensing abilities of T and of D in the transitional grammar of JLsE, as indicated in (7.11) below:

(7.11) Acceptability of multiple Specs

L1 *Japanese*	JLsE's transitional grammar	L1 *English*
OK MNC	* MNC	* MNC
OK MGC	OK MGC	* MGC

The conclusion we have reached heretofore is that multiple Specs of D persist in the transitional grammar of JLsE, whereas those of T can never manifest themselves in their transitional grammar. To put it differently, English D in JLsE's transitional grammar retains its ability to license/project multiple Specs; however, English T in their transitional grammar has relinquished it.

This is particularly mysterious not only on empirical grounds but also on theoretical grounds because the two widely accepted hypotheses

CHAPTER 7   Φ-FEATURE SPECIFICATION OF T/D IN TRANSITIONAL GRAMMAR

we reviewed in § 7.1 (i.e., PRA and LTA), no matter which of them we may take, leads a wrong prediction that English T in the transitional grammar of JLsE are expected to behave syntactically the same as English D in their transitional grammar. Notice again that either of the two hypotheses cannot provide any sufficient explanation to the difference in the ability to license/ project multiple Specs between T and D in the transitional grammar of JLsE. We will show, in the next chapter, that this mystery can be unraveled appropriately with our FTFL.

CHAPTER 8

Crosslinguistic Investigations on Multiple Specifiers in Transitional Grammar

In this chapter, it will be demonstrated that FTFL can be crosslinguistically applied to the existence/absence of multiple Specs in transitional grammar. In what follows, we will examine the φ-feature specification of Japanese T/D in the transitional grammar of English learners of Japanese (ELsJ).

8.1. Multiple Specifiers in ELsJ's TG: Prediction by FTFL

First, we will apply FTFL to the φ-features in Japanese T and D in the transitional grammar of beginner/intermediate and in that of advanced ELsJ, as shown in (8.1) below:

(8.1) Prediction of the properties of T in the transitional grammar of beginner/intermediate and advanced ELsJ:

T	(L1) English	(TG) Beginner/ Intermediate	(TG) Advanced	(Target) Japanese
Person	{–}	–	∅	∅
Gender	{∅}	∅	∅	∅
Number	{–}	–	∅	∅
Multiple Specs	no	no	yes	yes

First, with respect to the *person-/number*-features, the markedness of the features of T in the L1 feature inventory of ELsJ is different from those of target ones in L1 Japanese; that is, the L1 features, being partially specified, count as unmarked, but the target features, being underspecified, are marked. Under FTFL, the *person-/number*-features in Japanese T in the transitional grammar of beginner/intermediate ELsJ are partially specified due to Feature Transfer, but those in L1 Japanese T in the transitional grammar of advanced ELsJ becomes underspecified thanks to Feature Learning.

With respect to the *gender*-feature, the specification of the L1 feature in T in their L1 feature inventory is the same as the target one in L1 Japanese; that is, the L1 feature and the target one are both underspecified. FTFL therefore demands that the *gender*-feature in Japanese T in the transitional grammar of beginner/intermediate ELsJ be underspecified due to Feature Transfer, and the *gender*-feature in Japanese T in the transitional grammar of advanced ELsJ should be the same. As a consequence, Japanese T at the later stage of the transitional grammar of ELsJ has the feature compoisition of {Ø,Ø,Ø}, as shown in (8.1) above. Notice here that this specification indicates that T in the transitional grammar of advanced ELsJ can project multiple Specs.

Next, the existence/absence of multiple Specs of Japanese D in the transitional grammar of beginner/intermediate and in that of advanced ELsJ can also be coherently accounted for under FTFL, as shown in (8.2) below:

(8.2) Prediction of the properties of D in the transitional grammar of beginner/intermediate and advanced ELsJ:

D	(L1) English	(TG) Beginner/ Intermediate	(TG) Advanced	(Target) Japanese
Person	{+} ⟶	+	+	+
Gender	{Ø} ⟶	Ø	Ø	Ø
Number	{+} ⟶	+ ⟶	(+)	−
Multiple Specs	*no*	*no*	*yes*	*yes*

With respect to the *person-/number*-features, the strictly specified features in the L1 feature inventory of ELsJ should be transferred to their transitional grammar, and they are the same in the transitional grammar of advanced ELsJ, because the markedness of the L1 features is the same as the target ones. To be more specific, the *number*-feature in D in the L1 feature inventory of ELsJ is strictly specified and the corresponding one in D in L1 Japanese is partially specified, but both of them are the same in terms of the markedness of their specification because both are unmarked. Accordingly, under FTFL, non-application of Feature Learning is predicted.

With respect to the *gender*-feature, the specification of the L1 feature is the same as that of the relevant feature in the target grammar; that is, both of the L1 feature and the target one are underspecified. FTFL therefore demands that the *gender*-feature in Japanese D in the transitional grammar of beginner/intermediate ELsJ be underspecified due to Feature Transfer, and the *gender*-feature in Japanese D in the transitional grammar of advanced ELsJ should be the same.

As a consequence of FTFL, Japanese D in the transitional grammar of advanced ELsJ has the feature composition of $\{+,\emptyset,+\}$, as shown in (8.2). Given this, we can reach the conclusion that D in the transitional grammar of advanced ELsJ cannot project multiple Specs. In the next section, we will conduct small experimental surveys in order to investigate whether multiple Specs of Japanese T and/or D are allowed or not in the transitional grammar of ELsJ.

8.2. Experiments

The group of beginner/intermediate ELsJ who participated in our experimental surveys consists of 11 university students, all of whom were native English speakers and had stayed in Japan as exchange students. At the time of our experiment, they had studied Japanese at university for two to three years. An advanced ELJ who participated in our experimental surveys was an English teacher who had lived in Japan for more than ten years. We had a control group consisting of 20 native speakers of Japanese, all of whom were undergraduate students at college. In order to disclose the existence/ absence of multiple Specifiers of Japanese T and of D in their transitional grammar, we set out the following two surveying tests and examined (i) whether ELsJ regard MNC as acceptable or not in their transitional grammar, and (ii) whether ELsJ regard MGC as acceptable or not in their transitional grammar.

First, in order to detect whether more than one DP within a single clause can be assigned nominative Case or not, our experimental subjects were asked whether multiple subjects within a single clause are acceptable or not in L1 Japanese. We adopted the test sentences in (8.3), (8.4), and (8.5) below:

(8.3) ^{OK}[$_{TP}$ Zoo-**ga** hana-**ga** [$_{T'}$ nagai T]] (koto).
elephant-NOM nose-NOM long (fact)
Lit. '(the fact that) elephants' noses are long.'

(8.4) ^{OK}[$_{TP}$ John-**ga** imooto-**ga** [$_{T'}$ kawai-i T]] (koto).
John-NOM sister-NOM pretty (fact)
Lit. '(the fact that) John's sister is pretty.'

(8.5) ^{OK}[$_{TP}$ John-**ga** imooto-**ga** ke-**ga** [$_{T'}$ naga-i T]] (koto).
John-NOM sister-NOM hair-NOM long (fact)
Lit. '(the fact that) John's sister's hair is long.'

Notice that the sentences in (8.3), (8.4) and (8.5) are acceptable in the grammar of L1 Japanese. The results of the above tests are shown in Table 7.1:

TABLE 7.1. Acceptalibity of MNC

(%)	Beginner/ intermediate ELsJ[a]	Advanced ELJ[b]	Control[c]
acceptable	0.0	**100.0**	*100.0*
unacceptable	**100.0**	*0.0*	*0.0*

[a]n=11. [b]n=1. [c]n=20.

CHAPTER 8 CROSSLINGUISTIC INVESTIGATIONS ON MULTIPLE SPECIFIERS IN TRANSITIONAL GRAMMAR

As shown in Table 7.1, 100% of the beginner/intermediate ELJ subjects in our experiment mistakenly recognized that multiple subjects in a single clause are disallowed in Japanese. Now we can conclude that beginner/intermediate ELsJ in their transitional grammar mistakenly regard MNC as unacceptable in Japanese. On the other hand, the advanced ELJ can correctly allowed MNC in Japanese. These results were empirically on par with what FTFL predicts.

Next, in order to detect whether more than one DP within a single DP can be assigned genitive Case or not, our experimental subjects were asked whether MGC in Japanese is acceptable or not. We adopted the test sentences in (8.6), (8.7), and (8.8) below:

(8.6) ^{OK} Watasi-wa [$_{DP}$ Mary-**no** sorera-**no** [$_{D'}$ inu D]]-o mi-ta.
I-TOP   Mary-GEN   these-GEN   dogs-ACC   see-PAST
Lit. 'I saw these dogs that Mary had.'

(8.7) ^{OK}John-wa [$_{DP}$ ko-**no**   watasi-**no** [$_{D'}$ kuruma D]]-ni
John-TOP   this-GEN   I-GEN   car-DAT
not-ta.
ride-PAST
Lit. 'John has ridden in this car of mine.'

(8.8) ^{OK}John-wa [$_{DP}$ sorera-**no**   anata-no   [$_{D'}$ hon D]]-o   yon-da.
John-TOP   these-GEN   you-GEN   books-ACC   read-PAST
Lit. 'John has read these books of yours.'

Note that all of the given test sentences in (8.6), (8.7) and (8.8) are acceptable in the grammar of L1 Japanese. The results of the above tests are shown in Table 7.2:

TABLE 7.2. Acceptalibity of MGC

(%)	Beginner/intermediate ELsJ[a]	Advanced ELJ[b]	Control[c]
acceptable	27.3	0.0	100.0
unacceptable	**72.7**	**100.0**	0.0

[a]$n=11$. [b]$n=1$. [c]$n=20$.

As shown in Table 7.2, 72.7% of the beginner/intermediate ELJ subjects in our experiment mistakenly recognized that D cannot project multiple Specs in Japanese. The advanced ELJ also erroneously rejected MGC in Japanese. We have thus far observed, through our experimental surveys, that beginner/intermediate ELsJ mistakenly regard MNC and MGC as unacceptable in Japanese, but advanced ELsJ correctly regard MNC as acceptable, but mistakenly regard MGC as unacceptable. It should be noted here that FTFL correctly predicts that even advanced ELsJ are expected to disallow MGC in Japanese, because the specification of the *number*-feature of D in L1 English cannot change to the target specification.

CHAPTER 9

Split Binding in Transitional Grammar

In Part I, we have thus far demonstrated that the syntactic properties of reflexive binding can be theoretically accounted for if we apply FTFL to each φ-feature in the L1 feature inventory of reflexive items and each φ-feature in a reflexive in learners' target language. Then it has been revealed, for example, that a reflexive in the transitional grammar of JLsE shows *φ-defective*. If a reflexive is φ-defective, its syntactic properties are explainable through ATRB, the properties to which our experimental surveys to JLsE have provided an empirical support. In Part II, it has been demonstrated that T and D can project more than one Specifier when they have particular φ-feature composition. We have argued that both of English T and D in the transitional grammar of JLsE can project multiple Specs.

Finally, in this chapter, we will give a theoretical account to the syntactic mechanism of split binding in transitional grammar. Of theoretically/empirically particular importance throughout this dissertation is that syntactic parameters can be reduced with the idea of the φ-feature (de)composition. Then, we assume, following Ishino and Ura (2011a), that the parametric difference between the existence/absence of the split binding of a reflexive can be attributed to the following two conditions:

(9.1) A plural reflexive form R in language L can be split bound
  (α) iff R is φ-defective, and
  (β) iff T in L has multiple feature checking ability.

It follows that if we apply a theoretical explanation with FTFL to both our experimental observations concerning the φ-property of a reflexive item and our experimental observations concerning the φ-property of T in transitional grammar, we can give a natural/coherent explanation to the existence/absence of the split binding of a reflexive in transitional grammar. Before presenting our empirical observations of the split binding in transitional grammar, we will outline the recent *Agree*-based account for the split binding (Ishino and Ura 2011a).

9.1. Split Binding through *Agree*

It has been observed that the L1 English locally-bound plural reflexive *themselves* cannot permit the split binding, as exemplified by the ill-formedness of (9.2) below:

(9.2) a. *John$_k$ told Bill$_h$ about *themselves*$_{k+h}$. (Lebeaux 1984)
 b. *John$_k$ made Bill$_h$ understand *themselves*$_{k+h}$.
  (Fiengo and May 1994)

As for the Japanese complex plural reflexives *zibun-tati-zisin* and *kare-ra-zisin*, both of which show the same locality when they are embedded in a tensed clause (i.e., they must be bound within the clause containing them), it has been observed in the literature that *zibun-tati-zisin* is likely to allow the split binding, but *kare-ra-zisin* is not, as exemplified in (9.3) and (9.4) below:[1]

(9.3) ^{OK}John-ga Bill-ni *zibun-tati-zisin* nituite katat-ta.
  John-NOM Bill-DAT SELF-PL-self about tell-PAST
  Lit. 'John told Bill about John and Bill.'

(9.4) *John-ga Bill-ni *kare-ra-zisin* nituite katat-ta.
  John-NOM Bill-DAT he-PL-self about tell-PAST
  Lit. 'John told Bill about John and Bill.'

CHAPTER 9   SPLIT BINDING IN TRANSITIONAL GRAMMAR

Here, as we have argued in Chapter 6, it is presumed that the φ-features of T[+tense] in L1 Japanese is capable of multiple feature checking. It has been argued in the literature that T[+tense] in L1 Japanese has the ability of agreeing with more than one Goal in addition to its canonical subject DP (cf. Ura 1996, and Hiraiwa 2005). The syntactic mechanism of the split binding through *Agree* can be explicated, as shown in (9.5) below:

(9.5) a. John$_k$-ga Bill$_h$-ni *zibun-tati-zisin*$_{k+h}$-nituite katat-ta.
       John-NOM Bill-DAT SELF-PL-self about tell-PST
       Lit. 'John$_k$ told Bill$_h$ about themselves$_{k+h}$.'

   b. [$_{TP}$ John$_{[\text{NOM}, \varphi]}$-ga [$_{vP}$ Bill-ni *zibun-tati-zisin*-nituite V] T$_{[\text{Case}, \varphi]}$]
      ⌜——— φ (at narrow syntax) ———⌝

   c. [$_{TP}$ John$_k$-ga [$_{vP}$ Bill$_h$-ni *zibun-tati-zisin*$_{k+h}$-nituite V] T$_{[\varphi]}$]
      ⌜——— φ (at narrow syntax) ———⌝
                   └———√φ (at LF)———┘
         └—————————√φ (at LF)—————————┘

As illustrated in (9.5b), T[+tense] agrees with the subject DP *John* to provide it with the nominative Case. Then, in (9.5c), at LF, √φ in T[+tense] agrees with a φ-defective reflexive within its clause to supply it with φ-features. (9.5c) illustrates that √φ in T can agree *optionally* with another DP *Bill*, when the DP is in the same clause thanks to the multiple feature checking ability of √φ in T in L1 Japanese. As a result, T with the whole φ-feature amalgam mediates three Goals; namely, the subject DP (before Spell-Out), the φ-defective reflexive, and the non-subject DP within its clause (at LF), as illustrated in (9.5c). This gives rise to a situation where the φ-defective reflexive is syntactically bound by the subject DP and another DP within the clause; whence, split-binding emerges, as required.[2]

Let us precisely explain the existence/absence of the multiple feature checking ability in φ and √φ in T from the perspective of crosslinguistically parametric differences: In Chapter 6, it was argued that L1 Japanese allows multiple subject construction because the φ-feature of T in L1 Japanese can have the multiple checking ability; however, in § 5.2, it was proposed that *zibun* in L1 Japanese optionally allows the long-distant binding in a tensed clause because the √φ-feature of T in L1 Japanese can have the multiple checking ability, whereas *sich* in L1 German does not allow the long-distant binding in a tensed clause. That is, the allowance of multiple Specs and that of the split binding each stems from the different property of T (i.e., φ vs. √φ). We can schematize the parametric differences, as shown in Chart 6 below:

CHART 6. The Parametric Differences of Multiple Feature Checking Ability

L1 *Japanese*
  a. Ordinary Binding

  [TP Subj   T   .... Reflexive]
        └─φ(in narrow syntax)──┘
                              └─√φ(at LF)─┘

  b. Multiple Specs (multiple checking ability (more than one) in φ in T)

  [TP Subj   Subj   T   ....]
              └─φ(at narrow syntax)─┘
        └──────φ(in narrow syntax)──┘

  c. Null Subject (multiple checking ability (none) in φ in T)

  [TP Subj   T   ....]

  d. Split Binding (multiple checking ability (more than one) in √φ in T)

                               ┌─────√φ(at LF)─────────┐
                                         ┌─√φ(at LF)─┐
  [TP Subj   T   .... DP   ....(plural)Reflexive]
        └─φ(in narrow syntax)──┘

  e. Long-distant Binding of *zibun* (multiple checking ability (none) in √φ in T$_1$)

  [TP Subj T ... Reflexive$_k$ [TP Subj T$_1$ ..... t_k]
        └─φ─┘   └─φ─┘

                              move at LF

CHAPTER 9   SPLIT BINDING IN TRANSITIONAL GRAMMAR

As shown in Chart 6, we assume that both φ and √φ of T in L1 Japanese can have the multiple feature checking ability. As precisely discussed in § 3.4, ATRB proposed in Ishino and Ura (2011a) demands that the scheme in (a) depict the ordinary binding dependency in L1 Japanese; that is, T agrees with a Subject at its Spec in the φ-feature in narrow syntax (i.e., before Spell-Out), and T also agrees with a φ-defective reflexive in the √φ-feaute at LF.

As stated above, φ of T in L1 Japanese is assumed to have the multiple checking ability. As a result, the scheme in (b) indicates that T agrees with more than one subject at its Specs in the φ-feature in narrow syntax, resulting in multiple subject construction, as argued in Chapter 6. More importantly, the term *multiple feature checking* implies *no feature checking*. To put it differently, the relevant head is allowed to agree with no goal. This gives rise to a situation where T agrees with no subject, resulting in null subject construction, as shown in (c).

On the analogy of the assumption that φ of T in L1 Japanese has the multiple checking ability, it is also conceived that √φ of T in L1 Japanese has the multiple checking ability. As a result, the scheme in (d) indicates that T agrees with more than one goal (i.e., a φ-defective reflexive and a non-subject DP in the same clause) in the √φ-feature at LF, resulting in the split binding, as proposed in Ishino and Ura (2011a). What is more, the scheme in (e) indicates that if a situation rises where there is no feature checking in √φ thanks to the multiple checking ability of √φ, the relevant head is allowed to agree with no goal. As shown in (e), when √φ in T_1 does not agree with the reflexive *zibun* in the same clause, *zibun* can move at LF to the higher clause because it needs to be supplied with its φ-features by T in the superordinate/matrix clause. Then the long-distant binding of *zibun* in L1 Japanese emerges as required.

On the other hand, if we take into consideration the abovementioned explanations to the multiplicity in the feature checking in L1 Japanese, we can consistently explain the local binding of the German reflexive *sich* in a tensed clause, as we have argued in § 5.2. Now we can attribute its local dependency to the non-multiple checking ability in √φ of T in L1 German, as shown in Chat 6.1 below:

CHART 6.1. The Parametric Differences of Multiple Feature Checking Ability

L1 *German*

a. Local Binding of *sich* (non multiple checking ability in $\sqrt{\varphi}$ in T_1)

$$[_{TP} \text{ Subj } T \ldots [_{TP} \text{ Subj } T_1 \overbrace{\ldots\ldots \text{Reflexive}}^{\sqrt{\varphi}(\text{at LF})}]$$
$$\underbrace{}_{\varphi} \quad\quad \underbrace{}_{\varphi}$$

In L1 German, it is stipulated that $\sqrt{\varphi}$ of T does not have the multiple checking ability (that is, $\sqrt{\varphi}$ of T obligatorily checks a φ-defective reflexive if there is one in the same clause). Accordingly, $\sqrt{\varphi}$ of T in L1 German is not allowed to agree with more than one goal either, resulting in the ban on the split binding in L1 German. We see that the multiplicity in the feature checking of φ and $\sqrt{\varphi}$ is closely interlinked; that is, if $\sqrt{\varphi}$ in a language *L* has the multiple feature checking ability, we predict that φ in *L* also has the multiple checking ability, but it is not necessarily the case that if φ in language *L* has the multiple feature checking ability, $\sqrt{\varphi}$ in *L* also has the multiple checking ability. As stated in footnote 7 in Chapter 5, the relevancy of the feature checking ability of φ and that of $\sqrt{\varphi}$ should be investigated in greater detail on empirical grounds in a future research.

In Chapter 6, we have demonstrated the existence/absence of the multiple feature checking ability in terms of the φ-features. Strictly speaking, the feature which we have examined in the previous experimental research in Chapter 6 is not the feature that is concerned with the split binding because the split binding is assumed to be materialized due to the multiple checking ablity of $\sqrt{\varphi}$. As stated above, it is plausible that the multiplicity in the feature checking of φ and that of $\sqrt{\varphi}$ are closely interlinked. Thus, we will use the term *multiple feature checking* with no distinction between φ and $\sqrt{\varphi}$ in what follows.

Returning to the discussion of the syntactic mechanism for split binding, Ishino and Ura (2011a) deduce the contrast between languages which allow the split binding and those disallowing it from some independently motivated parameters. It is predicted that the split binding is materialized in a language L iff (α) T in L is capable of multiple feature checking, and (β) L has a φ-defective reflexive (as shown in (9.6)).

(9.6) Split-binding is materialized in a language L
iff (α) T in L is capable of multiple feature checking, and
(β) L has a φ-defective reflexive. (Ishino and Ura 2011a)

The split binding is allowed in L1 Japanese because *zibun-tati(-zisin)* is φ-defective (as observed in Chapter 3) and L1 Japanese T has the ability of multiple feature checking due to its φ-feature compoisition (as observed in Chapter 6); that is, L1 Japanese is compliant with both condition (α) and (β). On the other hand, the split binding is not allowed in L1 English because *themselves* is φ-complete (as observed in Chapter 3) and L1 English T does not allow multiple feature checking due to its φ-feature compoisition (as observed in Chapter 6); that is, L1 English is deviant from both condition (α) and (β). Moreover, for example, the split binding is not allowed in L1 Chinese because *tamen-ziji* (i.e., a plural form of *ta-ziji*) is φ-defective (as observed in Chapter 5), but L1 Chinese T does not allow multiple feature checking due to its φ-feature composition (see Ishino and Ura (2011b) for the comparative study on the existence/absence of multiple Specs and the φ-feature composition of T and D, as indicated in Chart 5); that is, L1 Chinese is compliant with condition (α), but deviant from condition (β).

A theoretically interesting question from the perspective of SLA is: Do JLsE allow the split binding or not with respect to the English reflexives in their transitional grammar? And, do JLsC allow the split binding or not with respect to the Chinese reflexives in their transitional grammar? Before demonstrating that FTFL can apply simultaneously to the L2 learning of reflexive binding and functional categories (such as T), we will first report an empirically interesting observation concerning the availability of the split binding in our experimental surveys to JLsE and JLsC.

9.2. Experiments

We will demonstrate in detail that JLsE disallow the split binding of the English reflexives in their transitional grammar, whereas JLsC are mistakenly apt to allow the Chinese reflexives to be split bound. The difference between the existence/absence of the split binding of their English reflexives and their Chinese reflexives is very interesting on empirical grounds.

9.2.1. Subjects and Procedures

254 college students, all of whom were native Japanese and had studied English as a second language for more than seven years at the time of our experiment, participated in our experiments. Their average score of TOEFL(P) (TOEFL Papre-based Test) was approximately 505. They were regarded as high-intermediate learners of English. We set out the following test and examined whether JLsE in their transitional grammar allow split binding or not. We had a control group consisting of 20 undergraduate students, all of whom were native English.

In addition to the JLsE, 16 college students, all of whom were native Japanese and had studied Chinese for one to four years, also participated in our experimental surveys. They were regarded as beginner/intermediate learners of Chinese. None of them had lived in Chinese-speaking countries at the time of our experiment. We had a control group consisting of 12 undergraduate students, all of whom were native Chinese.

9.2.2. Results

In order to examine whether the English plural reflexive *themselves* in the transitional grammar of JLsE allows the split binding or not, we adopted the test sentence in (9.7), which is unacceptable in the grammar of L1 English:

(9.7)   *John told Bill about *themselves*.

The result of this survey is delineated in Table 8.1 below:

TABLE 8.1. Acceptalibity of Split Binding (English Reflexive (*themselves*))

(%)	High-intermediate JLsE[a]	Control[b]
acceptable	36.3	20.7
unacceptable	**63.7**	79.3

[a]$n=254$. [b]$n=20$.

CHAPTER 9 SPLIT BINDING IN TRANSITIONAL GRAMMAR

As shown above, 63.7% of our JLE subjects disallow the split binding of the English reflexives in their transitional grammar. This result indicates that the English reflexives in the transitional grammar of high-intermediate JLsE are deviant either from condition (α) or from condition (β), or both.

Next, in order to examine whether the Chinese plural reflexive *tamen-ziji* in the transitional grammar of JLsC allows the split binding or not, we adopted the test sentence in (9.8), which is also unacceptable in the grammar of L1 Chinese:

(9.8) *Zhangsan gaosu Lisi youguan *tamen-ziji*.
 Zhangsan tell Lisi about he-PL-SELF
 Lit. 'Zhangsan tells Lisi about themselves.'

The result of this survey is delineated in Table 8.2 below:

TABLE 8.2. Acceptabilty of Split Binding (Chinese Reflexive (*tamen-ziji*))

(%)	Beginner/intermediate JLsC[a]	Control[b]
acceptable	**62.5**	*16.7*
unacceptable	*37.5*	*83.3*

[a]$n=16$. [b]$n=12$.

It is interesting to note that 62.5% of the total JLC subjects mistakenly regarded the Chinese plural reflexive *tamen-ziji* as allowing the split binding, even though (9.8) is ungrammatical in the grammar of L1 Chinese. This result indicates that the Chinese reflexives in the transitional grammar of beginner/intermediate JLsC are compliant with both condition (α) and condition (β).

Moreover, our 254 JLE subjects were also given the following sentence (as shown in (9.9)) and were asked whether the Japanese plural reflexive form *zibun-tati-zisin* having split antecedents is grammatical or not. They were asked to answer by their native intuition.

(9.9) ^{OK}Taro-wa Jiro-ni *zibun-tati-zisin*-o hihans-ase-ta.
Taro-TOP Jiro-DAT SELF-PL-self-ACC criticize-CAUSE-PAST
Lit. 'Taro made Jiro criticize themselves.'

The result of this survey is shown in Table 8.3 below:

TABLE 8.3. **Acceptalibity of Split Binding (Japanese Reflexive (*zibun-tati-zisin*))**

(%)	High-intermediate JLsE(Control)[a]
acceptable	*73.4*
unacceptable	*26.6*

[a]n=254.

An empirically interesting fact is that 73.4% of the total JLE subjects regarded *zibun-tati-zisin* as tolerating the split binding.[3] This result is compatible with our hypothesis that the split binding is allowed in the grammar of L1 Japanese because *zibun-tati(-zisin)* is a φ-defective reflexive and L1 Japanese T is capable of multiple feature checking; that is, L1 Japanese is compliant both with condition (α) and with condition (β).

9.3. Explanation

Now let us explain our experimental/empirical observation through FTFL. First, with respect to the English reflexives in the transitional grammar of high-intermediate JLsE, they have been argued (and empirically confirmed as well) to be *φ-defective* due to the defectiveness of the *number*-feature, as observed in (4.1) in Chapter 4 (repeated as (9.10) below).

CHAPTER 9 SPLIT BINDING IN TRANSITIONAL GRAMMAR

(9.10)

(i)	level	L1 Japanese	TG *himself*		Target English *himself*
			Beginner/ Intermediate	(High-intermediate) / Advanced	
(ii)	φ-features				
	person	{Ø} ⟶ Ø ⟹		+ ⟵----- +	
	gender	{Ø} ⟶ Ø ⟹		+ ⟵----- +	
	number	{−} ⟶ −		(−)	+
(iii)	φ-completeness		φ-defective	***φ-defective***	φ-complete

An observationary fact is that (I) the English reflexives in the transitional grammar of JLsE show φ-defective and satisfy condition (α).

In addition, the fact is revealed that English T in the transitional grammar of JLsE cannot retain the multiple feature checking ability, resulting in the absence of multiple Specs, as observed in (7.1) in Chapter 7 (repeated as (9.11) below).

(9.11)

T	(L1) Japanese	(TG) Beginner/ Intermediate	(TG) (High-intermediate) Advanced	(target) English
Person	{Ø} ⟶ Ø ⟹		− ⟵--- −	
Gender	{Ø} ⟶ Ø		Ø	Ø
Number	{Ø} ⟶ Ø ⟹		− ⟵--- −	
Multiple Specs	*yes*	*yes*	***no***	*no*

Another observationary fact is that (II) English T in the transitional grammar of high-intermediate JLsE has the feature composition of {−,Ø,−} and deviates from condition (β). Taking the fact (I) and the fact (II) into consideration, we are led to conclude that the English reflexives in the transitional grammar of JLsE disallow the split binding. What we have so far deductively demonstrated through FTFL is consistent perfectly with our experimental survey reported in Table 8.1.

Next, let us consider the Chinese reflexives in the transitional grammar of beginner/intermediate JLsC. In Chapter 5, FTFL predicts that they are φ-*defective*, as shown in (5.7) (repeated as (9.12) below).

(9.12)

		L1 Japanese	TG *ta (men)-ziji*		Target Chinese *ta (men)-ziji*
			Beginner/ Intermediate	Advanced	
(i)	level				
(ii)	φ-features				
	person	{Ø} ⟶	Ø ⟹	+ ⟵------	+
	gender	{Ø} ⟶	Ø	Ø	Ø
	number	{−} ⟶	−	(−)	+
(iii)	φ-completeness		**φ-*defective***	φ-defective	φ-defective

Accordingly, the fact follows that (III) the Chinese reflexives in the transitional grammar of beginner/intermediate JLsC show φ-defective and satisfy condition (α). With respect to the L2 learning of Chinese T by JLsC, FTFL stipulates that only Feature Transfer takes place at an early stage of the L2 learning; that is, T for beginner/intermediate JLsC is expected to have the feature compoisition of {Ø,Ø,Ø} and it indicates that their Chinese T can project multiple Specs. To put it differently, the fact follows that (IV) Chinese T in the transitional grammar of beginner/intermediate JLsC complies with condition (β). Taking the fact (III) and the fact (IV) into consideration, we are led to conclude that the Chinese reflexives in the transitional grammar of beginner/intermediate JLsC indeed allow the split binding. What FTFL so far deductively demonstrated with respect to the allowance of the split binding of the Chinese reflexive *tamen-ziji* for JLsC is also consistent appropriately with our experimental survey reported in Table 8.2.

CHAPTER 9   SPLIT BINDING IN TRANSITIONAL GRAMMAR

NOTES

1   The observations shown in (9.3) and (9.4) were reported in Katada (1990), who contended that *karera-zisin* as well as *zibun-tati-zisin* is perfectly acceptable in (9.4), the judgment which is endorsed by Kasai (2000). According to the experimental survey reported in Ishino and Ura (2011a), however, 102 out of the 116 native speakers of Japanese (i.e., 87.9%) allow the split binding of *zibun-tati-zisin*, but 41 out of the 116 Japanese (i.e., 35.3%) accept the split binding of *kare-ra-zisin*.

2   As we have argued through Chapter 6 to Chapter 8, we also assume that D has the φ-feature specification. It is also predicted that D, if it has an active φ-feature, counts as a Probe for a φ-defective reflexive to supply it with the φ-features. As a consequence, the split binding can occasionally be allowed in a DP containing *zibun-tati-zisin*. For example, look at (i):

(i) ^{OK}John$_k$-no   Mary$_h$-e-no   zibun-tazi-zisin$_{k+h}$-e-no   hihan
      John-GEN   Mary-to-COPULAR   SELF-PL-self-to-COPULAR   criticism

Given that the φ-feature of D in Japanese is active and has the multiple checking ability, it can be naturally predicted that the split binding in a DP is allowed in Japanese. We will leave it to future research to pursue this issue.

3   On the other hand, 64.7% of our JLE subjects disallowed split antecedents of PRONOUN+*zisin*. In the literature on Japanese syntax, it has been purportedly established (Nakamura 1989, Katada 1991, and Aikawa 2002, among others) that *zibun-tati-zisin*, the locally-bound plural reflexive form in Japanese, prohibit the split binding; however, the result in Table 8.3 has brought us not only an empirically interesting consequence but also a theoretically important consequence; that is, PRONOUN+*zisin*, which counts as φ-complete, does not need to agree with T under ATRB.

Conclusion

In this dissertation, we have argued that our newly introduced theory about the L2 learning (i.e., FTFL) is not only very pertinent to the empirical/experimental data, which were reported in the previous literature or obtained through our own experiments, but also superior theoretically to other major hypotheses proposed in the field of the L2 learning concerning reflexive binding, because all of the syntactic properties of reflexives in transitional grammar in the crosslinguistic L2 data can be coherently accounted for with FTFL, which is based on the idea with the φ-feature (de) composition. In addition, FTFL was shown to be applicable to the L2 learning concerning the presence/absence of multiple Specs, because the multiple feature checking ability can be attributed to the φ-feature composition of functional categories (such as T and D). Furthermore, we have given a lucid explanation to the syntactic mechanism of the split binding in transitional grammar through demonstrating that FTFL can be applied simultaneously to the mechanism for the L2 learning of the syntactic properties of reflexive binding and to that of the feature checking property of a functional category (such as T). A theoretically significant consequence of this dissertation is that FTFL demands that the syntactic mechanism for the L2 learning of a targe language be attributed to the L2 learning of the φ-features, which are inherent in a lexical item/functional category in the target language; that is, the mechanism for the L2 learning is recaptured by the idea that the φ-feature specification of an L1 item is overwritten or retained according to the markedness of the specification of the L1/L2 items: Consequently, FTFL is empirically further expandable without any additional stipulation. We of course need to proceed to a next step to make a more extensive research on L2 learning where L1 and/or L2 items/categories have other possible feature specification for the purpose of investigating whether FTFL can give a universally consistent account to these cases. We will, however, leave it to future research to pursue investigations into them.

Now, the conclusion is that FTFL, which is founded conceptually upon the well-motivated theory of learnability and the widely accepted theory of minimalist syntax, is remarkably pertinent to some crosslinguistic observations, which are resistant to the major previous approaches.

REFERENCES

Aikawa, Takako. 1993. Reflexivity in Japanese and LF-analysis of *zibun*-binding. Doctoral dissertation, Ohio State University, Columbus OH.
Aikawa, Takako. 1994. Logophoric use of the Japanese reflexive *zibun-zisin* 'self-self.' In *MIT working papers in linguistics* 24, 1–22. Cambridge, Mass.: MITWPL.
Aikawa, Takako. 1999. Reflexives. In *The handbook of Japanese linguistics*, ed. Natsuko Tsujimura, 154–190. Malden, MA: Blackwell.
Ayoun, Dalila. 2003. *Parameter setting in language acquisition*. London: Continuum.
Berwick, Robert. 1985. *The acquisition of syntactic knowledge*. Cambridge, Mass.: MIT Press.
Benett, Susan, and Ljiljana Progovac. 1998. Morphological status of reflexives in second language acquisition. In *The generative study of second language acquisition*, ed. Suzanne Flynn, Gita Martohardjono and Wayne O'Neil, 187–214. Mahwah, NJ: Lawrence Erlbaum.
Bennis, Hans, and Jan Koster. 1984. GLOW Colloquium 1984, Call for papers: Parametric typology. *GLOW Newsletter* 12, 6–7.
Bley-Vroman, Robert. 1988. The fundamental character of foreign language learning. In *Grammar and second language teaching*, ed. William E. Rutherford and Michael Sharwood Smith, 19–30. Newbury House Publishers.
Borer, Hagit. 1984. *Parametric syntax: Case studies in Semitic and Romance languages*. Dordrecht: Foris.
Borer, Hagit, and Kenneth Wexler. 1987. The maturation of syntax. In *Parameter setting*, ed. Thomas Roeper and Edwin Williams, 123–172. Dordrecht: Reidel.
Bouchard, Denis. 1984. *On the content of empty categories*. Dordrecht: Foris.
Büring, Daniel. 2005. *Binding theory*. Cambridge: Cambridge University Press.
Burzio, Luigi. 1991. The morphological basis of anaphora. *Journal of Linguistics* 27, 81–105.
Chomsky, Noam. 1955/75. *Logical structure of linguistic theory.* Ms., Harvard University [published from Plenum in 1975].
Chomsky, Noam. 1965. *Aspects of the theory of syntax*. Cambredge, Mass.: MIT Press.
Chomsky, Noam. 1981. *Lectures on government and binding*. Dordrecht: Foris.
Chomsky, Noam. 1988. *Generative grammar: Its basis, development and prospects. Studies in English linguistics and literature,* Special Issue. University of Foreign Studies, Kyoto.
Chomsky, Noam. 1989. Some notes on economy of derivation and representation. In

MIT working papers in linguistics 10, 43–74.
Chomsky, Noam. 1995. *The minimalist program*. Cambridge, Mass.: MIT Press.
Chomsky, Noam. 2004. Beyond explanatory adequacy. In *Structures and beyond, Vol. 3*, ed. Adriana Belletti, 104–131. Oxford: Oxford University Press.
Chomsky, Noam, and Howard Lasnik. 1993. The theory of principles and parameters. In *Syntax: An international handbook of contemporary research, Vol. 1*, ed. Joachim Jacobs et al., 506–569. Berlin: Walter de Gruyter.
Clahsen, Harald, Sonja Eisenbeiß, and Anne Vainikka. 1994. The seeds of structure: A syntactic analysis of the acquisition of Case marking. In *Language acquisition studies in generative grammar*, ed. Teun Hoekstra and Bonnie D. Schwartz, 85–118. Amsterdam: John Benjamins.
Cole, Peter, Gabriella Hermon, and Li-May Sung. 1990. Principles and parameters of long-distance reflexives. *Linguistic Inquiry* 21, 1–22.
Cole, Peter, and Li-May Sung. 1994. Head movement and long-distance reflexives. *Linguistic Inquiry* 25, 355–406.
Crain, Stephen, and Diane Lillo-Martin. 1999. *An introduction to linguistic theory and language acquisition*. Oxford: Blackwell.
Everaert, Martin. 1986. *The syntax of reflexivization*. Dordrecht: Foris.
Epstein, Samuel David, Suzanne Flynn, and Gita Martohardjono. 1996. Second language acquisition: Theoretical and experimental issues in contemporary research. *Brain and behavioural sciences* 19, 677–714.
Eubank, Lynn. 1994. Optionality and the initial state in L2 development. In *Language acquisition studies in generative grammar*, ed. Teun Hoekstra and Bonnie D. Schwartz, 369–388. Amsterdam: John Benjamins.
Eubank, Lynn. 1996. Negetion in early German-English interlanguage: More valueless features in the L2 initial state. *Second Language Research* 12, 73–106.
Eubank, Lynn, Janine Bischof, April Huffstutler, Patricia Leek, and Clint West. 1997. Tom eats slowly cooked eggs: Thematic-verb raising in L2 knowledge. *Language Acquisition* 6, 171–199.
Faltz, Leonard. 1977. *Reflexivization: A study in universal syntax*, Doctoral dissertation, University of California, Berkeley [Published by Garland, New York, 1985].
Fiengo, Robert, and Robert May. 1994. *Indices and identity*. Cambridge, Mass.: MIT Press.
Finer, Daniel, and Ellen Broselow. 1986. Second language acquisition of reflexive binding. *NELS* 16, 154–168.
Fischer, Silke. 2004. Optimal binding. *Natural Language & Linguistic Theory* 22, 481–526.
Fukui, Naoki. 1986. *A theory of category projection and its applications*. Doctoral dissertation, MIT.
Fukui, Naoki. 1988. Deriving the differences between English and Japanese: A case study in parametric syntax. *English Linguistics* 5, 249–270.
Gallego, Ángel J. 2010. Binding through Agree. *Linguistic Analysis* 34, 163–192.
Gallmann, Peter. 2009. Erweiterte Bindungsdomäne bei schwachen Reflexiva. Ms.,

References

Friedrich Schiller Universität Jena.
Gair, James. 1988. Kinds of markedness. *Linguistic Theory in Second Language Acquisition*, ed. Suzanne Flynn and Wayne O'Neil, 225–250. Dordrecht, Kluwer.
García Mayo, María del Pilar, and Roger Hawkins. 2009. *Second language acquisition of articles: Empirical findings and theoretical implications*. Amsterdam: John Benjamins.
Gast, Volker and Florian Haas. 2008. On reciprocal and reflexive uses of anaphors in German and other European languages, *Reciprocals and reflexives: Theoretical and typological explorations*, ed. Ekkehard Konig and Volker Gast, 307–346. Berlin: Mouton de Gruyter.
Hawkins, Roger, and Cecilia Y.-h. Chan. 1997. The partial availability of Universal Grammar in second language acquisition: The 'Failed Functional Features Hypothesis.' *Second Language Research* 13, 187–226.
Heim, Irene. 2008. Features on bound pronouns. In *Phi Theory*, ed. Daniel Harbour, David Adger and Susana Béjar, 35–56. Oxford: Oxford University Press.
Heim, Irene, Howard Lasnik, and Robert May. 1993. Reciprocity and plurality. *Linguistic Inquiry* 22, 63–101.
Heinat, Fredrik. 2008. *Probes, pronouns, and binding in the minimalist program*. VDM Verlag.
Hicks, Glyn. 2009. *The derivation of anaphoric relations*. Amsterdam: John Benjamins.
Hiraiwa, Ken. 2005. *Dimensions of symmetry in syntax: Agreement and clausal architecture*. Doctoral dissertation, MIT.
Hirakawa, Makiko. 1990. A study of the L2 acquisition of English reflexives. *Second Language Research* 6, 60–85.
Huang, C.-T. James. 1982. *Logical relations in Chinese and the theory of grammar*. Doctoral dissertation, MIT [Published by Garland, New York, 1998].
Huang, C.-T. James. 2001. Distributivity and reflexivity. In *On the formal way to Chinese languages*, ed. Sze-Wing Tang and C.-S. Luther Liu. Cambridge: CSLI and Cambridge University Press.
Huang, C.-T. James, Y.-H. Audrey Li, and Yafei Li. 2009. *The syntax of Chinese*. Cambridge: Cambridge University Press.
Huang, C.-T. James, and C.-C. Jane Tang. 1991. On the local nature of the long-distance reflexive in Chinese. In *Long-distance anaphora*, ed. Jan. Koster and Eric. Reuland, 263–282. Cambridge, Cambridge University Press.
Huang, Yan. 1994. *The syntax and pragmatics of anaphora: A study with special reference to Chinese*. Cambridge: Cambridge University Press.
Ishino, Nao. 2010. Selective transfer of *zibun-zisin* and the L2 acquisition of reflexives. *Kansai English Studies* 4, 87–111.
Ishino, Nao. 2011a. Feature composition of reflexives in interlanguage grammar. *Proceedings of the 35th annual meeting of the Kansai Linguistic Society* 31, 156–167.
Ishino, Nao. 2011b. Multiple specifier parameter and φ-feature specification in SLA.

Paper presented at the 143rd biannual meeting of the Linguistic Society of Japan.

Ishino, Nao. 2012. Syntactic feature transfer and reflexive binding in interlanguage. *English Linguistics* 29.1, 1–37.

Ishino, Nao, and Hiroyuki Ura. 2009. Exclusively Selective Transfer Hypothesis in L2 acquisition and multiple parameters for Japanese reflexives. Paper presented at the 139th biannual meeting of the Linguistic Society of Japan.

Ishino, Nao, and Hiroyuki Ura. 2010. Feature transfer in L2 acquisition: With special reference to reflexive binding. In *The proceedings of the eleventh Tokyo Conference on Psycholinguistics*, ed. Yukio Otsu, 141–160. Tokyo: Hituzi Syobo.

Ishino, Nao, and Hiroyuki Ura. 2011a. Split-bound anaphora and binding chain through Agree. Paper presented at Chains in Minimalism, held at Yokohama National University.

Ishino, Nao, and Hiroyuki Ura. 2011b. Featural specification for multiple specifiers in Universal Grammar. Ms., Kwansei Gakuin University.

Ishino, Nao, and Hiroyuki Ura. 2011c. Φ-features and locality for binding: A comparative study on Germanic/east Asian languages. Ms., Kwansei Gakuin University.

Ishino, Nao, and Hiroyuki Ura. 2011d. Syntactic feature transfer in L2 acquisition: Reflexive binding in Chinese and Japanese. Paper presented at the 11th annual meeting of the Japan Second Language Association.

Jiang, Lin. 2009. A referential/quantified asymmetry in the second language acquisition of English reflexives by Chinese-speaking learners. *Second Language Research* 25, 469–491.

Jiang, Zhao-zi, and Shao Chang-zhong. 2006. Markedness in Universal Grammar and second language acquisition. *US-China Education Review* 21, 77–79.

Kasai, Hironobu. 2000. Some split antecedents are not split. *Linguistic Research* 17, 47–60.

Katada, Fusa. 1991. The LF representation of anaphors. *Linguistic Inquiry* 22, 287–314.

Kitagawa, Yoshihisa. 1986. *Subjects in Japanese and English*. Doctoral dissertation, University of Massachusetts, Amherst [Published by Garland, New York, 1994].

Kuroda, Sige-Yuki. 1965. *Generative grammatical studies in the Japanese language*. Doctoral dissertation, MIT [Published by Garland, New York, 1979].

Kuroda, Sige-Yuki. 1988. Whether we agree or not: A comparative syntax of English and Japanese. *Linguistic Investigations* 12, 1–47.

Langendoen, Terence. 1978. The logic of reciprocity. *Linguistic Inquiry* 9, 177–197.

Langendoen, Terence, and Joel Magloire. 2003. The logic of reflexivity and reciprocity. In *Anaphora*, ed. Andrew Barss, 237–263. Oxford: Blackwell.

Lardiere, Donna. 2008. Feature assembly in second language acquisition. In *The role of formal features in second language acquisition*, ed. Juana M. Liceras et al, 106–40. New York: Laurence Erlbaum Associates.

References

Lardiere, Donna. 2009. Some thoughts on the contrastive analysis of features in second language acquisition. *Second Language Research* 25, 173–227.
Lebeaux, David. 1984. Locality and anaphoric binding. *The Linguistic Review* 4, 343–363.
Lee-Schoenfeld, Vera. 2008. Binding, phases, and locality. *Syntax* 11, 281–298.
Lennenberg, Eric Heinz. 1967. *Biological foundations of language.* John Wiley & Sons.
Liceras, Juana M., Helmut Zobl, and Helen Goodluck. 2008. *The role of formal features in second language acquisition.* Mahwah, New Jersey: Lawrence Erlbaum Associates.
MacLaughlin, Dawn. 1995. Language acquisition and the subset principle. *Linguistic Review* 12, 143–191.
MacLaughlin, Dawn. 1998. The acquisition of the morphosyntax of English reflexives by non-native speakers. In *Morphology and its interfaces in second language knowledge*, ed. Maria-Luise Beck, 195–226. Amsterdam: John Benjamins.
Manning, Christopher, Ivan Sag, and Masayo Iida. 1999. The lexical integrity of Japanese causatives. In *Readings in HPSG*, ed. Georgia Green and Robert Levine, 39–79. Cambridge: Cambridge University Press.
Nakamura, Masaru. 1987. Parametrized extention of binding theory. In *MIT working papers in linguistics* 9, 193–223. Cambridge, Mass.: MITWPL.
Nakamura, Masaru. 1989. Reflexives in Japanese. *Gengo Kenkyu* 95, 206–230.
Ogawa, Yoshiki. 1996. Word order, object shift and multiple specifiers. *English Linguistics* 13, 63–92.
Ouhalla, Jamal. 1991. *Functional categories and parametric variation.* London/New York: Routledge.
Partee, Barbara H, Alice ter Meulen, and Robert E. Wall. 1990. *Mathematical methods in linguistics.* Dordrecht: Kluwer.
Pica, Pierre. 1987. On the nature of the reflexivization cycle. *NELS* 17, 483–499.
Pinker, Steven. 1984. *Language learnability and language development.* Cambridge, Mass.: Harvard University Press.
Progovac, Ljiljana. 1992. Relativized SUBJECT: Long-distance reflexives without movement. *Linguistic Inquiry* 23, 671–680.
Progovac, Ljiljana. 1993. Long-distance reflexives: Movement-to-Infl vs. relativized subject. *Linguistic Inquiry* 24, 755–772.
Quicolli, A. Carlos. 2008. Anaphora by phase. *Syntax* 11, 299–329.
Radford, Andrew. 1997. *Syntax: A minimalist introduction.* Cambridge, Cambridge University Press.
Reinhart, Tanya, and Eric Reuland. 1991. Anaphors and logophors: An argument structure perspective. In *Long distance anaphora,* ed. Jan Koster and Eric Reuland, 283–321. Cambridge: Cambridge University Press.
Reinhart, Tanya, and Eric Reuland. 1993. Reflexivity. *Linguistic Inquiry* 24, 657–720.
Reuland, Eric. 2005. Agreeing to bind. In *Organizing grammar: Studies in honor*

of Henk van Riemsdijk, ed. Hans Broekhuis et al., 505–513. Berlin: Mouton de Gruyter.

Reuland, Eric. 2008. Anaphoric dependencies: How are they encoded? Towards a derivation-based typology. In *Reciprocals and reflexives: Theoretical and typological explorations,* ed. Ekkehard König and Volker Gast, 499–555. Berlin: Mouton de Gruyter.

Reuland, Eric. 2011. *Anaphora and language design.* Cambridge, Mass.: MIT Press.

Safir, Ken. 1987. Comments on Wexler and Manzini. In *Parameter setting*, ed. Thomas Roeper and Edwin Williams, 77–90. Dordrecht: Reidel.

Safir, Ken. 2004. *The syntax of anaphora.* New York: Oxford University Press.

Saleemi, Anjum Pervez. 1990. Null subjects, markedness, and implicit negative evidence. In *Logical issues in language acquisition*, ed. Iggy M. Roca, 235–258. Dordrecht: Foris.

Selinker, Larry. 1972. Interlanguage. *International Review of Applied Linguistics* 10, 209–31.

Shirahata, Tomohiko. 2007. Interpretation of English pronouns and reflexives by Japanese learners -A preliminary study-. *Shizuoka University Kyoiku Gakubu Kenkyuu Houkoku* 57, 141–155.

Schwartz, Bonnie D. 1996. Parameters in non-native language acquisition. In *Investigating second language acquisition*, ed. Peter Jordens and Josine Lalleman, 211–235. Berlin: Mouton de Gruyter.

Schwartz, Bonnie, D. 1998. On two hypotheses of 'Transfer' in L2A: Minimal trees and absolute L1 transfer. In *The generative study of second language acquisition*, ed. Suzanne Flynn, Gita Martohardjono and Wayne O'Neil. Mahwah, New Jersey: Lawrence Erlbaum Associates.

Schwartz, Bonnie D., and Rex Sprouse. 1994. Word order and nominative Case in nonnative language acquisition: A longitudinal study of (L1 Turkish) German interlanguage. In *Language acquisition studies in generative grammar*, ed. Teun Hoekstra and Bonnie D. Schwartz, 317–368. Amsterdam: John Benjamins.

Schwartz, Bonnie D., and Rex Sprouse. 1996. L2 cognitive states and the Full Transfer/Full Access Model. *Second Language Research* 12, 40–72.

Schwartz, Bonnie D., and Rex Sprouse. 2000. When syntactic theories evolve: Consequences for L2 acquisition research. In *Second language acquisition and linguistic theory*, ed. John Archibald, 156–186. Oxford: Blackwell.

Thomas, Margaret. 1995. Acquisition of the Japanese reflexive *zibun* and movement of anaphors in logical forml. *Second Language Research* 11, 206–234.

Travis, L. deMena. 2008. The role of features in syntactic theory and language variation. In *The role of formal features in second language acquisition*, ed. Liceras, Juana M., Helmut Zobl and Helen Goodluck, 22–47. New York: Lawrence Erlabum Associates.

Tsimpli, Ianthi-Maria, and Anna Roussou. 1991. Parameter resetting in L2? In *University College London working papers in linguistics* 3, 149–169.

Ura, Hiroyuki. 1994. *Varieties of raising and the feature-based bare phrase struc-*

REFERENCES

ture theory. MIT Occasional Papers in Linguistics 7. Cambridge, Mass.: MITWPL.

Ura, Hiroyuki. 1996. Multiple feature-checking: A theory of grammatical function splitting, Doctoral dissertation, MIT.

Ura, Hiroyuki. 2000. *Checking theory and grammatical functions in Universal Grammar.* New York: Oxford University Press.

Uriagereka, Juan, and Ángel J. Gallego. 2006. (Multiple) Agree as local (binding and) obviation. Paper presented at Going Romance XX, Vrije Universiteit Amsterdam.

Vainikka, Anna, and Martha Young-Scholten. 1994. Direct access to X' theory: evidence from Korean and Turkish adults learning German. In *Language acquisition studies in generative grammar*, ed. Teun Hoekstra and Bonnie D. Schwartz 265–316. Amsterdam, John Benjamins.

Vainikka, Anna, and Martha Young-Scholten. 1996. Gradual development of L2 phrase structure. *Second Language Research* 12, 7–39.

Wakabayashi, Shigenori. 1996. The nature of interlanguage: SLA of English reflexives. *Second Language Research* 12, 266–303.

Wakabayashi, Shigenori. 2002. The acquisition of non-null subjects in English: A minimalist account. *Second Language Research* 18, 28–71.

Watanabe, Eriko, Chisato Fujii, Yoshie Kabuto, and Keiko Murasugi. 2008. Experimental evidence for the Parameter Resetting Hypothesis: The second language acquisition of English reflexive-binding by Japanese speakers. *Nanzan Linguistics: Special Issue* 3, 263–283.

Wexler, Kenneth, and Rita Manzini. 1987. Parameters and learnability in binding theory. In *Parameter setting*, ed. Thomas Roeper and Edwin Williams, 41–76. Dordrecht: Reidel.

White, Lydia. 1986. Markedness and parameter setting: Some implications for a theory of adult second language acquisition. In *Markedness*, ed. Fred Eckman et al., 309–328. New York: Plenum Press.

White, Lydia. 2000. Second language acquisition: From initial to final state. In *Second language acquisition and linguistic theory*, ed. John Archibald 130–155. Oxford: Blackwell.

White, Lydia. 2003. *Second language acquisition and Universal Grammar*. Cambridge: Cambridge University Press.

William, O'Grady. 2000. A linguistic approach to the study of language acquisition. Invited keynote talk presented at the annual meeting of the Pan-Pacific Association of Applied Linguistics.

Xue, Ping. 1991. The distribution of Chinese reflexives. In *Working papers of the linguistic circle of the University of Victoria* 11, 101–109.

Yang, Dong-Whee. 1984. The extended binding theory of anaphors. *Theoretical Linguistic Research* 1, 195–218.

Yuan, Boping. 1994. Second language acquisition of reflexives revisited. *Language* 70, 539–545.

Yuan, Boping. 1998. Interpretation of binding and orientation of the Chinese reflexive 'ziji' by English and Japanese speakers. *Second Language Research* 14, 324–341.

Yusa, Noriaki. 1998. A minimalist approach to second language acquisition. In *The generative study of second language acquisition,* ed. Suzanne Flynn, Gita Martohardjono and Wayne O'Neil, 215–238. Mahwah, NJ: Lawrence Erlbaum.

INDEX

A

active 55, 124, 125, 130
Agree 51
Agree Theory of Reflexive Binding (ATRB) 51, 52, 69, 81, 120, 121
Aikawa, T. 52, 56
Arabic T 165

B

Bennis, H and J. Koster 7
Berwick, R. 18, 36
binding dependency 13, 101, 120, 123, 125, 127, 130, 136
binding domain 26, 53, 56, 72, 81
Binding Theory A 14
Binding Through *Agree* 23, 25, 26, 28, 47, 66, 124, 194
Bley-Vroman, R. 3
Borer, H. 6
Bouchard, D. 26, 51
Burzio, L. 22, 26, 50, 51, 60, 66, 80, 120, 162

C

Case feature checking 124
causative clause 54, 55, 69, 81, 126
causative constructions 121
causee 55
c-command 75, 84
Chinese D 165
Chinese reflexives 96
Chinese T 165
Chomsky, N. 6, 11, 14, 25, 35, 51, 53, 96, 123, 161
complex anaphor 14
composite dependency 121
Crain and Lillo-Martin 12
C-T Probe 27

D

D 161, 162, 165, 170, 178
discourse binding 14
distributive operator 49, 50
distributive reading 13, 16, 24, 47, 48, 49, 50, 58, 70, 78, 79, 99, 101, 106, 111, 142

E

English D 165
English reflexive 34, 83, 144
English T 165
Eubank, L. 9

F

Faltz' typological classification 15, 121
feature chain 121
feature composition 169
Feature Learning 22, 36
feature specification 37
Feature Transfer 22, 36
Finer, D and E. Broselow 17
finite/non-finite asymmetry 149
First Language Acquisition (FLA) 3, 40
French T 165
Fukui, N. 6
Full Transfer/Full Access Model 9
Full Transfer/Partial Access Model 9

G

Gallego, A. J. 23, 27, 51
García Mayo and R. Hawkins 8
gender 13, 33, 47, 50, 57, 58, 67, 77, 120, 129, 167, 172, 180
genitive Case 183
German reflexives 120, 144

Governing Category Parameter (GCP)   4, 18, 19, 29, 71, 95
grammatical judgement test   75
group reading   109, 141

H

Hawkins, R and C. Chan   9
Heim, I.   49
Heim, Lasnik, and May   50
Heinat, F.   23
himself   17, 50, 52, 57, 58, 69, 70, 89, 146
Hirakawa, M.   17, 18, 82, 95, 144

I

inactive   55, 124, 125, 131
in situ   70, 125
interlanguage grammar (IL grammar)   8, 10, 13
Ishino, N and H. Ura   17, 26, 51, 121, 165
Italian T   165

K

kare-ra-zisin   194
kare-zisin   14, 70, 105, 106, 134, 146
Katada, F.   55, 120
Korean T   165
Kuroda, S-Y.   54, 161

L

L1 feature inventory   38, 43, 61, 66, 129
Language Acquisition Device (LAD)   2, 3
Lardiere, D.   8
learnability   35, 43
Lexical Transfer Approach (LTA)   17, 20, 71, 72, 94, 95, 127, 177
LF   51
license   184
Liceras, Zobl, and Goodluck   8
local binding   14, 62

locality   26, 69, 71, 81
logophor   14
long-distant binding   14, 62, 196

M

MacLaughlin, D.   17, 20
marked   36, 37, 39
markedness   22, 35, 36, 37, 102
micro-parameter   71
minimalist framework   6
minimality condition   27
minimality effect   69
Minimal Trees Hypothesis   9
Modern Greek T   165
move   70, 93, 120, 121, 123, 130
multiple feature checking ability   193, 196, 198
Multiple Genitive Construction (MGC)   161, 182, 190
multiple licensing ability   162
Multiple Nominative Construction (MNC)   161, 182, 190
multiple Specs   162, 177, 196

N

neutral interpretation   16, 24, 32, 48, 93, 98, 120, 139, 140, 141
No Access Hypothesis   3
nominative Case   26, 52, 182, 195
non-tensed clause   57, 69, 82, 98, 120
No Transfer/Full Access Model   9
null subject   166, 196
Null Subject Parameter   5
number   13, 34, 47, 48, 49, 50, 68, 78, 98, 129, 168, 172, 179

O

Ouhalla, J.   6
overwritten   38, 39, 44

INDEX

P

parameter 4
Parameter Resetting Approach (PRA) 17, 18, 19, 71, 72, 94, 95, 127, 177
parameter setting 5
parameter value 71, 72, 127
partially specified 31, 34, 37, 39, 44, 49
Partial Transfer/Full Access Model 9
Partial Transfer/Partial Access Model 9
person 13, 32, 47, 50, 67, 76, 120, 129, 166, 170, 179
Perusian T 165
phase 26
phase edge 121
φ-complete 22, 25, 28, 58, 60, 106, 147
φ-completeness 135
φ-defective 22, 25, 26, 27, 28, 51, 52, 55, 69, 83, 98, 101, 106, 120, 130, 193
φ-feature checking ability 130
φ-feature decomposition 21, 23, 43, 74, 79, 87, 164, 165, 178, 193
φ-features 21, 22, 24, 25, 26, 28, 51, 55, 80, 123, 124, 195
φ-feature specification 16, 31, 35
Pica's generalization 14, 19, 120
Pinker, S. 9
plural antecedent 109
plural reflexive 193
positive evidence 36, 40, 43, 71
Principle A 84
Principle B 84
Probe 26, 51, 54, 55, 123, 124
Probe-Goal framework 25, 51
pronominal 84
PRONOUN+*zisin* 20, 28, 52
proper antecedent 82
Proper Antecedent Parameter (PAP) 19, 53
proper subset 178

Q

Quechua T 165
Quicolli, A. C. 23, 51

R

reflexive feature 121
reflexivizer 56, 57, 66
Reinhart, T and E. Reuland 56, 102, 120
retained 41, 42, 44
Reuland, E. 23, 51, 120, 121
Russian T 165

S

Saleemi, A.P. 5
Schwartz, B. 9
Schwartz, B and R. Sprouse 9
seg 13
seg selv 13
sich 52, 118, 122, 123
sich -selbst 52, 118
simplex anaphor 14, 28, 120, 123
Spell-Out 49, 123
split binding 193, 196, 198
strictly specified 31, 33, 34, 37, 39, 41, 44, 50, 58
subject orientation 13, 15, 23, 24, 52, 70, 80, 99, 101, 106, 120, 130, 143
Subset Principle 18, 36, 71, 177
subset relation 35
syntactic antecedent 49

T

T 26, 52, 55, 123, 124, 127, 130, 161, 162, 165, 169, 178, 195
tamen-ziji 93, 199, 204
ta-ziji 16, 52, 70, 91, 92, 93, 99, 100, 102, 108
tensed clause 57, 69, 82, 120, 122
themselves 194, 199
Thomas, M. 17
transitional grammar (TG) 8, 10, 11, 13, 21, 22, 36, 38, 79, 83, 89, 129, 145, 182
Travis, L. 8
Tsimli, I. M and A, Roussou 9

U

UG accessibility   3
underspecified   31, 32, 34, 35, 40, 44, 48, 120
uninterpretable feature   123
unmarked   35, 36, 37, 39, 41, 42
Ura, H.   162, 164, 165
Uriagereka and Gallego   25, 51

V

Valueless Feature Hypothesis   9
vP   54, 121, 126
vP phase edge   121
V-T complex   120

W

Wexler, K and R. Manzini   5, 18, 53, 71
White, L.   5, 36

Y

Yuan, B.   17, 20, 95

Z

zibun   14, 18, 20, 28, 32, 52, 55, 123
zibun-tati   48
zibun-tati-zisin   48, 194, 199
zibun-zisin   14, 20, 26, 27, 32, 48, 52, 53, 54, 55, 70, 103
zich   13
zichzelf   13
ziji   15, 52, 70, 91, 92, 93, 98, 102, 109

【著者略歴】

石野　尚（いしの・なお）

2012年、関西学院大学にて言語学博士号を取得。
現在は大手前大学総合文化学部講師。専門は、統語論、第二言語習得理論。

主要な著作：Syntactic Feature Transfer and Reflexive Binding in Interlanguage. *English Linguistics* 29 (1), 1-37, 2012.

Feature Transfer and Feature Learning in Universal Grammar

2019年12月15日初版第一刷発行

著　者	石野　尚
発行者	田村和彦
発行所	関西学院大学出版会
所在地	〒662-0891 兵庫県西宮市上ケ原一番町1-155
電　話	0798-53-7002
印　刷	株式会社クイックス

©2019 Nao Ishino
Printed in Japan by Kwansei Gakuin University Press
ISBN 978-4-86283-295-5
乱丁・落丁本はお取り替えいたします。
本書の全部または一部を無断で複写・複製することを禁じます。